S0-BNA-606

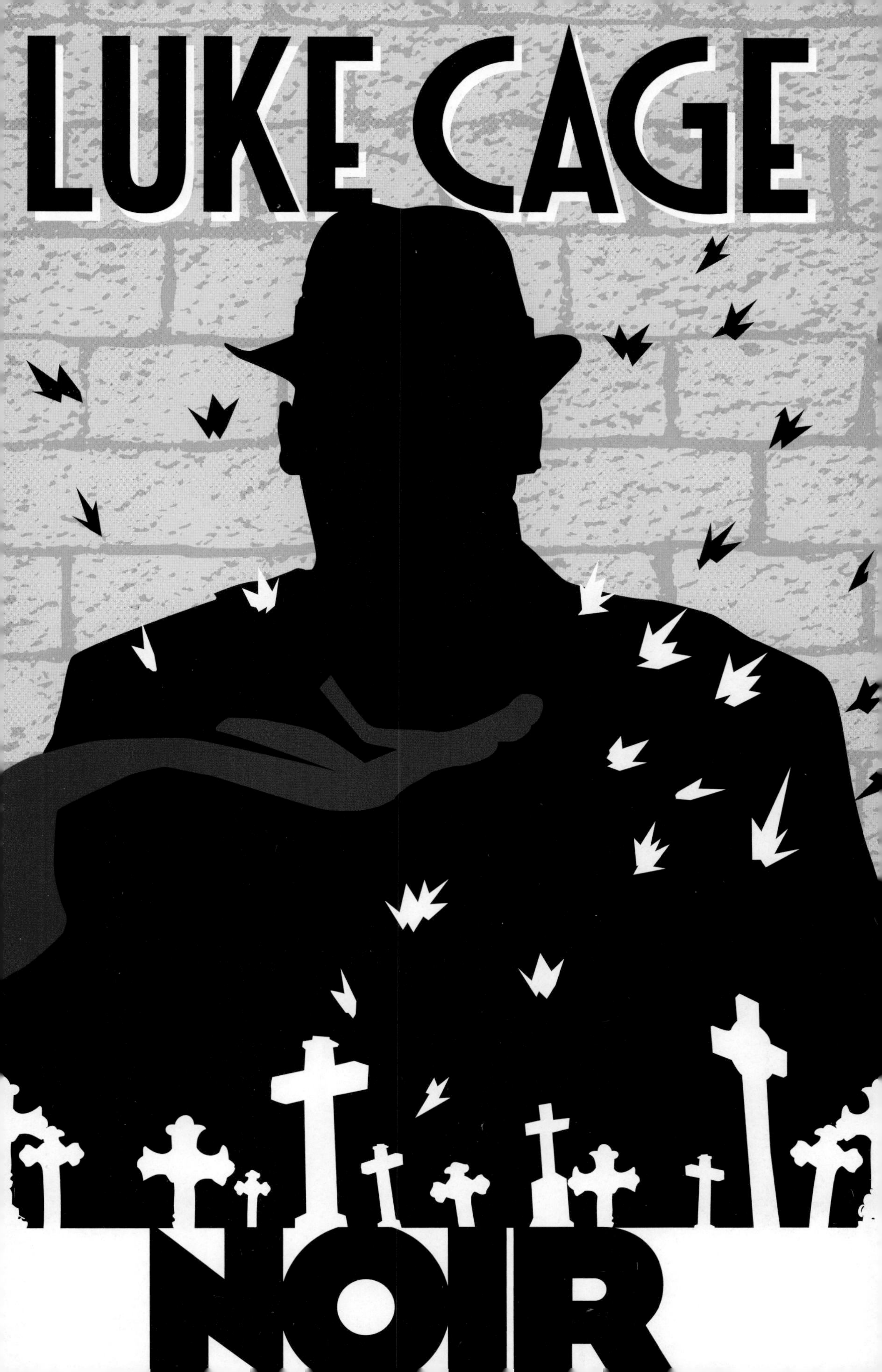
LUKE CAGE
NOIR

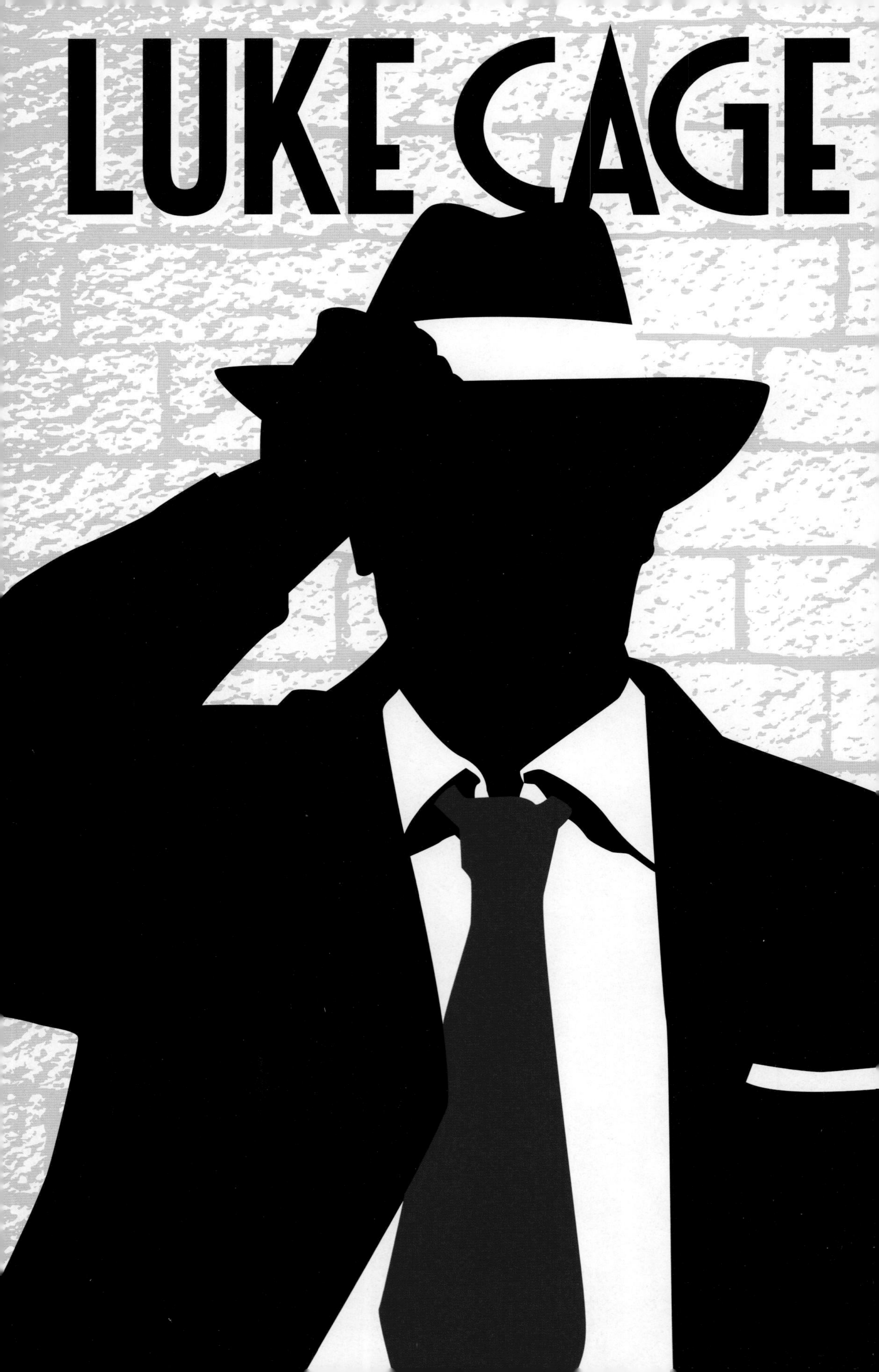
LUKE CAGE

WRITERS
**MIKE BENSON
& ADAM GLASS**

ARTIST
SHAWN MARTINBROUGH

COLORIST
NICK FILARDI

LETTERER
VC'S CORY PETIT

COVER ARTIST
TIM BRADSTREET

ASSISTANT EDITOR
SEBASTIAN GIRNER

EDITOR
AXEL ALONSO

COLLECTION EDITOR
JENNIFER GRÜNWALD
ASSISTANT EDITORS
ALEX STARBUCK & JOHN DENNING
EDITOR, SPECIAL PROJECTS
MARK D. BEAZLEY
SENIOR EDITOR, SPECIAL PROJECTS
JEFF YOUNGQUIST
SENIOR VICE PRESIDENT OF SALES
DAVID GABRIEL
BOOK DESIGN
JEFF POWELL

EDITOR IN CHIEF
JOE QUESADA
PUBLISHER
DAN BUCKLEY
EXECUTIVE PRODUCER
ALAN FINE

LUKE CAGE NOIR. Contains material originally published in magazine form as LUKE CAGE NOIR #1-4. First printing 2010. ISBN# 978-0-7851-3942-3. Published by MARVEL WORLDWIDE, INC., a subsidiary of MARVEL ENTERTAINMENT, LLC. OFFICE OF PUBLICATION: 417 5th Avenue, New York, NY 10016. Copyright © 2009 and 2010 Marvel Characters, Inc. All rights reserved. $19.99 per copy in the U.S. (GST #R127032852); Canadian Agreement #40668537. All characters featured in this issue and the distinctive names and likenesses thereof, and all related indicia are trademarks of Marvel Characters, Inc. No similarity between any of the names, characters, persons, and/or institutions in this magazine with those of any living or dead person or institution is intended, and any such similarity which may exist is purely coincidental. **Printed in the U.S.A.** ALAN FINE, EVP - Office of the President, Marvel Worldwide, Inc. and EVP & CMO Marvel Characters B.V.; DAN BUCKLEY, Chief Executive Officer and Publisher - Print, Animation & Digital Media; JIM SOKOLOWSKI, Chief Operating Officer; DAVID GABRIEL, SVP of Publishing Sales & Circulation; DAVID BOGART, SVP of Business Affairs & Talent Management; MICHAEL PASCIULLO, VP Merchandising & Communications; JIM O'KEEFE, VP of Operations & Logistics; DAN CARR, Executive Director of Publishing Technology; JUSTIN F. GABRIE, Director of Publishing & Editorial Operations; SUSAN CRESPI, Editorial Operations Manager; ALEX MORALES, Publishing Operations Manager; STAN LEE, Chairman Emeritus. For information regarding advertising in Marvel Comics or on Marvel.com, please contact Ron Stern, VP of Business Development, at rstern@marvel.com. For Marvel subscription inquiries, please call 800-217-9158. **Manufactured between 1/11/10 and 2/10/10 by R.R. DONNELLEY, INC., SALEM, VA, USA.**

10 9 8 7 6 5 4 3 2 1

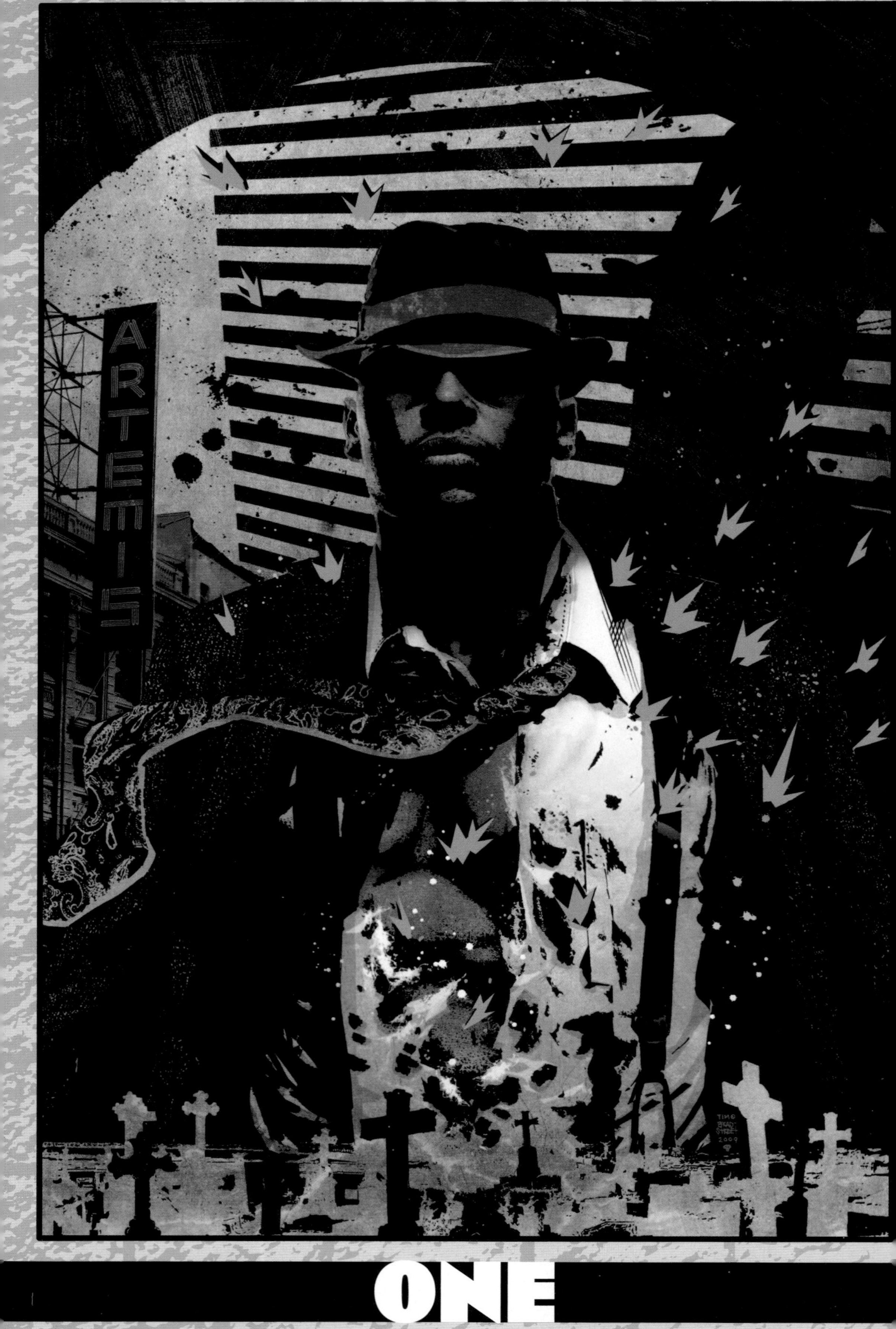
ARTEMIS
TIM BRADSTREET 2009

ONE

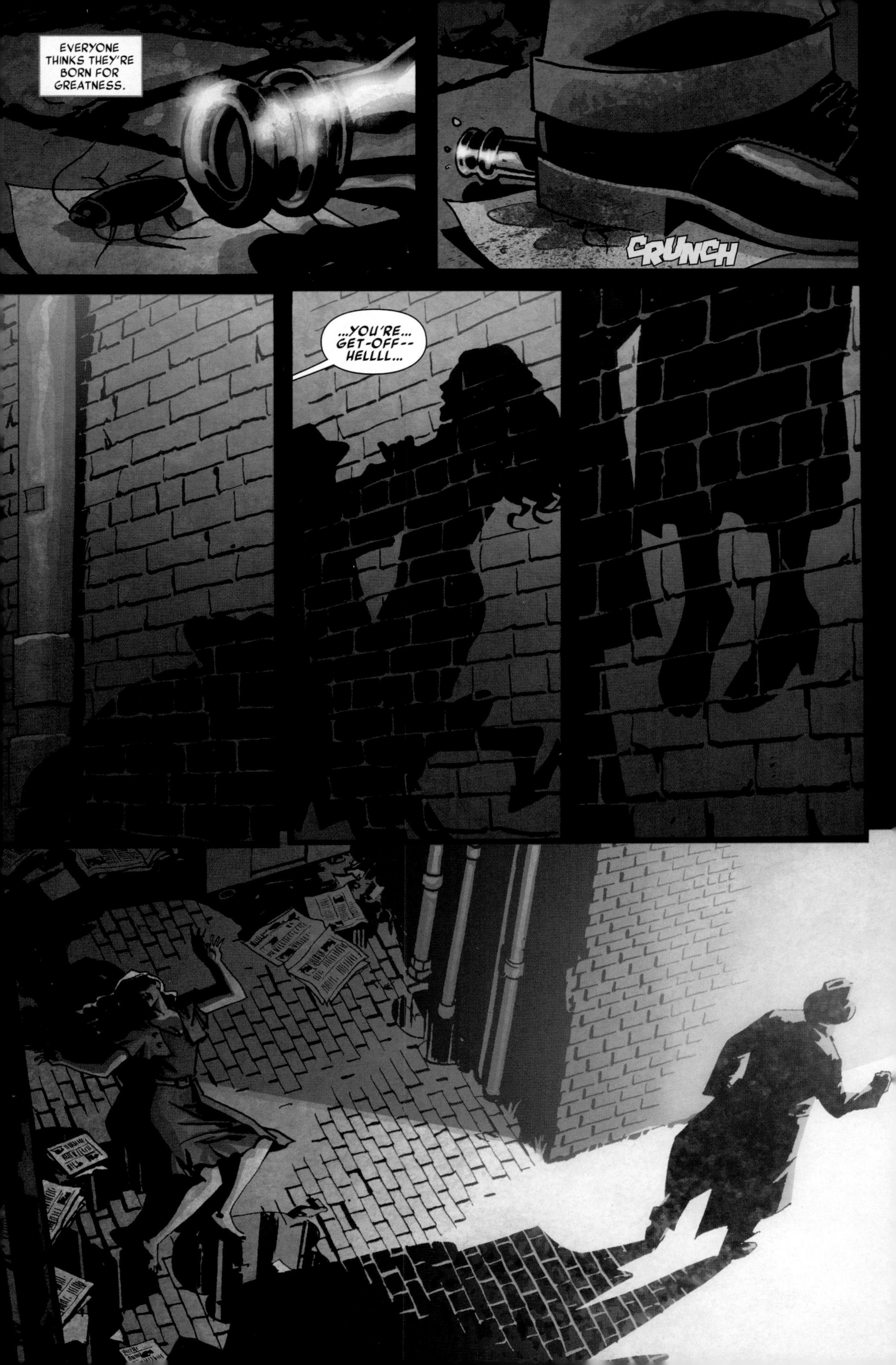
EVERYONE THINKS THEY'RE BORN FOR GREATNESS.
CRUNCH
...YOU'RE... GET-OFF-- HELLLL...

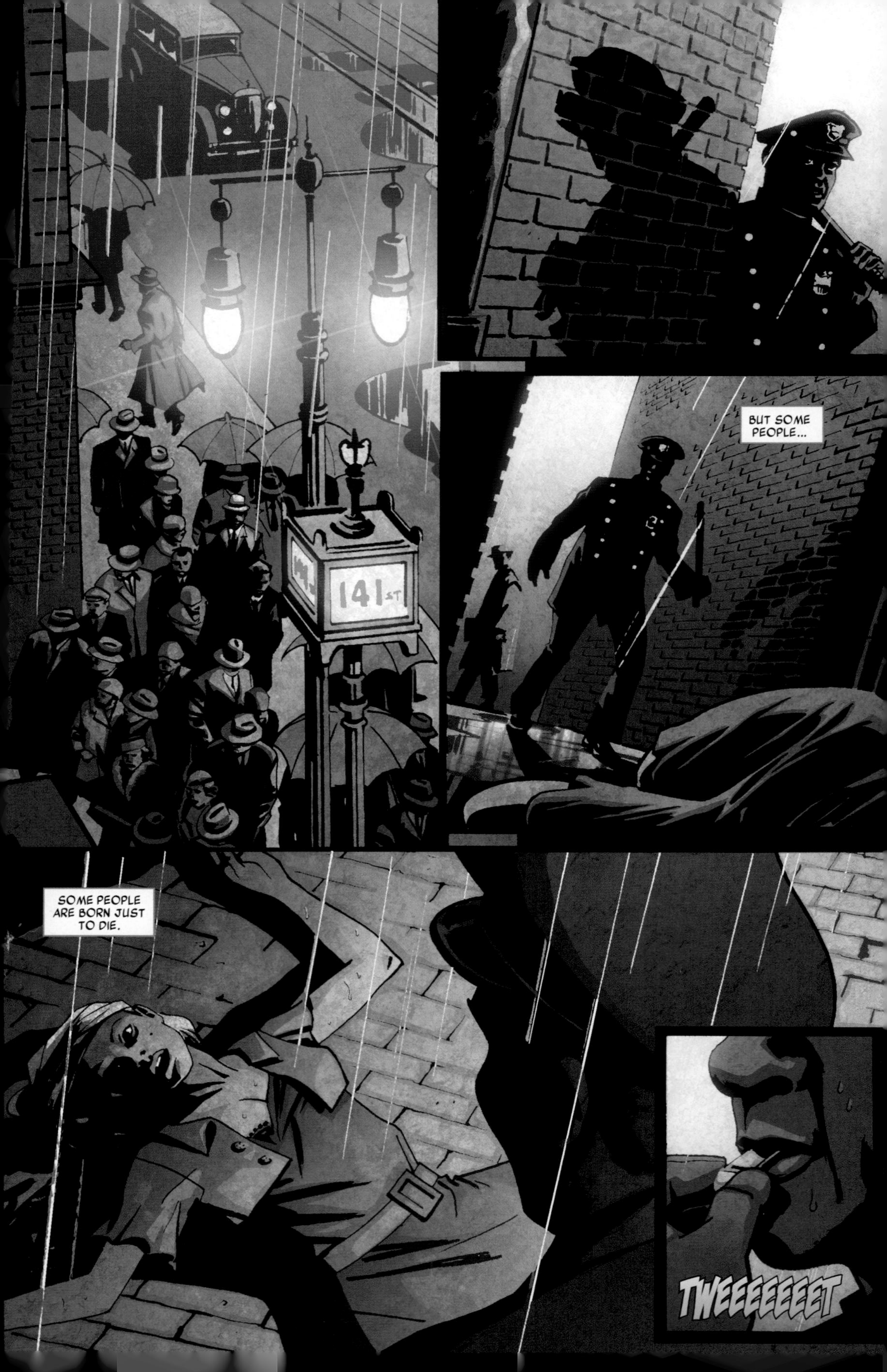
BUT SOME PEOPLE...
SOME PEOPLE ARE BORN JUST TO DIE.
TWEEEEEEET

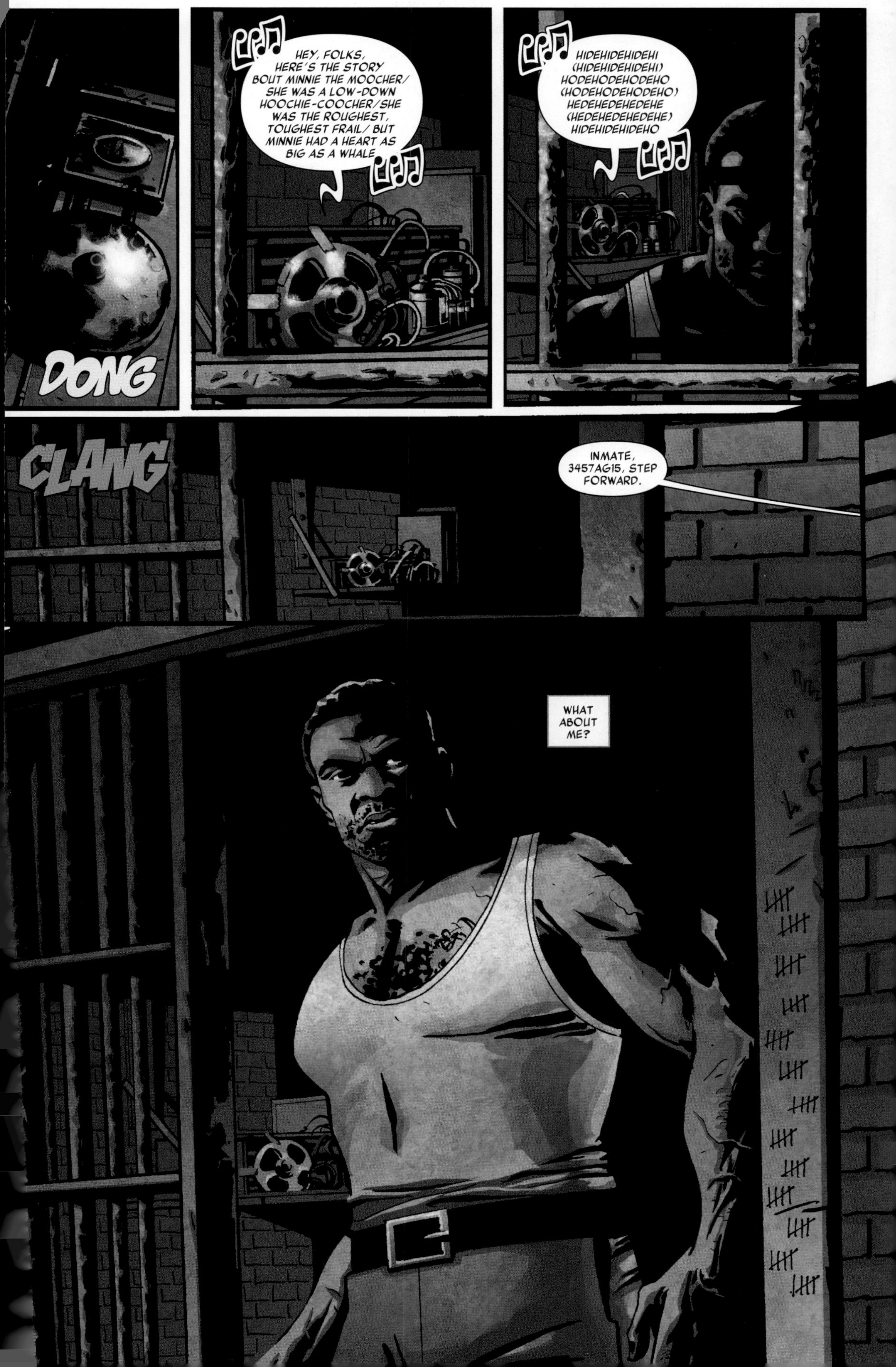
DONG
HEY, FOLKS, HERE'S THE STORY BOUT MINNIE THE MOOCHER/ SHE WAS A LOW-DOWN HOOCHIE-COOCHER/SHE WAS THE ROUGHEST, TOUGHEST FRAIL/ BUT MINNIE HAD A HEART AS BIG AS A WHALE
HIDEHIDEHIDEHI (HIDEHIDEHIDEHI) HODEHODEHODEHO (HODEHODEHODEHO) HEDEHEDEHEDEHE (HEDEHEDEHEDEHE) HIDEHIDEHIDEHO
CLANG
INMATE, 3457AG15, STEP FORWARD.
WHAT ABOUT ME?

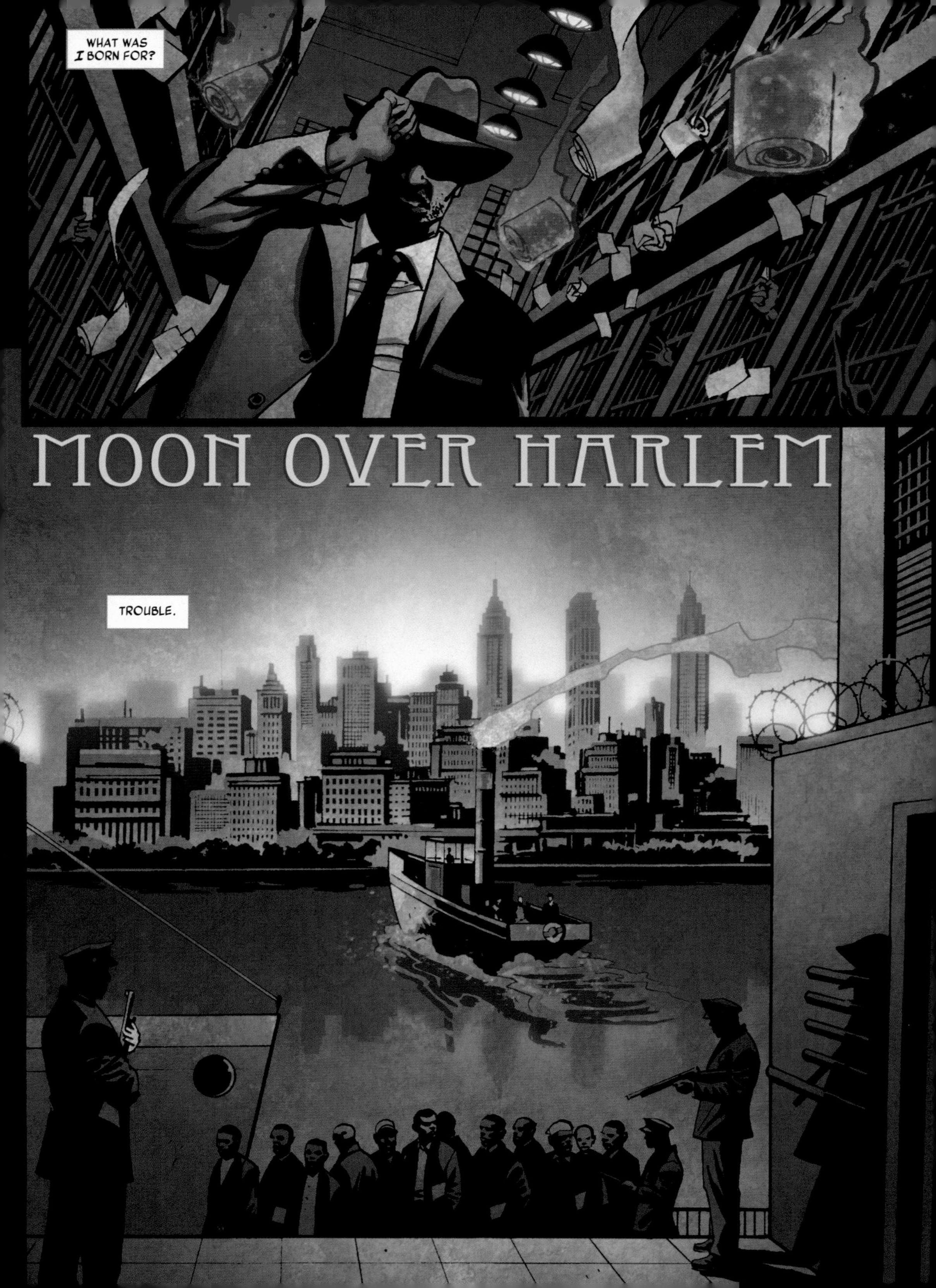
WHAT WAS I BORN FOR?
MOON OVER HARLEM
TROUBLE.

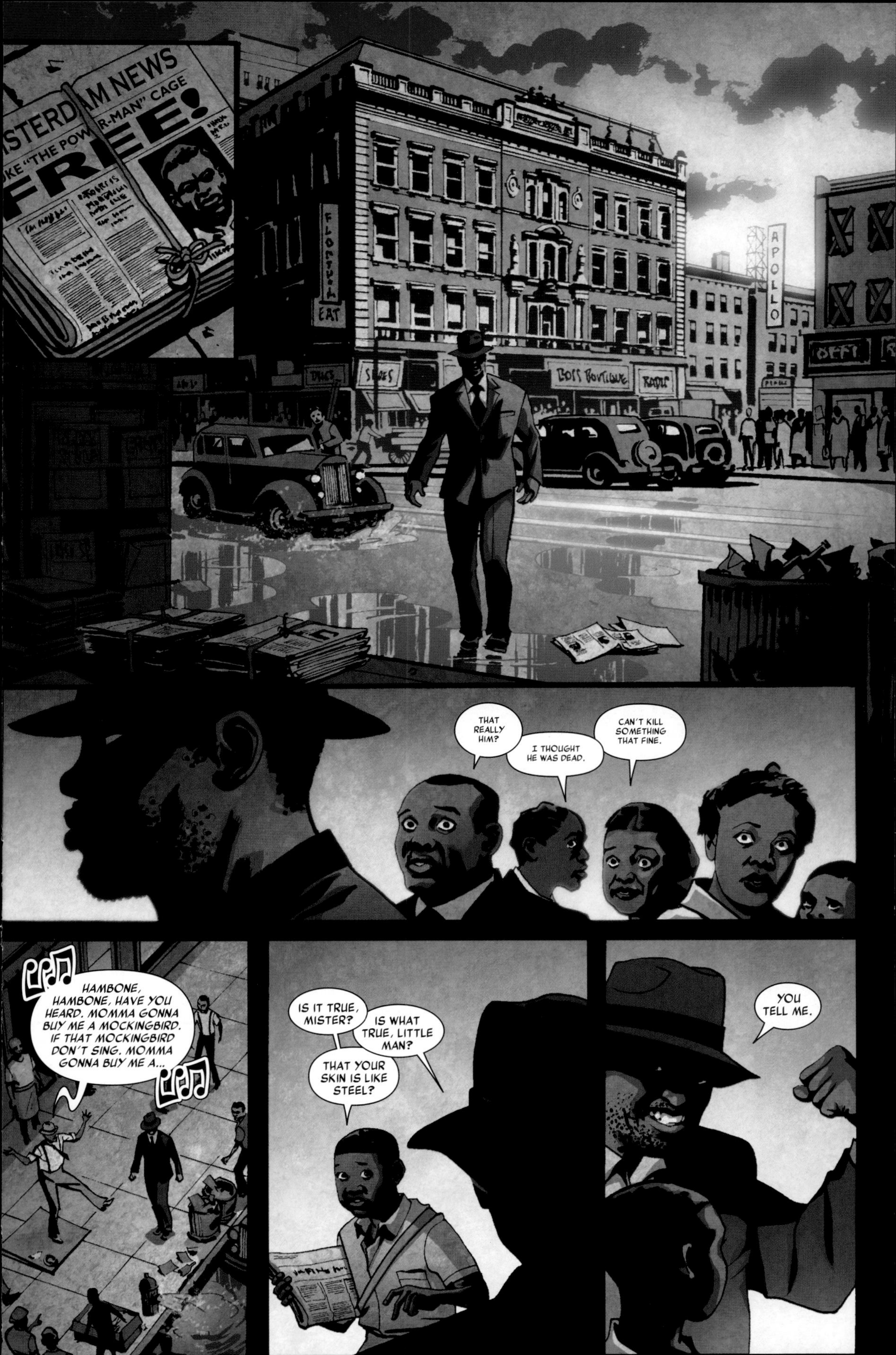
STERDAM NEWS
"THE POW R-MAN" CAGE
FREE!
APOLLO
EAT
THAT REALLY HIM?
I THOUGHT HE WAS DEAD.
CAN'T KILL SOMETHING THAT FINE.
HAMBONE, HAMBONE, HAVE YOU HEARD. MOMMA GONNA BUY ME A MOCKINGBIRD. IF THAT MOCKINGBIRD DON'T SING. MOMMA GONNA BUY ME A...
IS IT TRUE, MISTER?
IS WHAT TRUE, LITTLE MAN?
THAT YOUR SKIN IS LIKE STEEL?
YOU TELL ME.

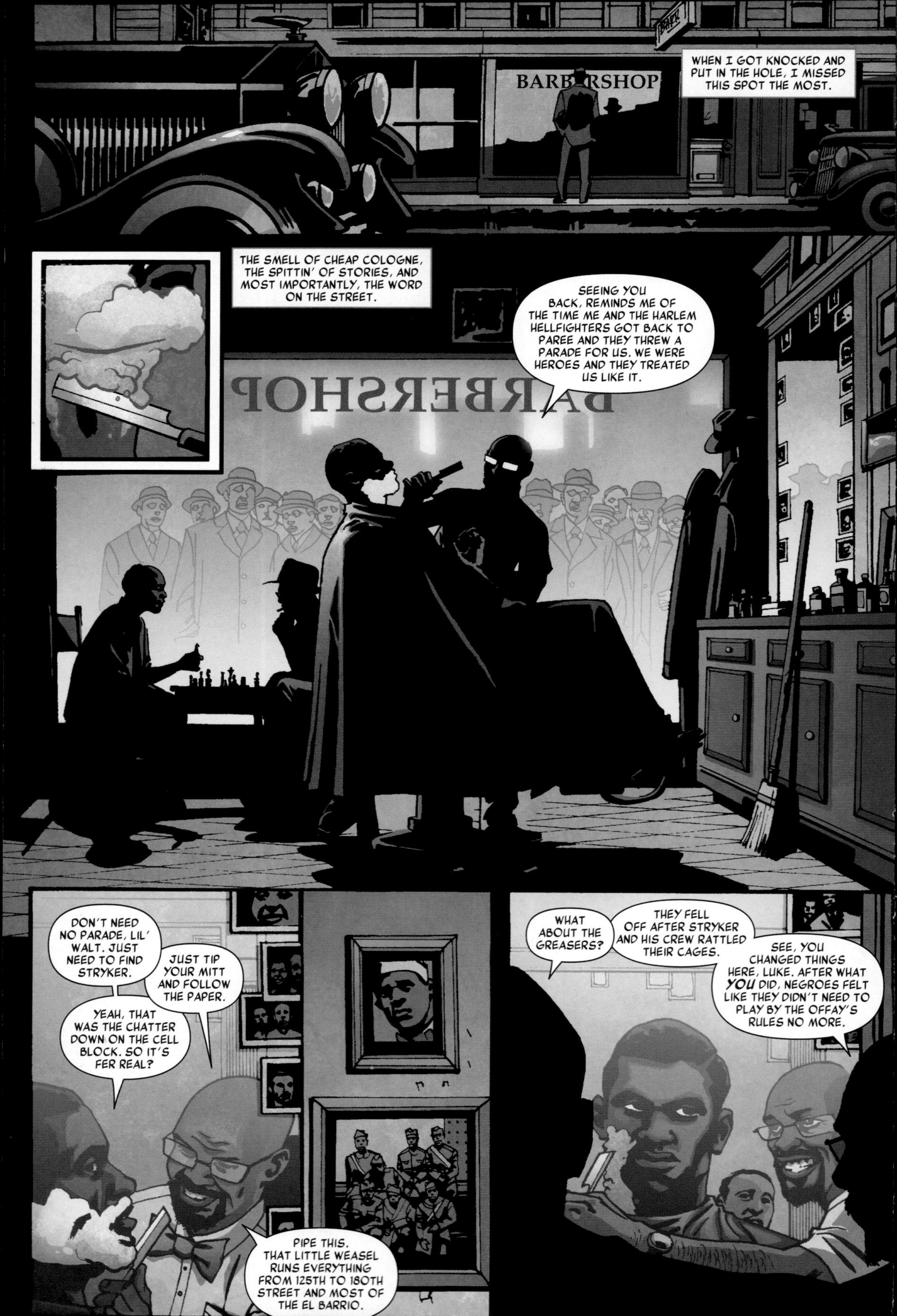
BARBERSHOP
WHEN I GOT KNOCKED AND PUT IN THE HOLE, I MISSED THIS SPOT THE MOST.
THE SMELL OF CHEAP COLOGNE, THE SPITTIN' OF STORIES, AND MOST IMPORTANTLY, THE WORD ON THE STREET.
SEEING YOU BACK, REMINDS ME OF THE TIME ME AND THE HARLEM HELLFIGHTERS GOT BACK TO PAREE AND THEY THREW A PARADE FOR US. WE WERE HEROES AND THEY TREATED US LIKE IT.
BARBERSHOP
DON'T NEED NO PARADE, LIL' WALT. JUST NEED TO FIND STRYKER.
JUST TIP YOUR MITT AND FOLLOW THE PAPER.
YEAH, THAT WAS THE CHATTER DOWN ON THE CELL BLOCK. SO IT'S FER REAL?
PIPE THIS. THAT LITTLE WEASEL RUNS EVERYTHING FROM 125TH TO 180TH STREET AND MOST OF THE EL BARRIO.
WHAT ABOUT THE GREASERS?
THEY FELL OFF AFTER STRYKER AND HIS CREW RATTLED THEIR CAGES.
SEE, YOU CHANGED THINGS HERE, LUKE. AFTER WHAT YOU DID, NEGROES FELT LIKE THEY DIDN'T NEED TO PLAY BY THE OFFAY'S RULES NO MORE.

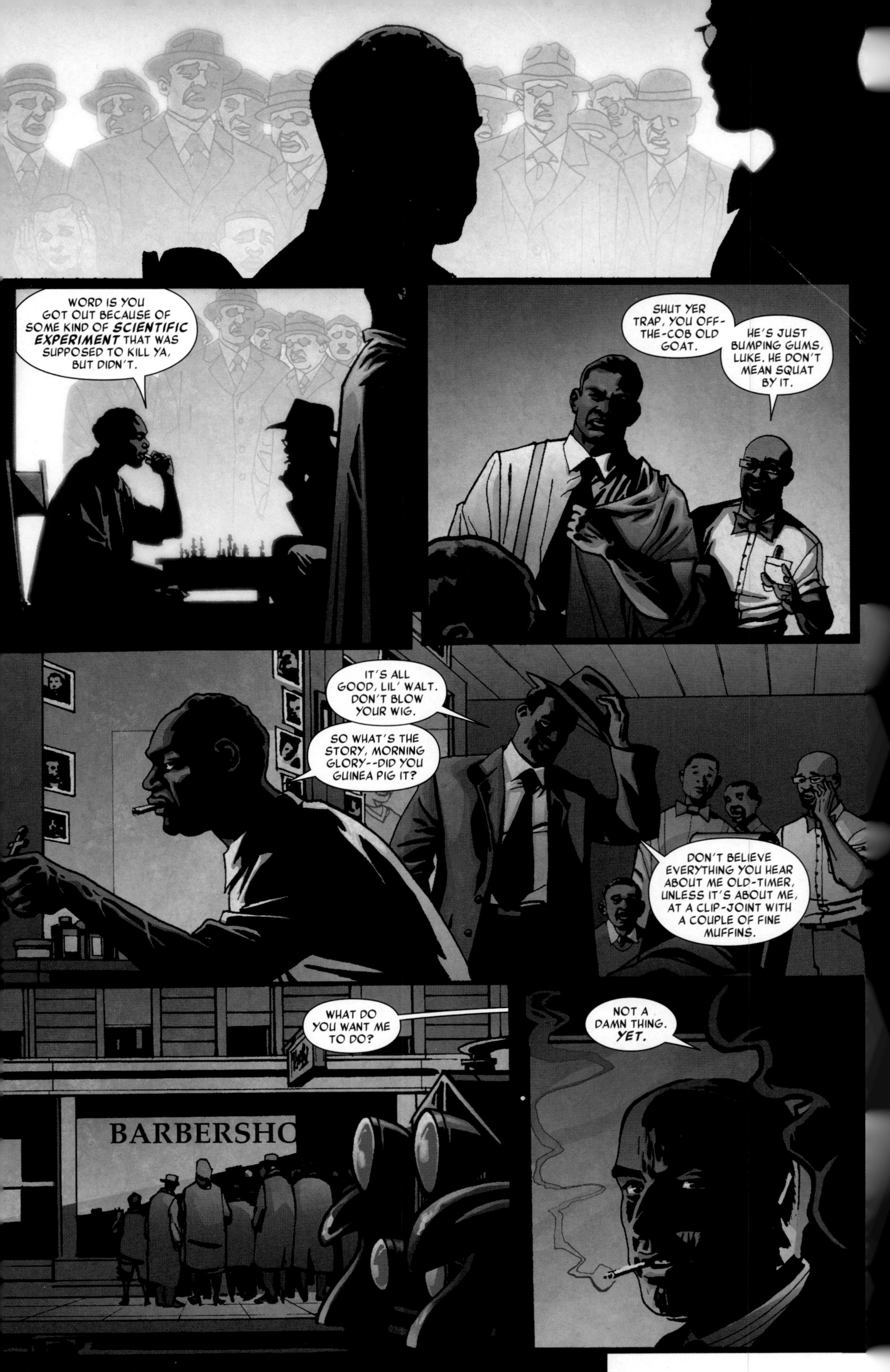
WORD IS YOU GOT OUT BECAUSE OF SOME KIND OF SCIENTIFIC EXPERIMENT THAT WAS SUPPOSED TO KILL YA, BUT DIDN'T.
SHUT YER TRAP, YOU OFF-THE-COB OLD GOAT.
HE'S JUST BUMPING GUMS, LUKE. HE DON'T MEAN SQUAT BY IT.
IT'S ALL GOOD, LIL' WALT. DON'T BLOW YOUR WIG.
SO WHAT'S THE STORY, MORNING GLORY--DID YOU GUINEA PIG IT?
DON'T BELIEVE EVERYTHING YOU HEAR ABOUT ME OLD-TIMER, UNLESS IT'S ABOUT ME, AT A CLIP-JOINT WITH A COUPLE OF FINE MUFFINS.
BARBERSHO
WHAT DO YOU WANT ME TO DO?
NOT A DAMN THING. YET.

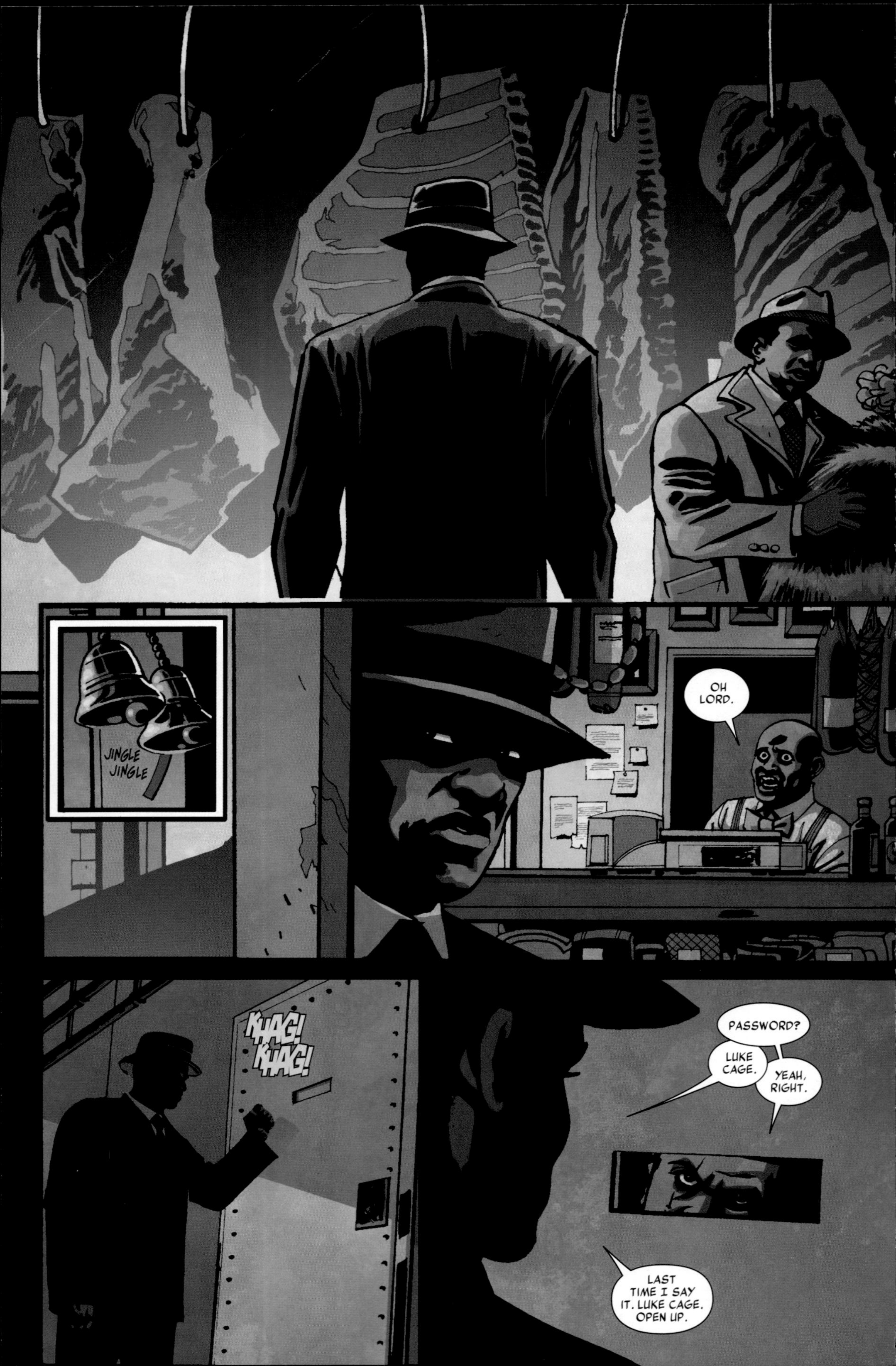
JINGLE JINGLE
OH LORD.
KHAG! KHAG!
PASSWORD?
LUKE CAGE.
YEAH, RIGHT.
LAST TIME I SAY IT. LUKE CAGE. OPEN UP.

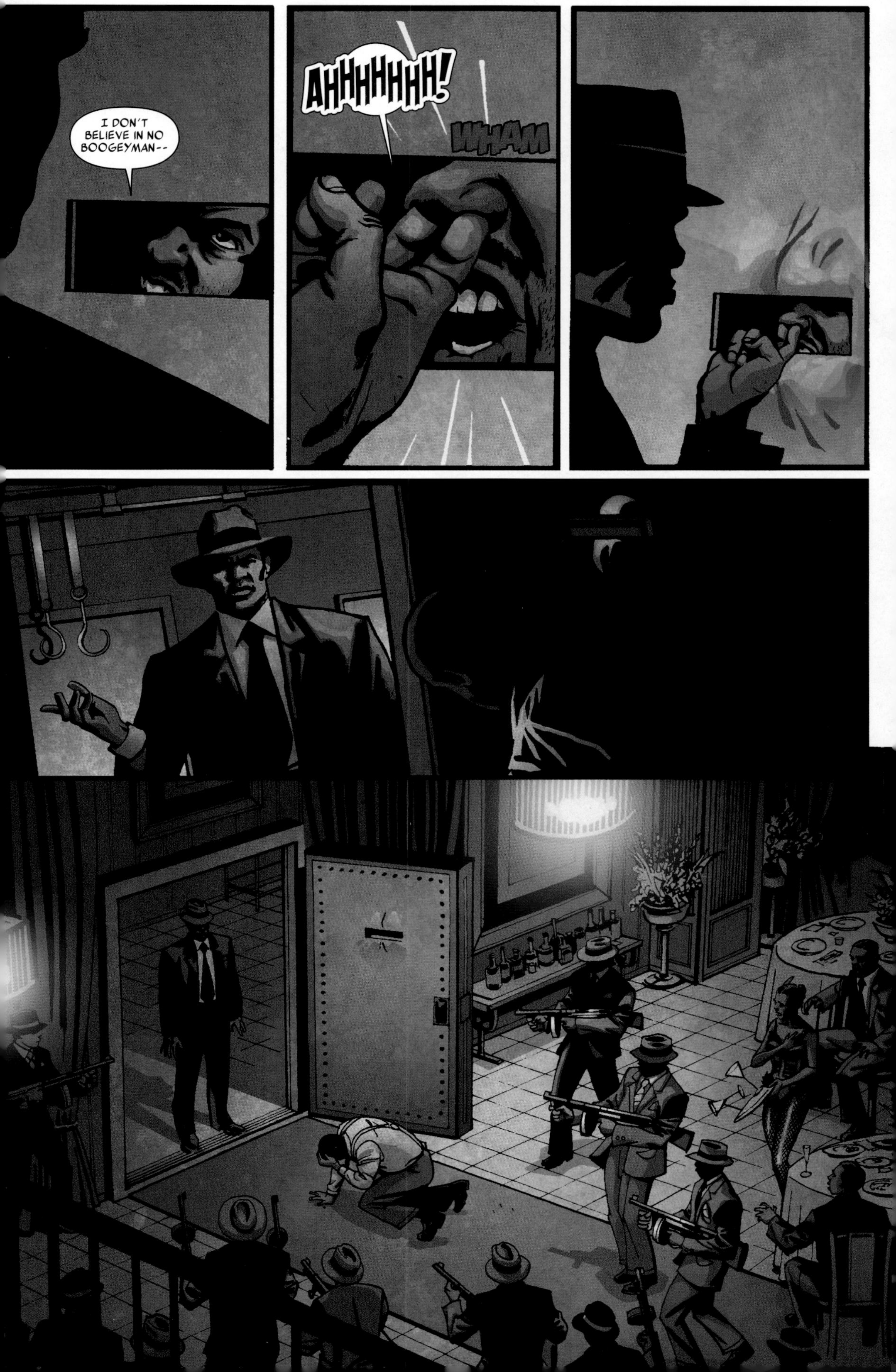

I DON'T BELIEVE IN NO BOOGEYMAN--
AHHHHHHH!
WHAM

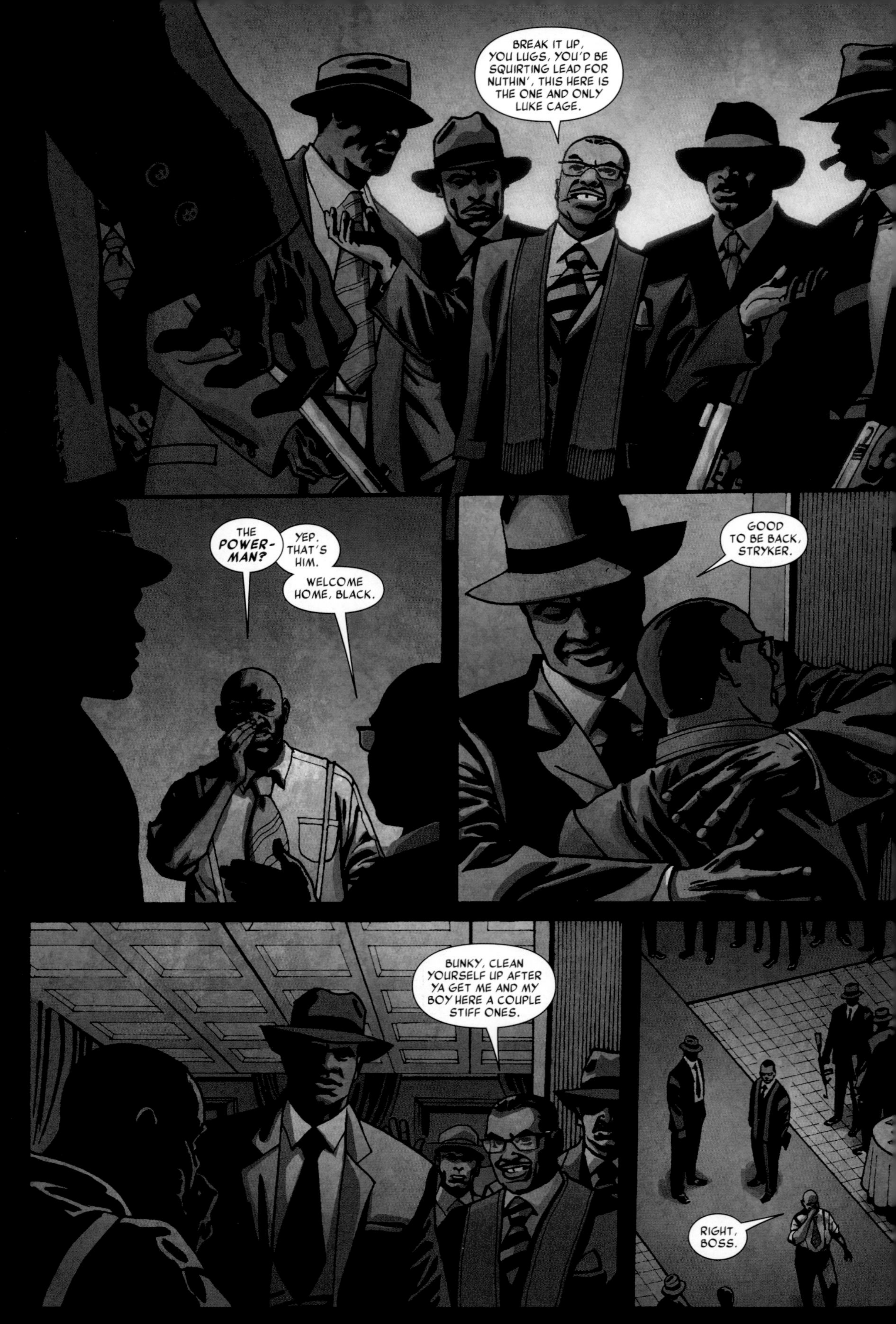
BREAK IT UP, YOU LUGS, YOU'D BE SQUIRTING LEAD FOR NUTHIN', THIS HERE IS THE ONE AND ONLY LUKE CAGE.
THE POWER-MAN?
YEP. THAT'S HIM.
WELCOME HOME, BLACK.
GOOD TO BE BACK, STRYKER.
BUNKY, CLEAN YOURSELF UP AFTER YA GET ME AND MY BOY HERE A COUPLE STIFF ONES.
RIGHT, BOSS.

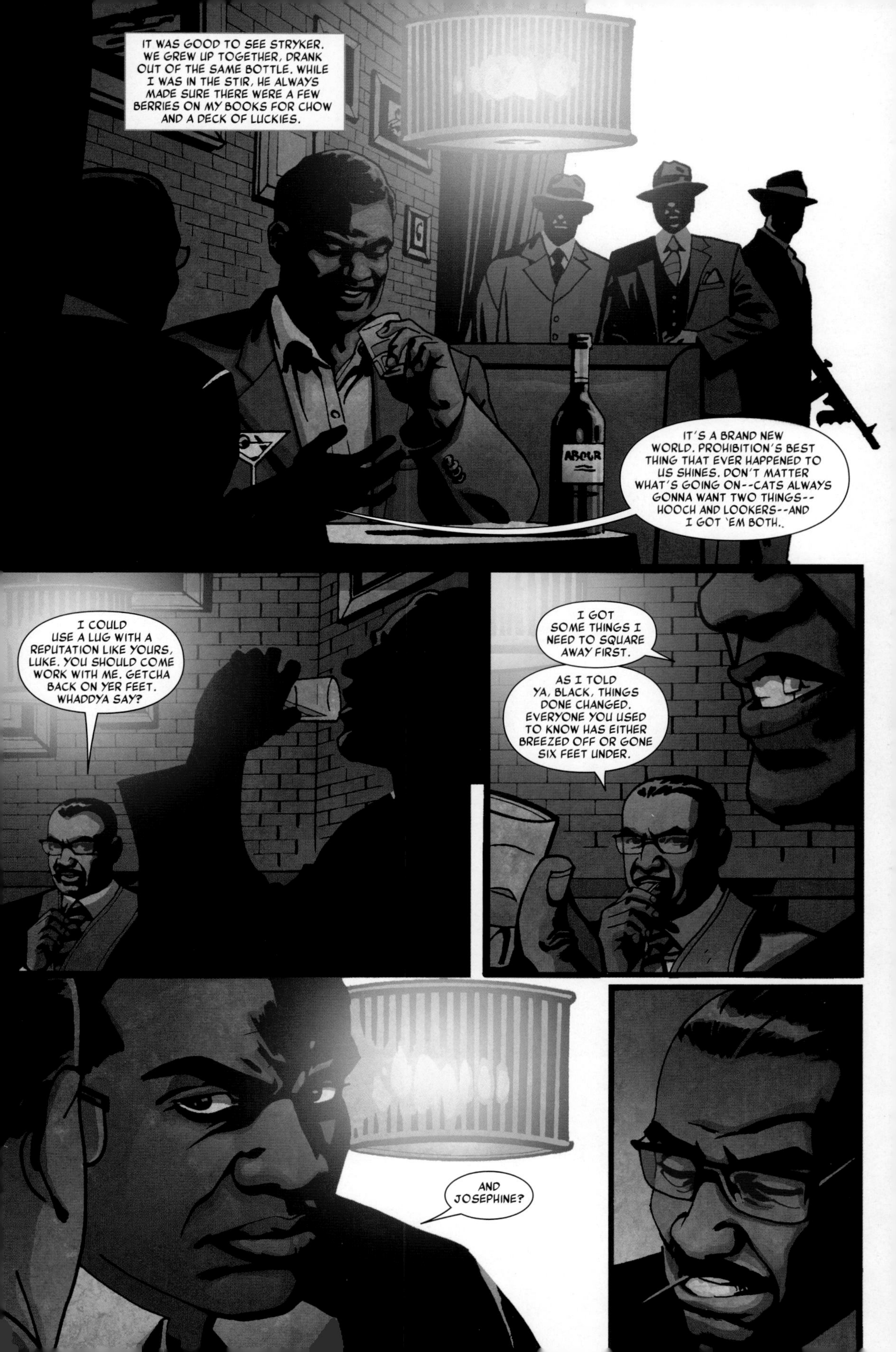
IT WAS GOOD TO SEE STRYKER. WE GREW UP TOGETHER, DRANK OUT OF THE SAME BOTTLE. WHILE I WAS IN THE STIR, HE ALWAYS MADE SURE THERE WERE A FEW BERRIES ON MY BOOKS FOR CHOW AND A DECK OF LUCKIES.
IT'S A BRAND NEW WORLD. PROHIBITION'S BEST THING THAT EVER HAPPENED TO US SHINES. DON'T MATTER WHAT'S GOING ON--CATS ALWAYS GONNA WANT TWO THINGS--HOOCH AND LOOKERS--AND I GOT 'EM BOTH.
I COULD USE A LUG WITH A REPUTATION LIKE YOURS, LUKE. YOU SHOULD COME WORK WITH ME. GETCHA BACK ON YER FEET. WHADDYA SAY?
I GOT SOME THINGS I NEED TO SQUARE AWAY FIRST.
AS I TOLD YA, BLACK, THINGS DONE CHANGED. EVERYONE YOU USED TO KNOW HAS EITHER BREEZED OFF OR GONE SIX FEET UNDER.
AND JOSEPHINE?

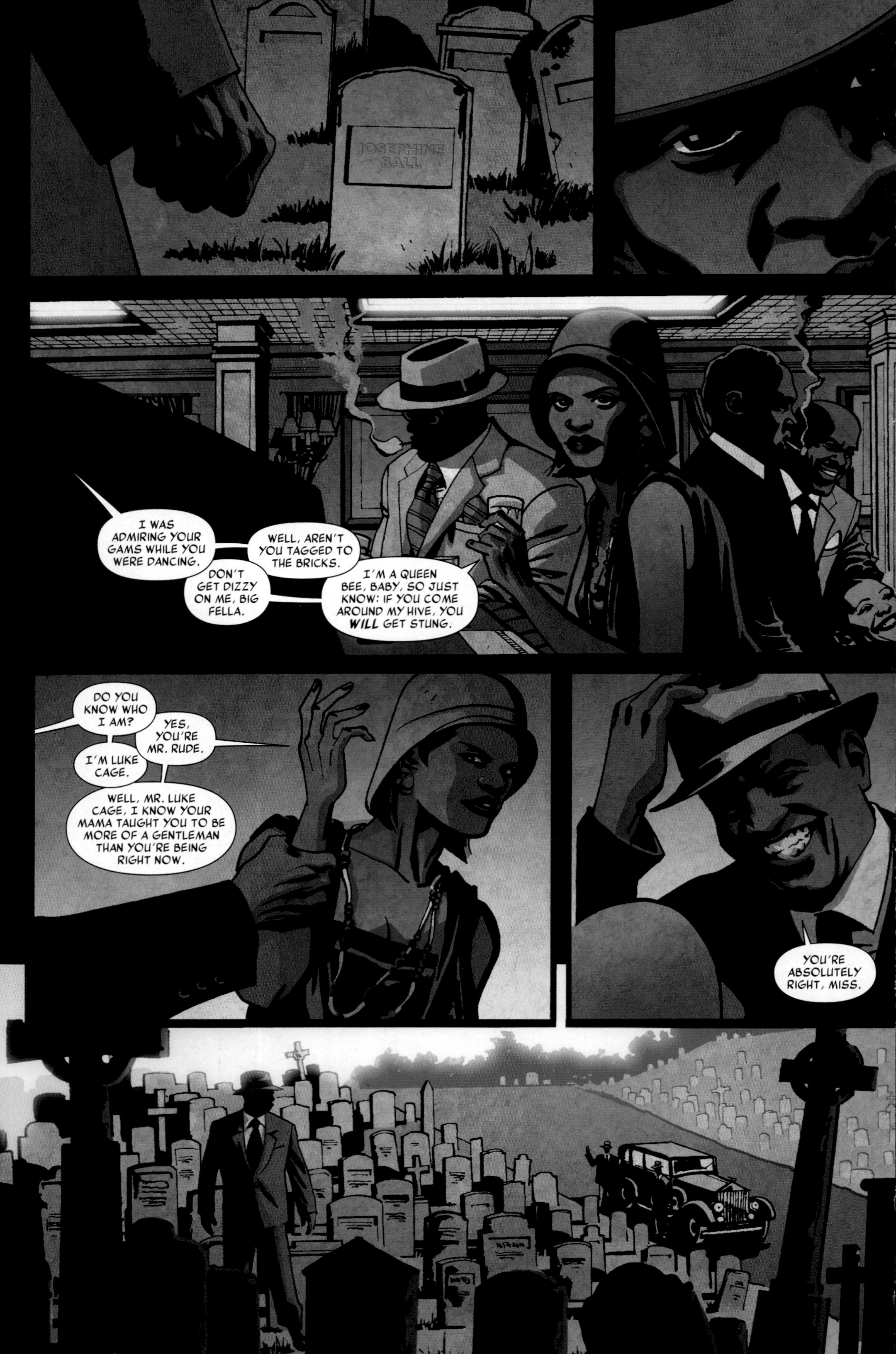
JOSEPHINE BALL
I WAS ADMIRING YOUR GAMS WHILE YOU WERE DANCING.
WELL, AREN'T YOU TAGGED TO THE BRICKS.
DON'T GET DIZZY ON ME, BIG FELLA.
I'M A QUEEN BEE, BABY, SO JUST KNOW: IF YOU COME AROUND MY HIVE, YOU WILL GET STUNG.
DO YOU KNOW WHO I AM?
YES, YOU'RE MR. RUDE.
I'M LUKE CAGE.
WELL, MR. LUKE CAGE, I KNOW YOUR MAMA TAUGHT YOU TO BE MORE OF A GENTLEMAN THAN YOU'RE BEING RIGHT NOW.
YOU'RE ABSOLUTELY RIGHT, MISS.

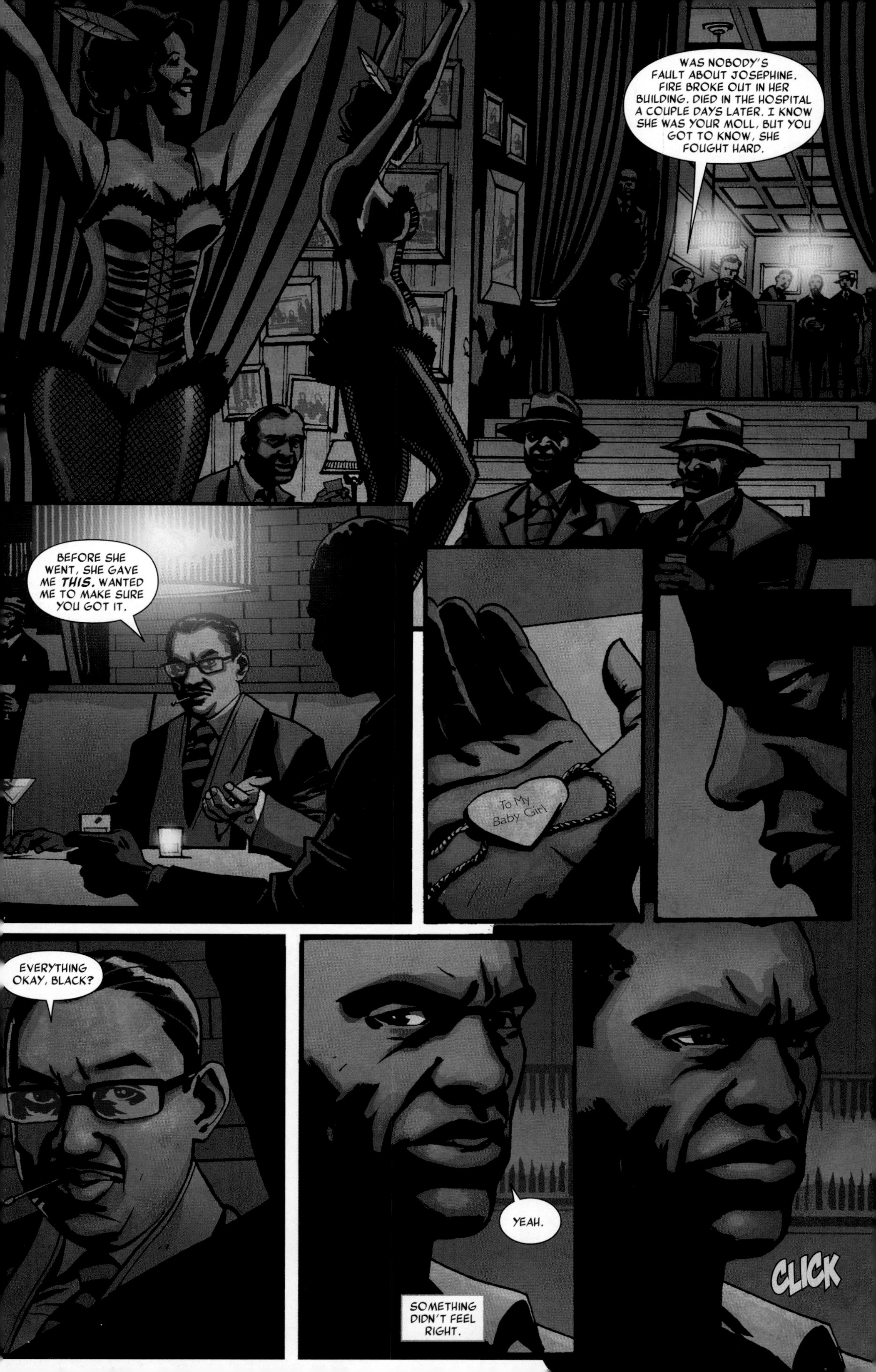
WAS NOBODY'S FAULT ABOUT JOSEPHINE. FIRE BROKE OUT IN HER BUILDING. DIED IN THE HOSPITAL A COUPLE DAYS LATER. I KNOW SHE WAS YOUR MOLL, BUT YOU GOT TO KNOW, SHE FOUGHT HARD.
BEFORE SHE WENT, SHE GAVE ME *THIS.* WANTED ME TO MAKE SURE YOU GOT IT.
To My Baby Girl
EVERYTHING OKAY, BLACK?
YEAH.
SOMETHING DIDN'T FEEL RIGHT.
CLICK

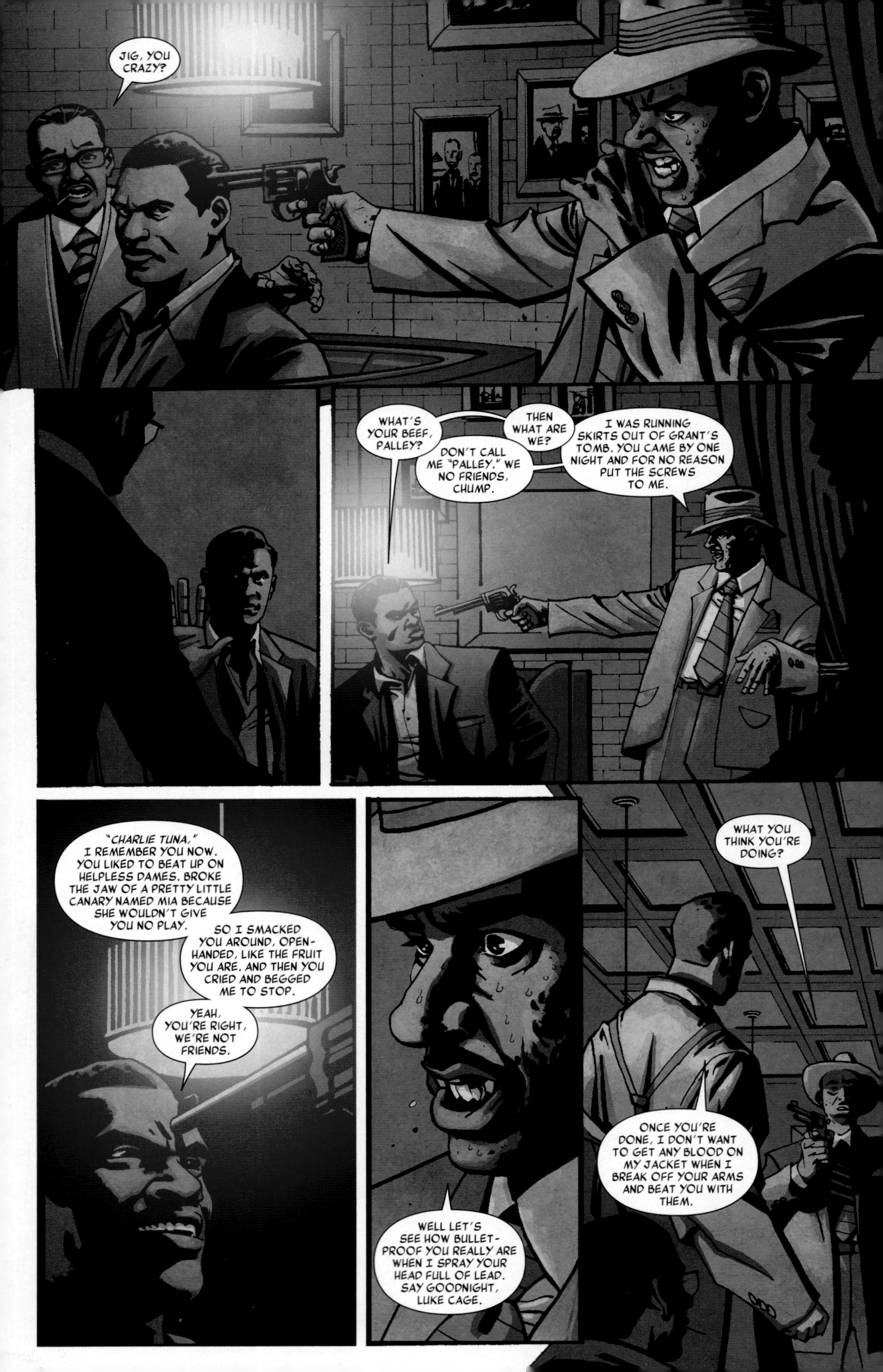
JIG, YOU CRAZY?
WHAT'S YOUR BEEF, PALLEY?
DON'T CALL ME "PALLEY." WE NO FRIENDS, CHUMP.
THEN WHAT ARE WE?
I WAS RUNNING SKIRTS OUT OF GRANT'S TOMB. YOU CAME BY ONE NIGHT AND FOR NO REASON PUT THE SCREWS TO ME.
"CHARLIE TUNA," I REMEMBER YOU NOW. YOU LIKED TO BEAT UP ON HELPLESS DAMES. BROKE THE JAW OF A PRETTY LITTLE CANARY NAMED MIA BECAUSE SHE WOULDN'T GIVE YOU NO PLAY.
SO I SMACKED YOU AROUND, OPEN-HANDED, LIKE THE FRUIT YOU ARE. AND THEN YOU CRIED AND BEGGED ME TO STOP.
YEAH, YOU'RE RIGHT, WE'RE NOT FRIENDS.
WHAT YOU THINK YOU'RE DOING?
ONCE YOU'RE DONE, I DON'T WANT TO GET ANY BLOOD ON MY JACKET WHEN I BREAK OFF YOUR ARMS AND BEAT YOU WITH THEM.
WELL LET'S SEE HOW BULLET-PROOF YOU REALLY ARE WHEN I SPRAY YOUR HEAD FULL OF LEAD. SAY GOODNIGHT, LUKE CAGE.

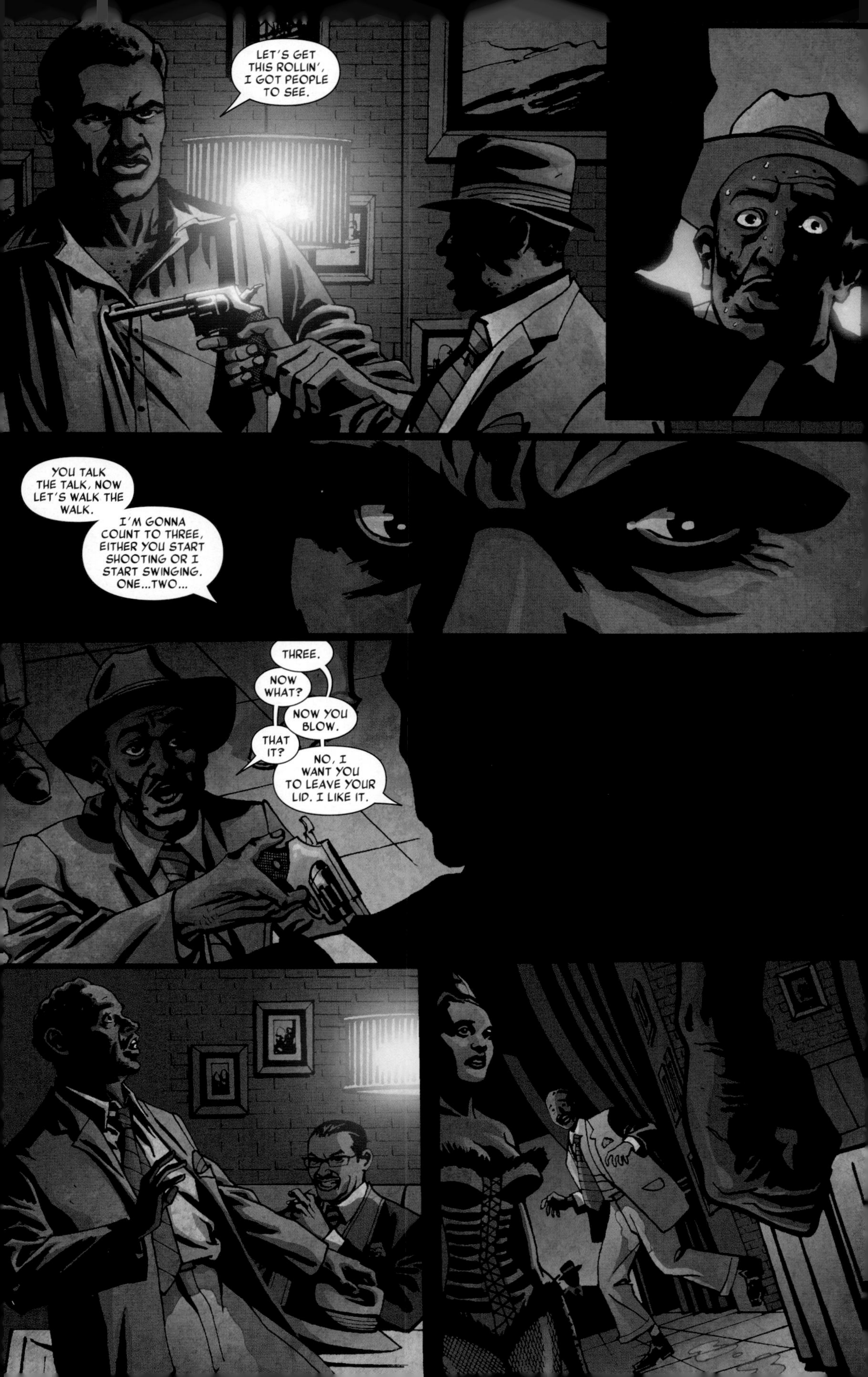
LET'S GET THIS ROLLIN', I GOT PEOPLE TO SEE.
YOU TALK THE TALK, NOW LET'S WALK THE WALK.
I'M GONNA COUNT TO THREE, EITHER YOU START SHOOTING OR I START SWINGING. ONE...TWO...
THREE.
NOW WHAT?
NOW YOU BLOW.
THAT IT?
NO, I WANT YOU TO LEAVE YOUR LID. I LIKE IT.

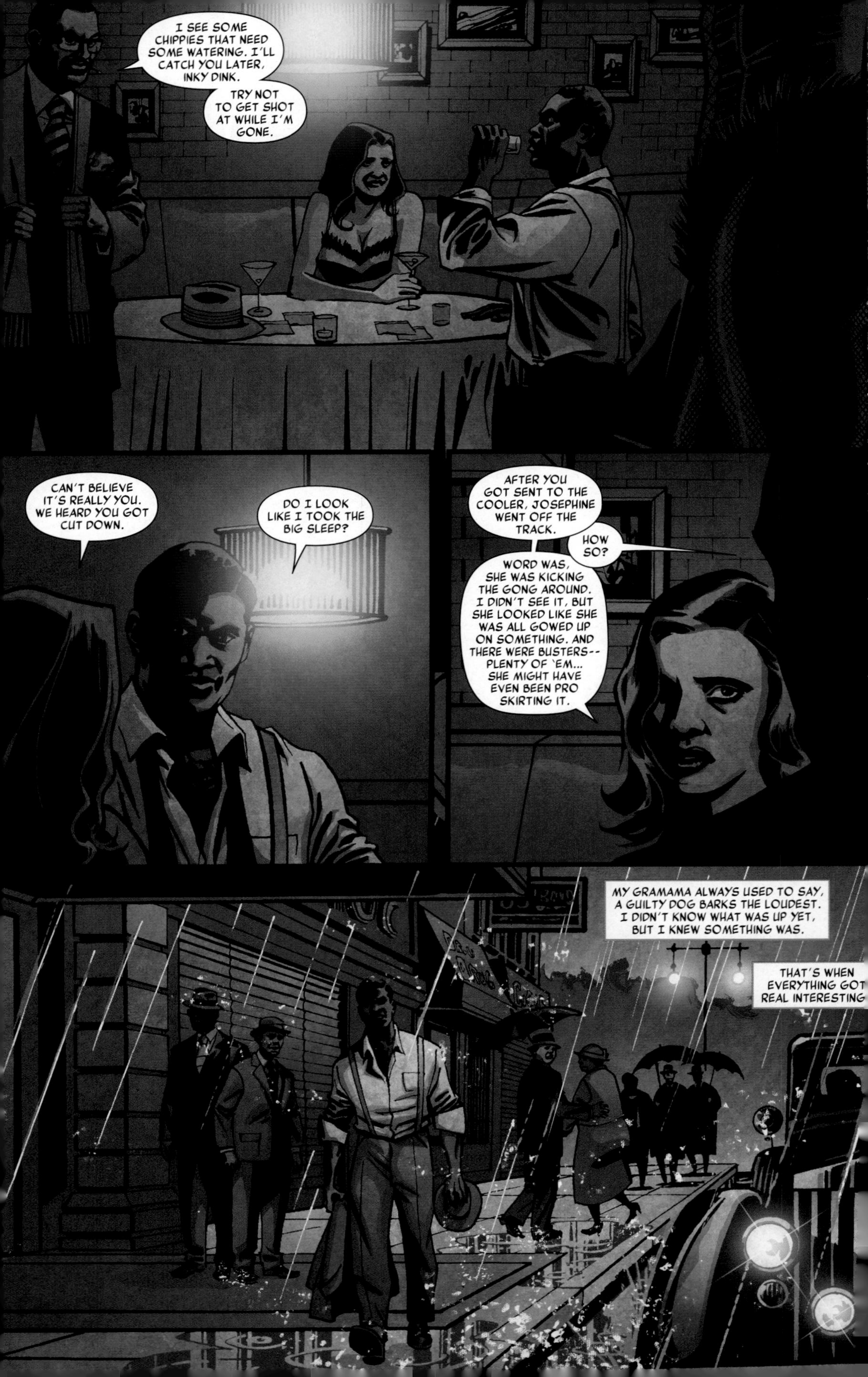
I SEE SOME CHIPPIES THAT NEED SOME WATERING. I'LL CATCH YOU LATER, INKY DINK.
TRY NOT TO GET SHOT AT WHILE I'M GONE.
CAN'T BELIEVE IT'S REALLY YOU. WE HEARD YOU GOT CUT DOWN.
DO I LOOK LIKE I TOOK THE BIG SLEEP?
AFTER YOU GOT SENT TO THE COOLER, JOSEPHINE WENT OFF THE TRACK.
HOW SO?
WORD WAS, SHE WAS KICKING THE GONG AROUND. I DIDN'T SEE IT, BUT SHE LOOKED LIKE SHE WAS ALL GOWED UP ON SOMETHING. AND THERE WERE BUSTERS-- PLENTY OF 'EM... SHE MIGHT HAVE EVEN BEEN PRO SKIRTING IT.
MY GRAMAMA ALWAYS USED TO SAY, A GUILTY DOG BARKS THE LOUDEST. I DIDN'T KNOW WHAT WAS UP YET, BUT I KNEW SOMETHING WAS.
THAT'S WHEN EVERYTHING GOT REAL INTERESTING

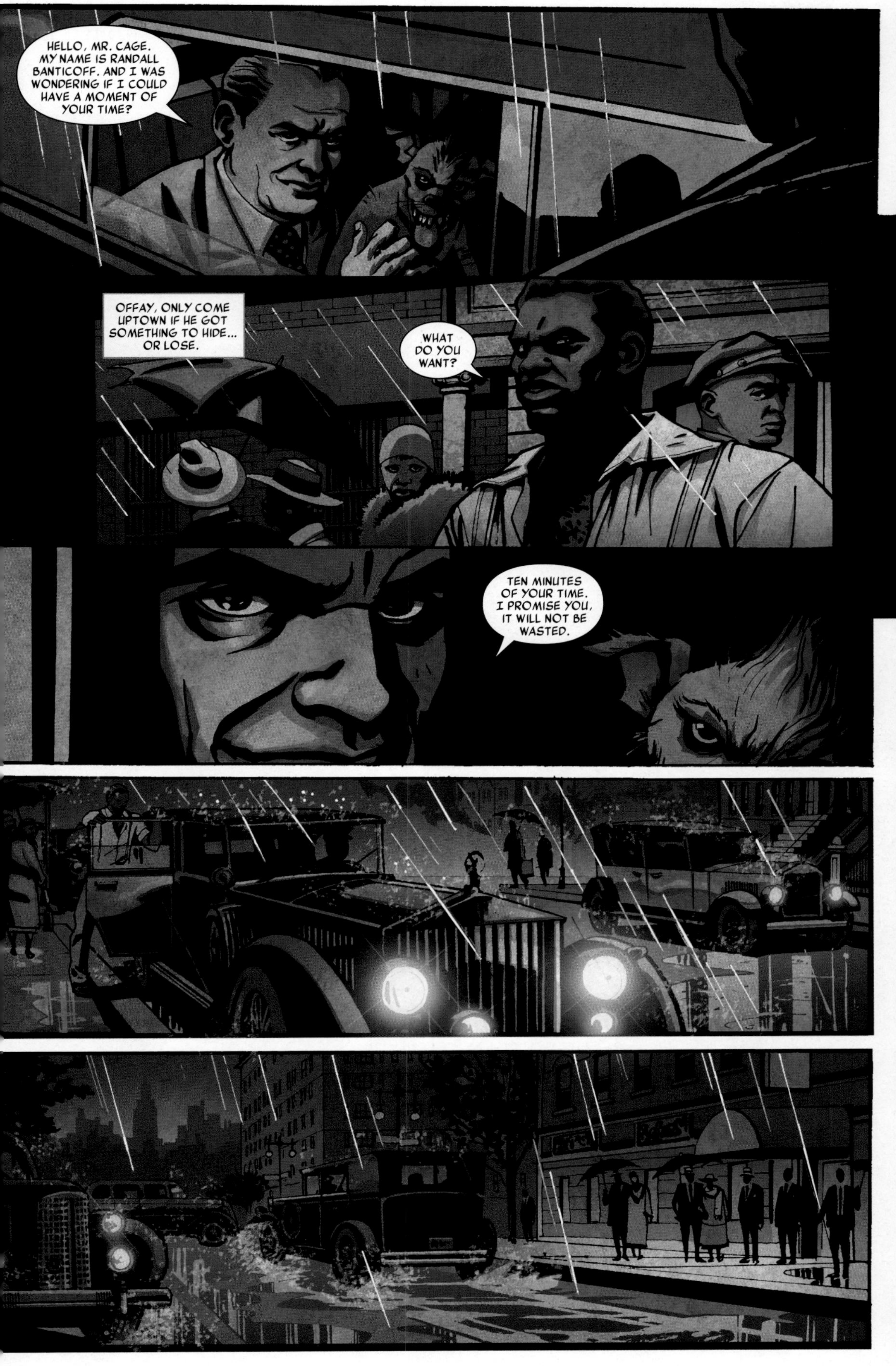
HELLO, MR. CAGE. MY NAME IS RANDALL BANTICOFF. AND I WAS WONDERING IF I COULD HAVE A MOMENT OF YOUR TIME?
OFFAY, ONLY COME UPTOWN IF HE GOT SOMETHING TO HIDE... OR LOSE.
WHAT DO YOU WANT?
TEN MINUTES OF YOUR TIME. I PROMISE YOU, IT WILL NOT BE WASTED.

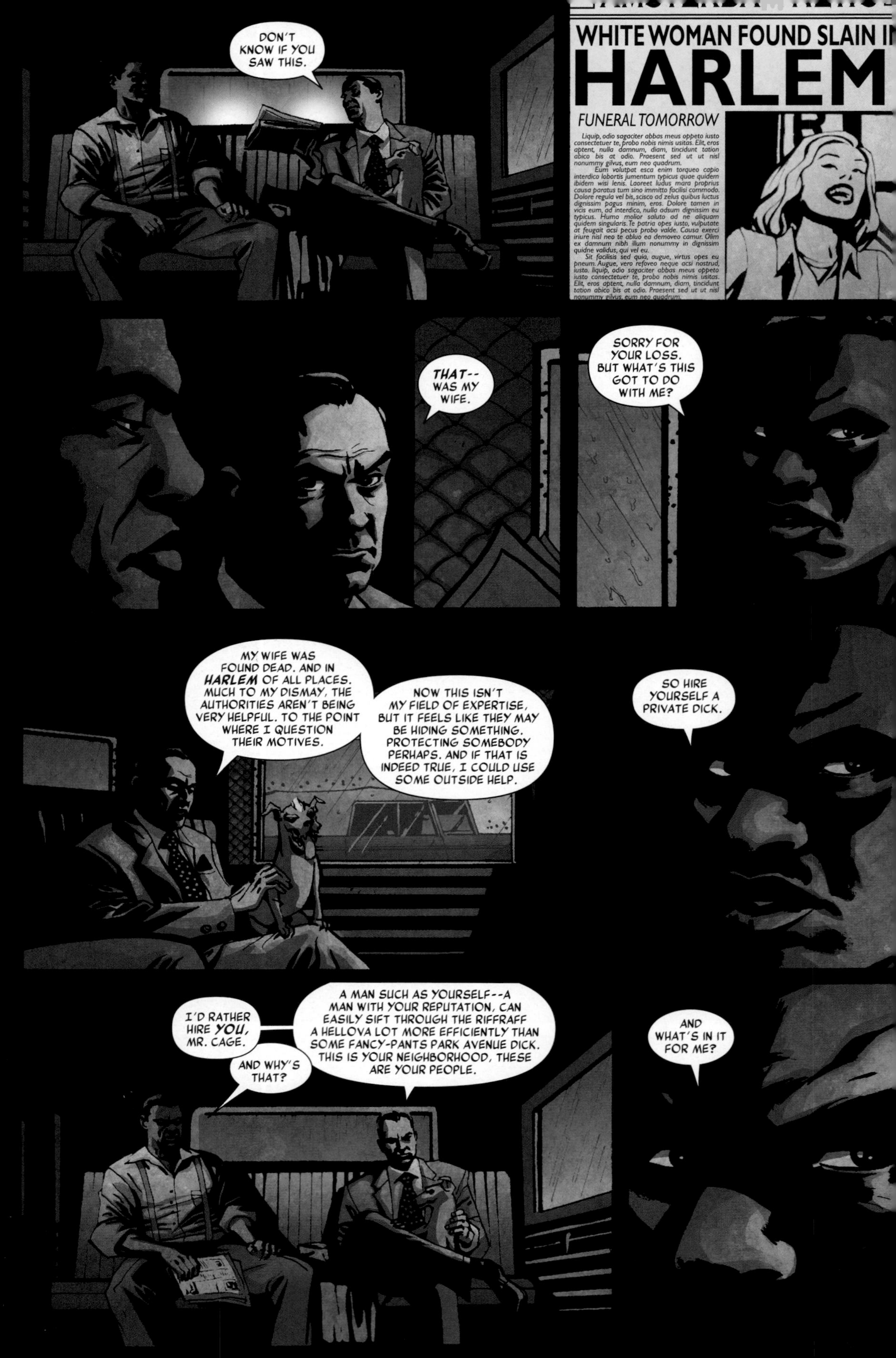
DON'T KNOW IF YOU SAW THIS.
WHITE WOMAN FOUND SLAIN IN
HARLEM
FUNERAL TOMORROW
THAT-- WAS MY WIFE.
SORRY FOR YOUR LOSS. BUT WHAT'S THIS GOT TO DO WITH ME?
MY WIFE WAS FOUND DEAD. AND IN HARLEM OF ALL PLACES. MUCH TO MY DISMAY, THE AUTHORITIES AREN'T BEING VERY HELPFUL. TO THE POINT WHERE I QUESTION THEIR MOTIVES.
NOW THIS ISN'T MY FIELD OF EXPERTISE, BUT IT FEELS LIKE THEY MAY BE HIDING SOMETHING. PROTECTING SOMEBODY PERHAPS. AND IF THAT IS INDEED TRUE, I COULD USE SOME OUTSIDE HELP.
SO HIRE YOURSELF A PRIVATE DICK.
I'D RATHER HIRE YOU, MR. CAGE.
AND WHY'S THAT?
A MAN SUCH AS YOURSELF--A MAN WITH YOUR REPUTATION, CAN EASILY SIFT THROUGH THE RIFFRAFF A HELLOVA LOT MORE EFFICIENTLY THAN SOME FANCY-PANTS PARK AVENUE DICK. THIS IS YOUR NEIGHBORHOOD, THESE ARE YOUR PEOPLE.
AND WHAT'S IN IT FOR ME?

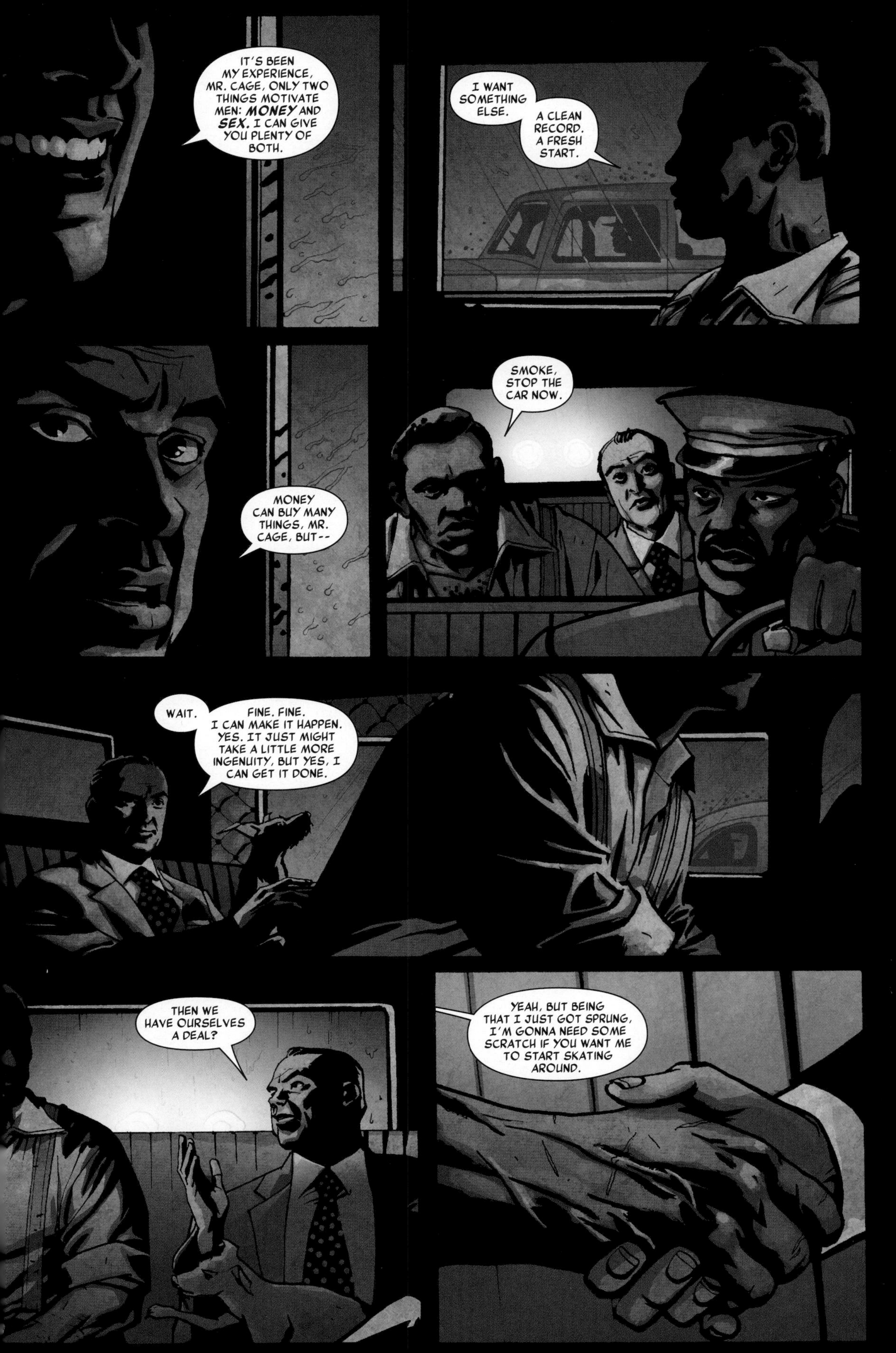
IT'S BEEN MY EXPERIENCE, MR. CAGE, ONLY TWO THINGS MOTIVATE MEN: **MONEY** AND **SEX.** I CAN GIVE YOU PLENTY OF BOTH.
I WANT SOMETHING ELSE.
A CLEAN RECORD. A FRESH START.
MONEY CAN BUY MANY THINGS, MR. CAGE, BUT--
SMOKE, STOP THE CAR NOW.
WAIT.
FINE. FINE. I CAN MAKE IT HAPPEN. YES. IT JUST MIGHT TAKE A LITTLE MORE INGENUITY, BUT YES, I CAN GET IT DONE.
THEN WE HAVE OURSELVES A DEAL?
YEAH, BUT BEING THAT I JUST GOT SPRUNG, I'M GONNA NEED SOME SCRATCH IF YOU WANT ME TO START SKATING AROUND.

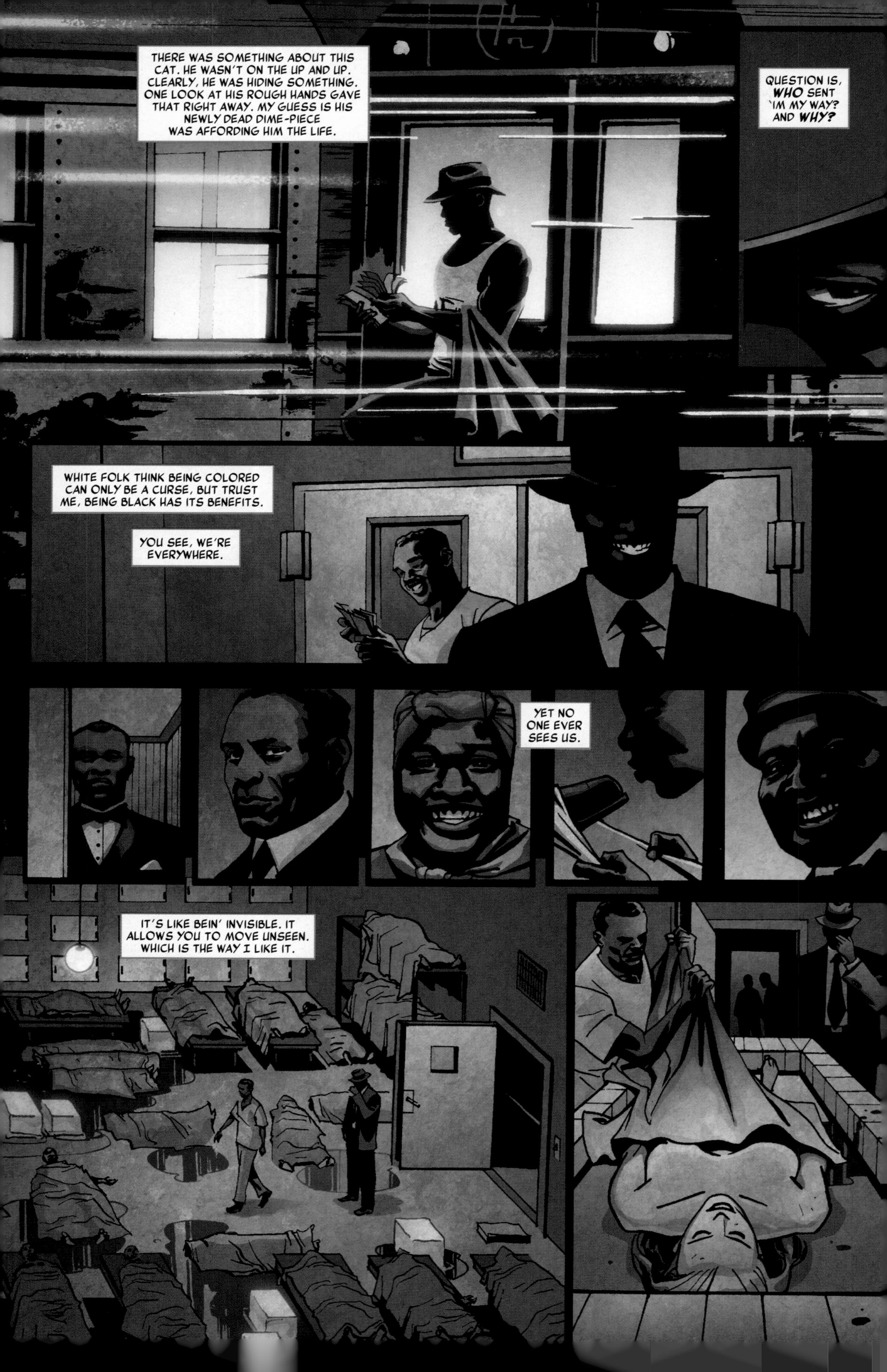
THERE WAS SOMETHING ABOUT THIS CAT. HE WASN'T ON THE UP AND UP. CLEARLY, HE WAS HIDING SOMETHING. ONE LOOK AT HIS ROUGH HANDS GAVE THAT RIGHT AWAY. MY GUESS IS HIS NEWLY DEAD DIME-PIECE WAS AFFORDING HIM THE LIFE.
QUESTION IS, WHO SENT 'IM MY WAY? AND WHY?
WHITE FOLK THINK BEING COLORED CAN ONLY BE A CURSE, BUT TRUST ME, BEING BLACK HAS ITS BENEFITS.
YOU SEE, WE'RE EVERYWHERE.
YET NO ONE EVER SEES US.
IT'S LIKE BEIN' INVISIBLE. IT ALLOWS YOU TO MOVE UNSEEN. WHICH IS THE WAY I LIKE IT.

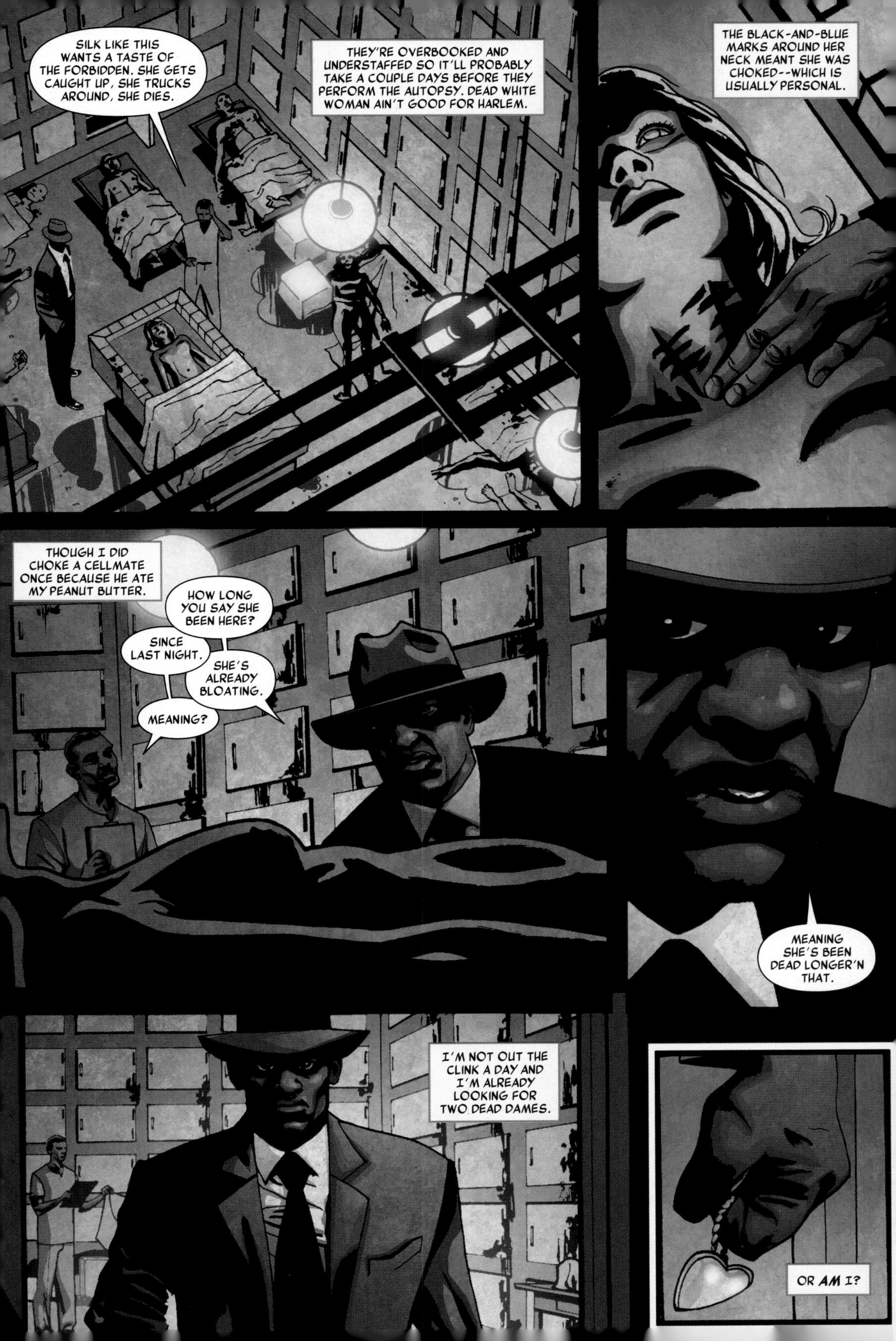
SILK LIKE THIS WANTS A TASTE OF THE FORBIDDEN. SHE GETS CAUGHT UP, SHE TRUCKS AROUND, SHE DIES.
THEY'RE OVERBOOKED AND UNDERSTAFFED SO IT'LL PROBABLY TAKE A COUPLE DAYS BEFORE THEY PERFORM THE AUTOPSY. DEAD WHITE WOMAN AIN'T GOOD FOR HARLEM.
THE BLACK-AND-BLUE MARKS AROUND HER NECK MEANT SHE WAS CHOKED--WHICH IS USUALLY PERSONAL.
THOUGH I DID CHOKE A CELLMATE ONCE BECAUSE HE ATE MY PEANUT BUTTER.
HOW LONG YOU SAY SHE BEEN HERE?
SINCE LAST NIGHT.
SHE'S ALREADY BLOATING.
MEANING?
MEANING SHE'S BEEN DEAD LONGER'N THAT.
I'M NOT OUT THE CLINK A DAY AND I'M ALREADY LOOKING FOR TWO DEAD DAMES.
OR ***AM*** I?

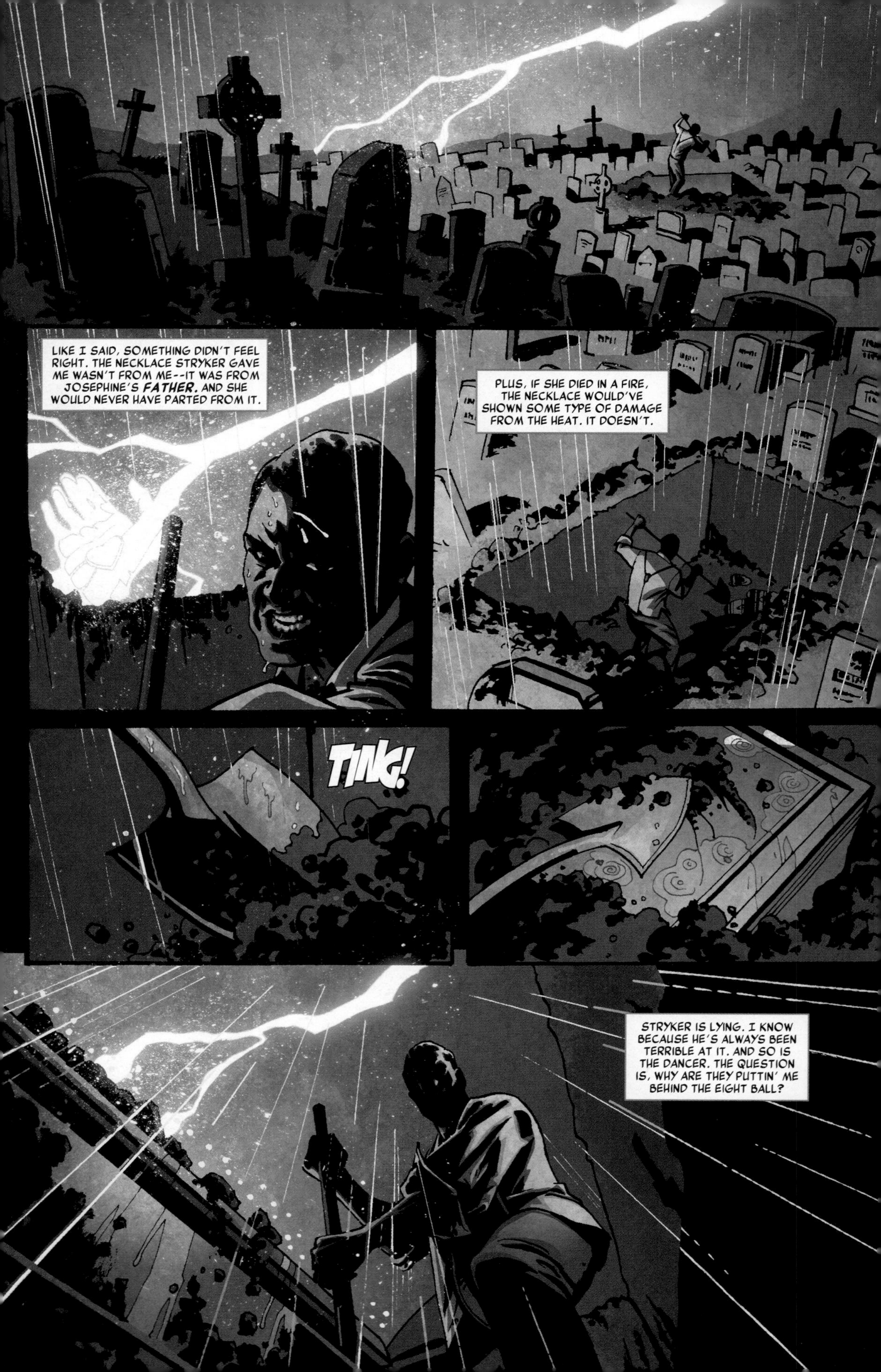
LIKE I SAID, SOMETHING DIDN'T FEEL RIGHT. THE NECKLACE STRYKER GAVE ME WASN'T FROM ME--IT WAS FROM JOSEPHINE'S FATHER. AND SHE WOULD NEVER HAVE PARTED FROM IT.
PLUS, IF SHE DIED IN A FIRE, THE NECKLACE WOULD'VE SHOWN SOME TYPE OF DAMAGE FROM THE HEAT. IT DOESN'T.
TING!
STRYKER IS LYING. I KNOW BECAUSE HE'S ALWAYS BEEN TERRIBLE AT IT. AND SO IS THE DANCER. THE QUESTION IS, WHY ARE THEY PUTTIN' ME BEHIND THE EIGHT BALL?

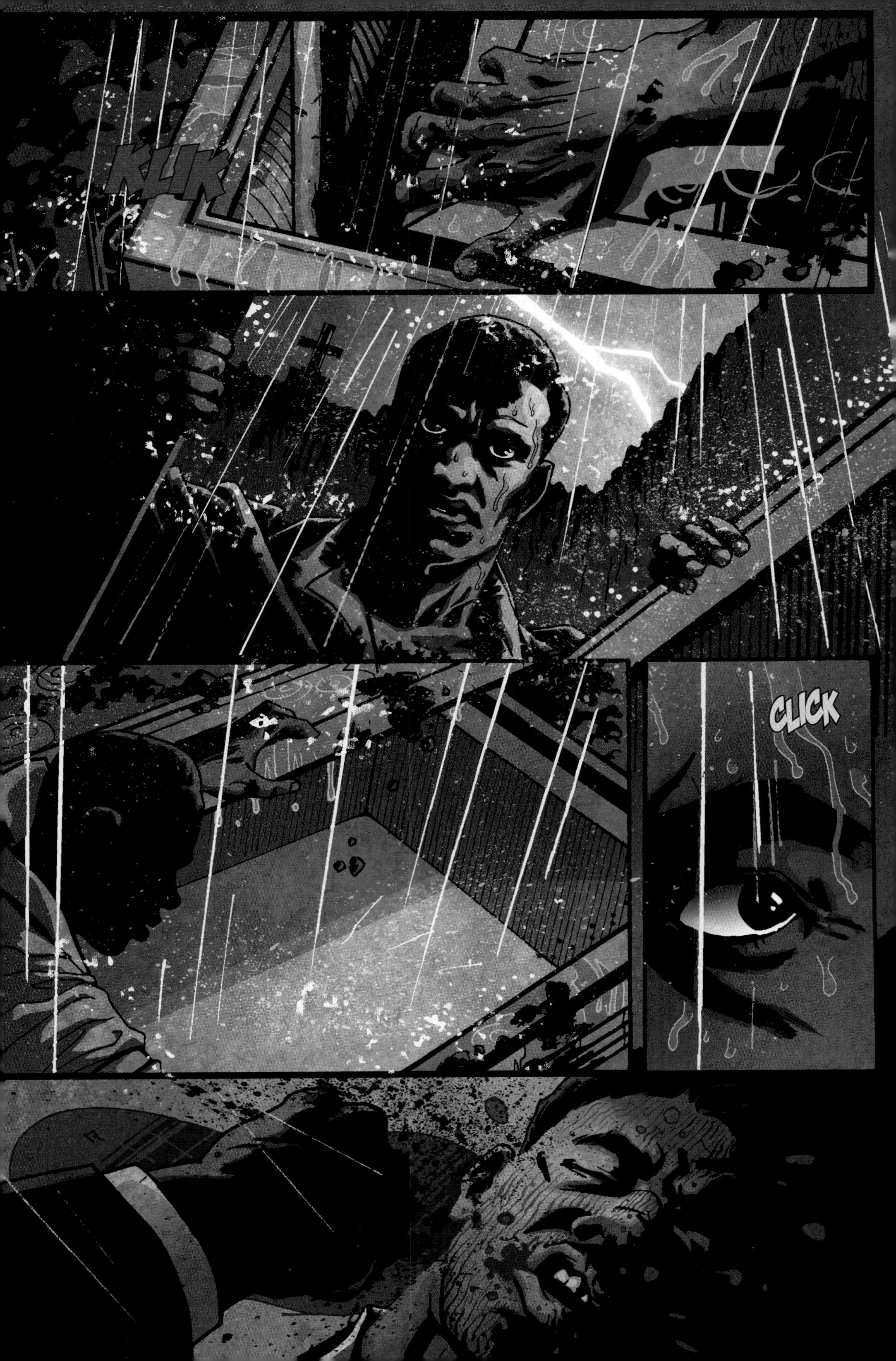
KLIK
CLICK

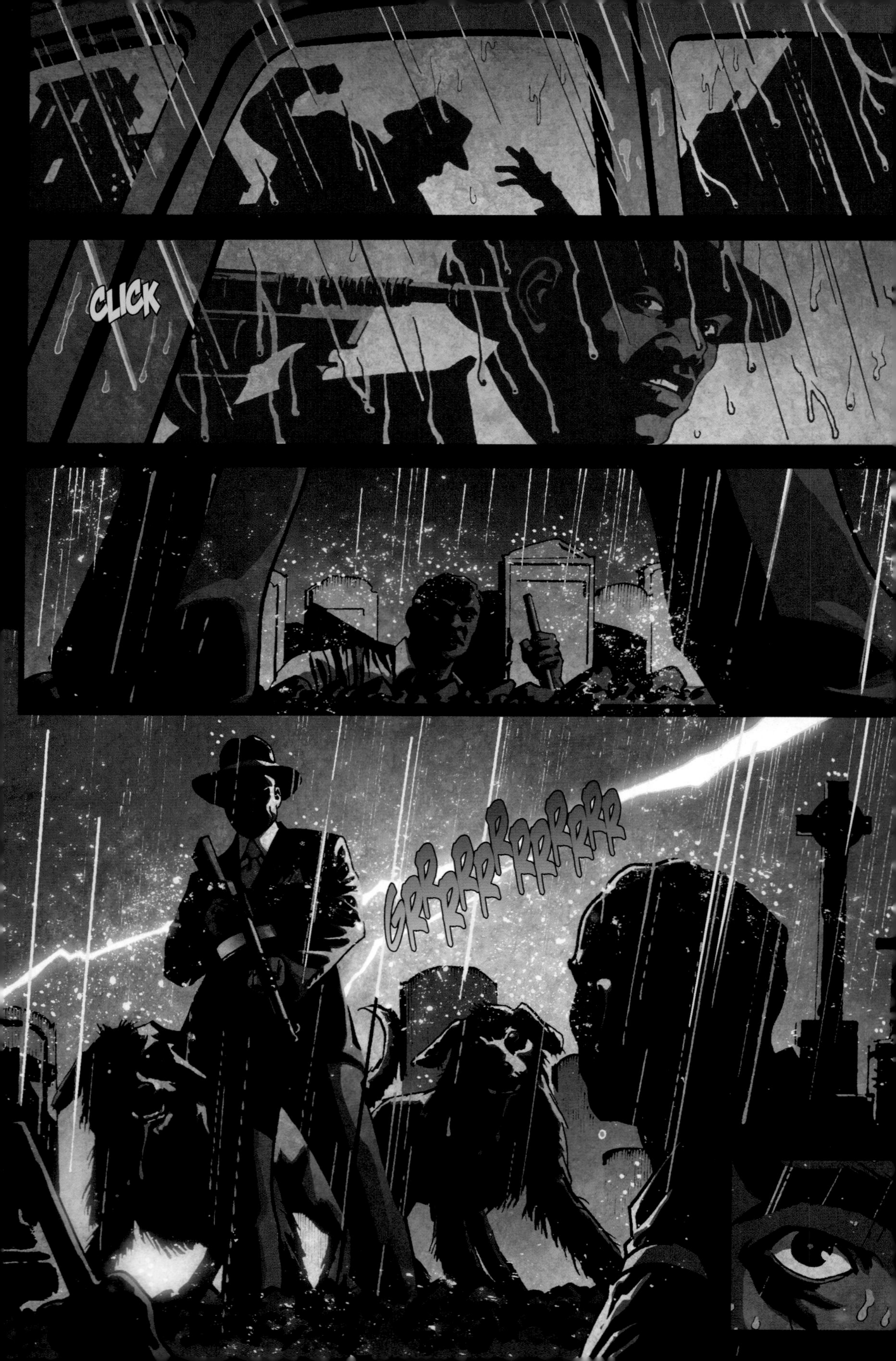
CLICK
GRRRRRRRRRRR

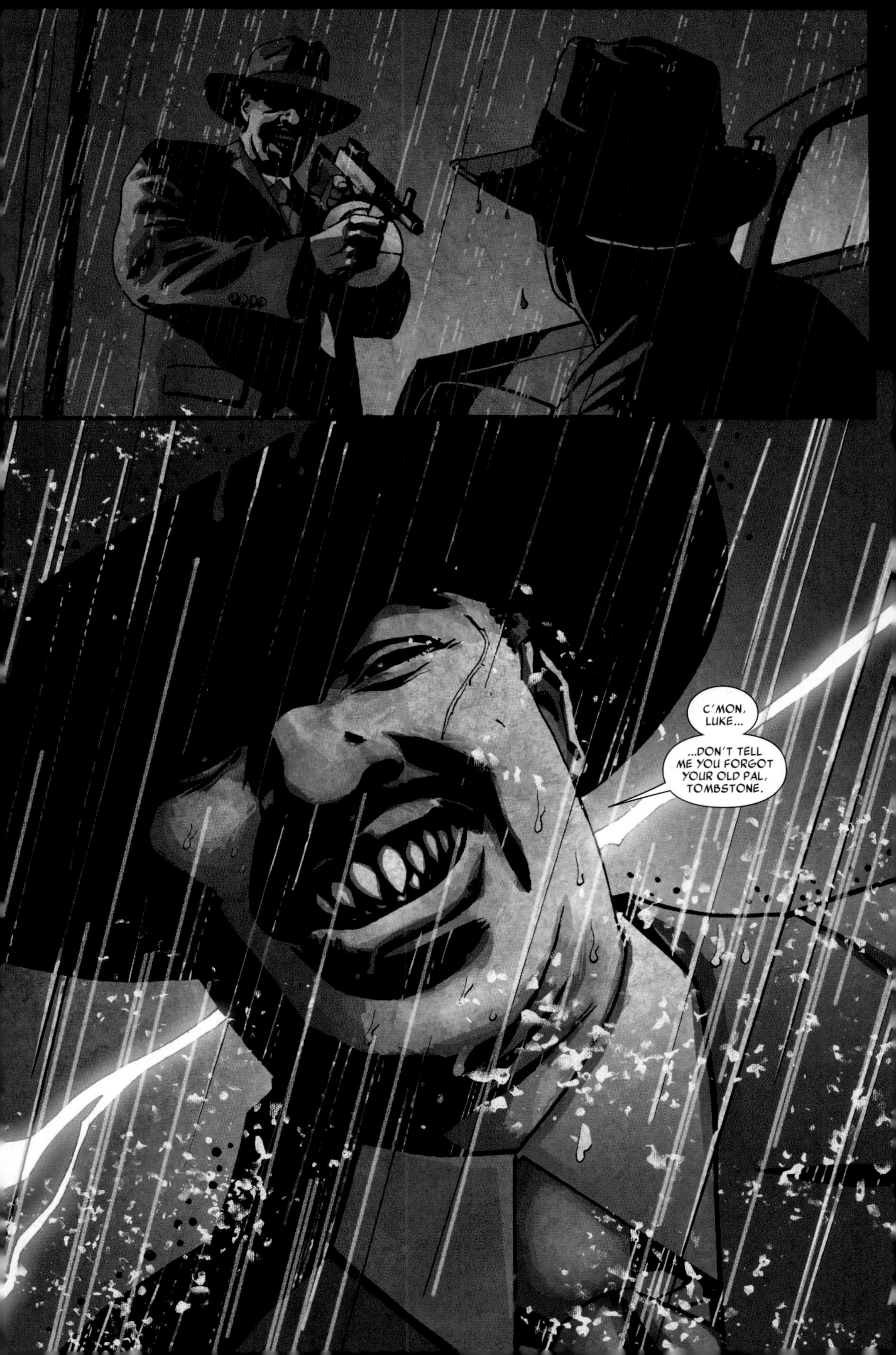
C'MON, LUKE...
...DON'T TELL ME YOU FORGOT YOUR OLD PAL, TOMBSTONE.

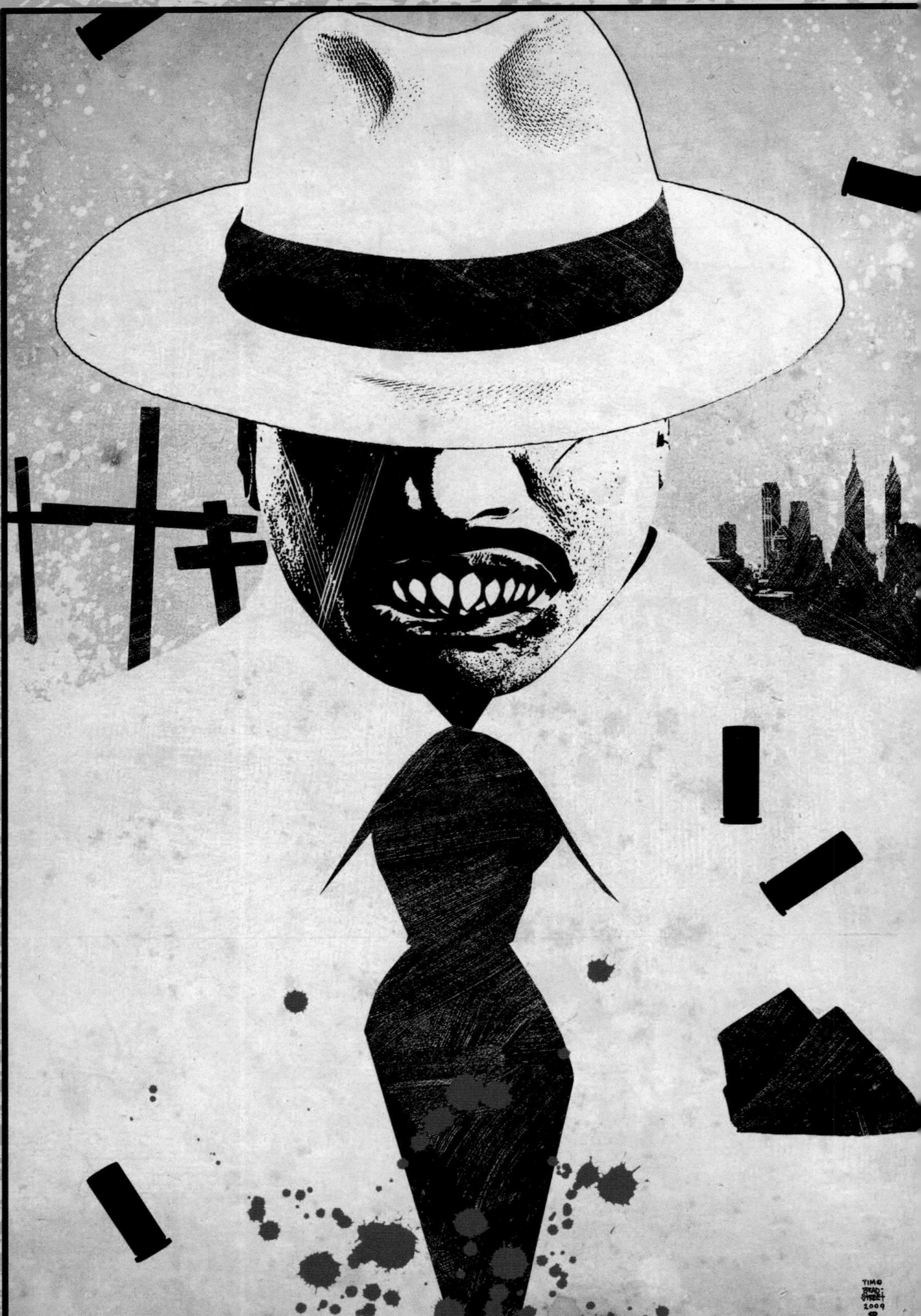
TIM BRADSTREET 2009

TWO

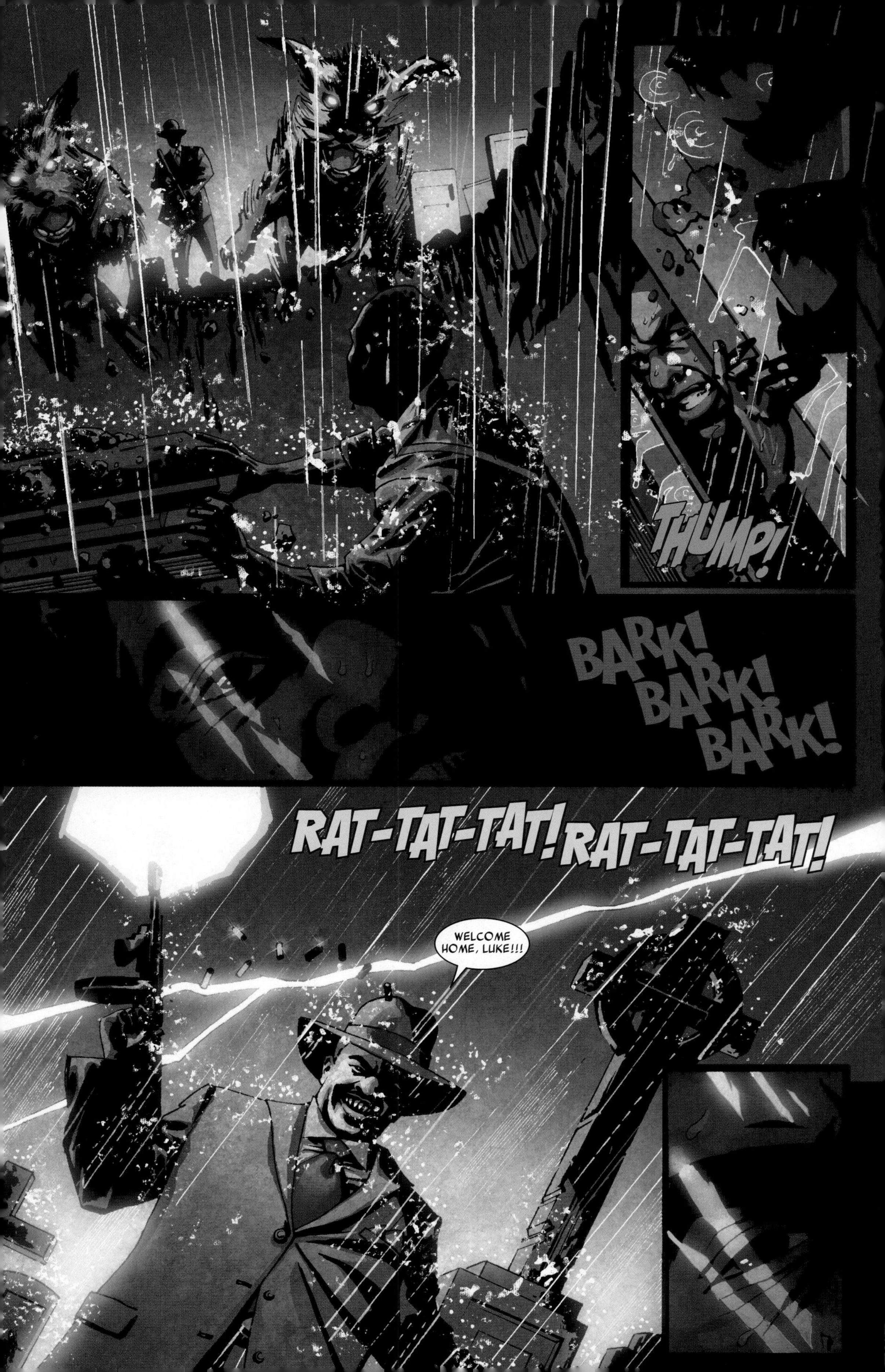
THUMP!
BARK!
BARK!
BARK!
RAT-TAT-TAT! RAT-TAT-TAT!
WELCOME HOME, LUKE!!!

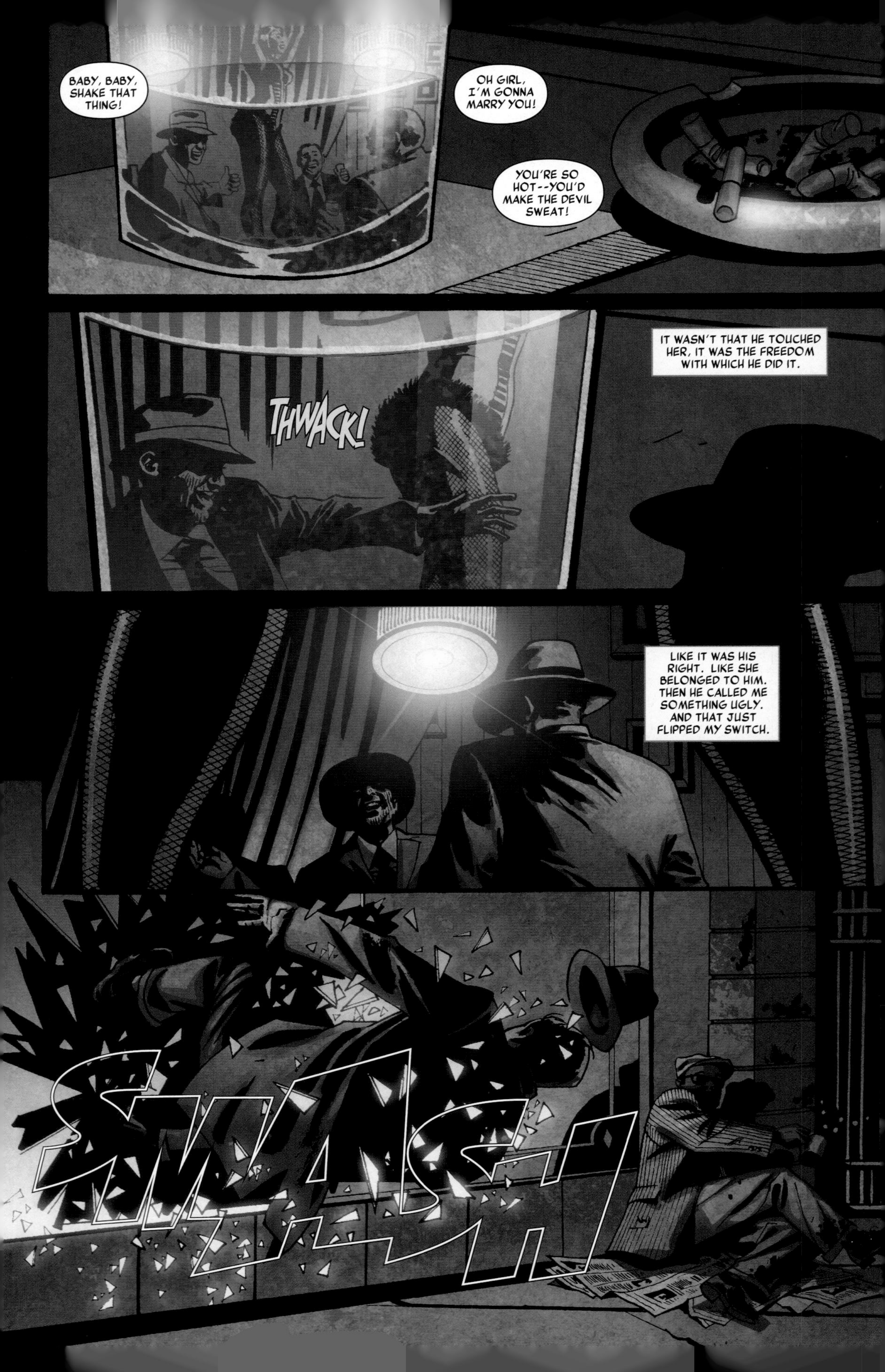
BABY, BABY, SHAKE THAT THING!
OH GIRL, I'M GONNA MARRY YOU!
YOU'RE SO HOT--YOU'D MAKE THE DEVIL SWEAT!
IT WASN'T THAT HE TOUCHED HER, IT WAS THE FREEDOM WITH WHICH HE DID IT.
THWACK!
LIKE IT WAS HIS RIGHT. LIKE SHE BELONGED TO HIM. THEN HE CALLED ME SOMETHING UGLY. AND THAT JUST FLIPPED MY SWITCH.
SMASH

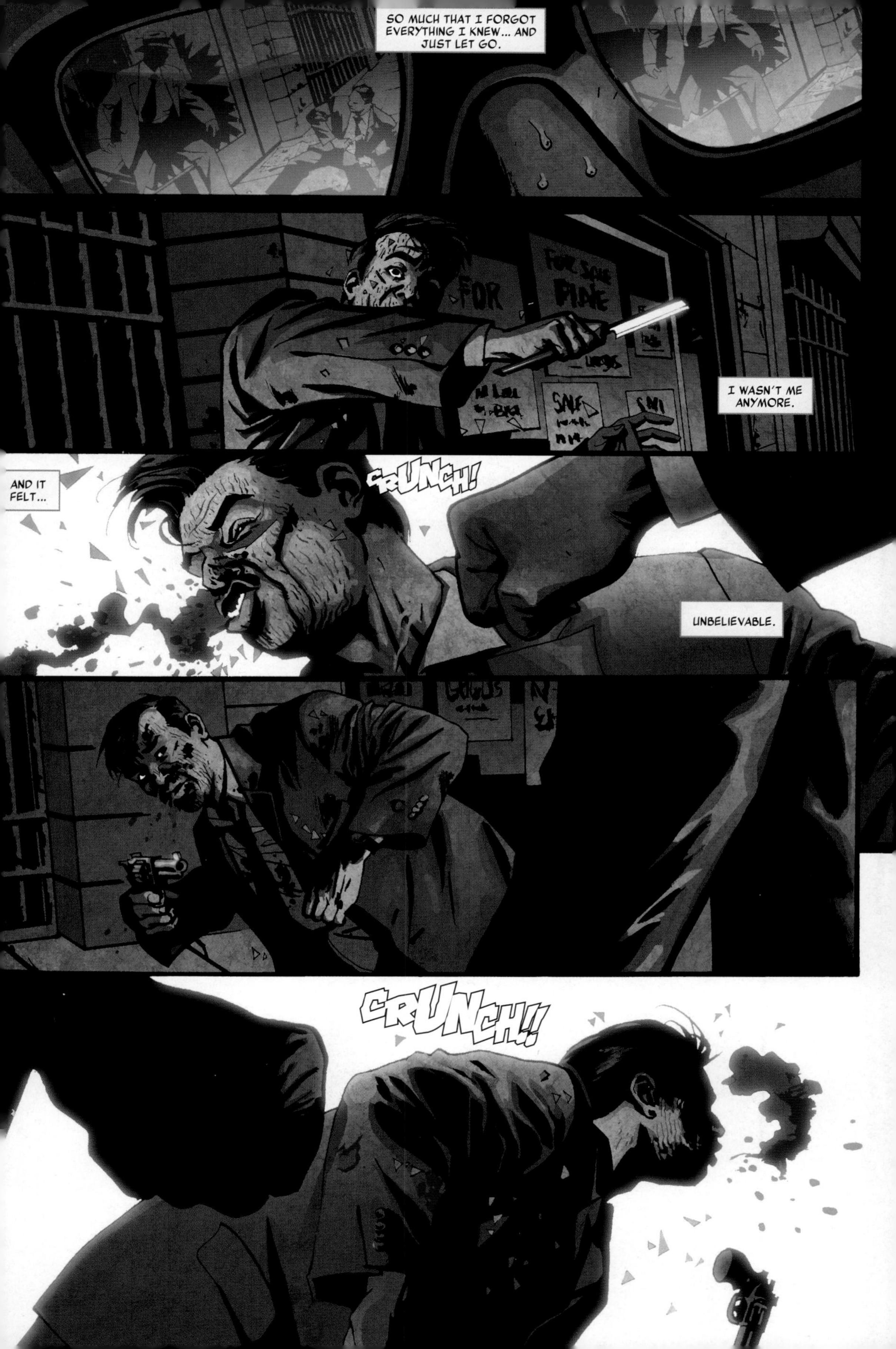
SO MUCH THAT I FORGOT EVERYTHING I KNEW... AND JUST LET GO.
I WASN'T ME ANYMORE.
AND IT FELT...
CRUNCH!
UNBELIEVABLE.
CRUNCH!!

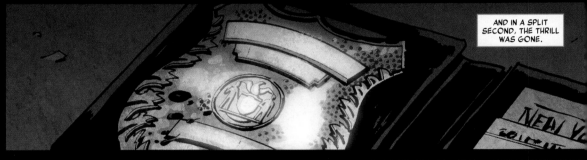

AND IN A SPLIT SECOND, THE THRILL WAS GONE.

AND I WAS AS GOOD AS DEAD.

BLAM BLAM

RAT-TAT-TAT!

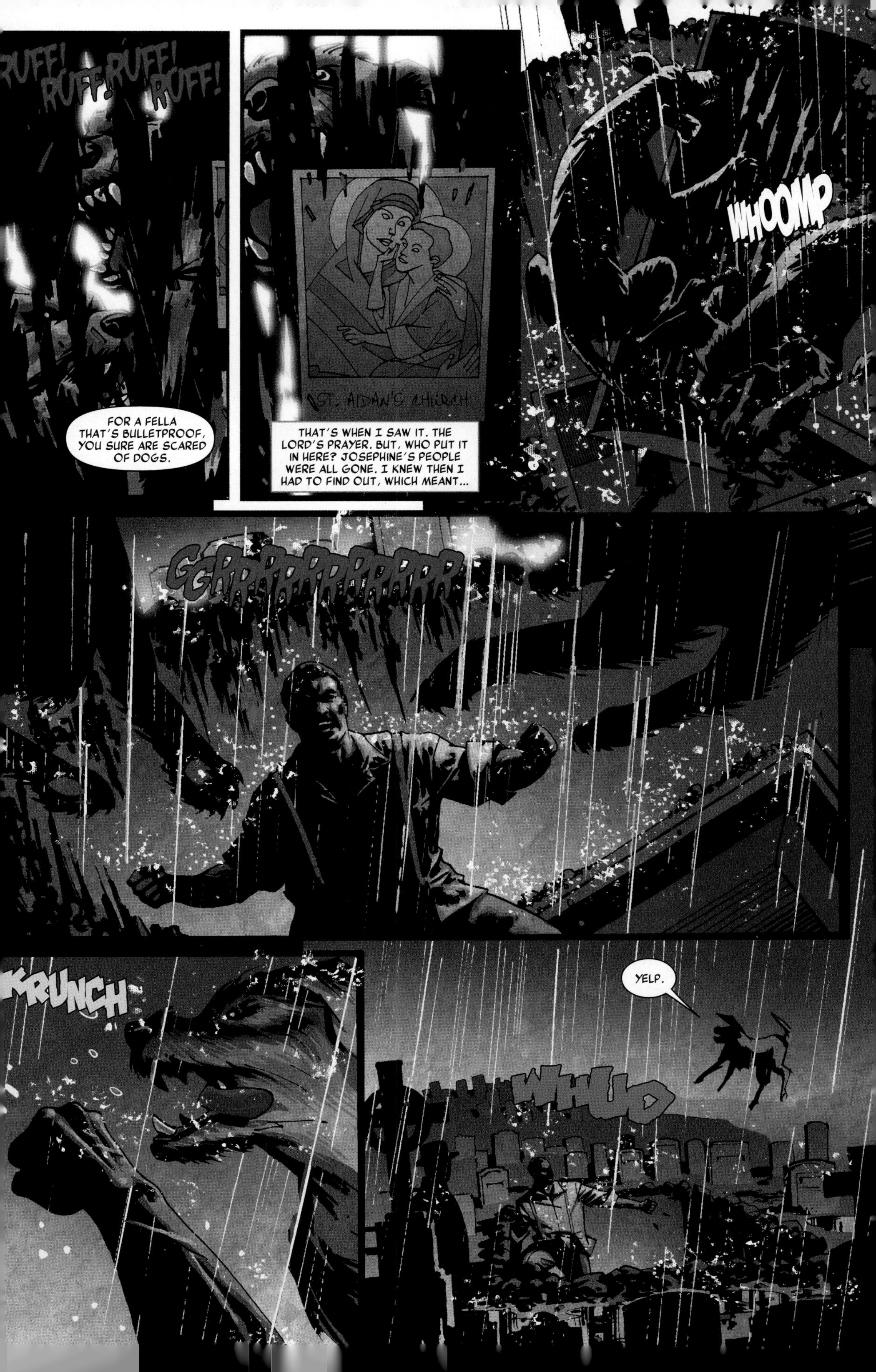
RUFF! RUFF! RUFF! RUFF!
FOR A FELLA THAT'S BULLETPROOF, YOU SURE ARE SCARED OF DOGS.
ST. AIDAN'S CHURCH
THAT'S WHEN I SAW IT. THE LORD'S PRAYER. BUT, WHO PUT IT IN HERE? JOSEPHINE'S PEOPLE WERE ALL GONE. I KNEW THEN I HAD TO FIND OUT, WHICH MEANT...
WHOOMP
GGRRRRRRRRRRRR
KRUNCH
YELP.
WHUD

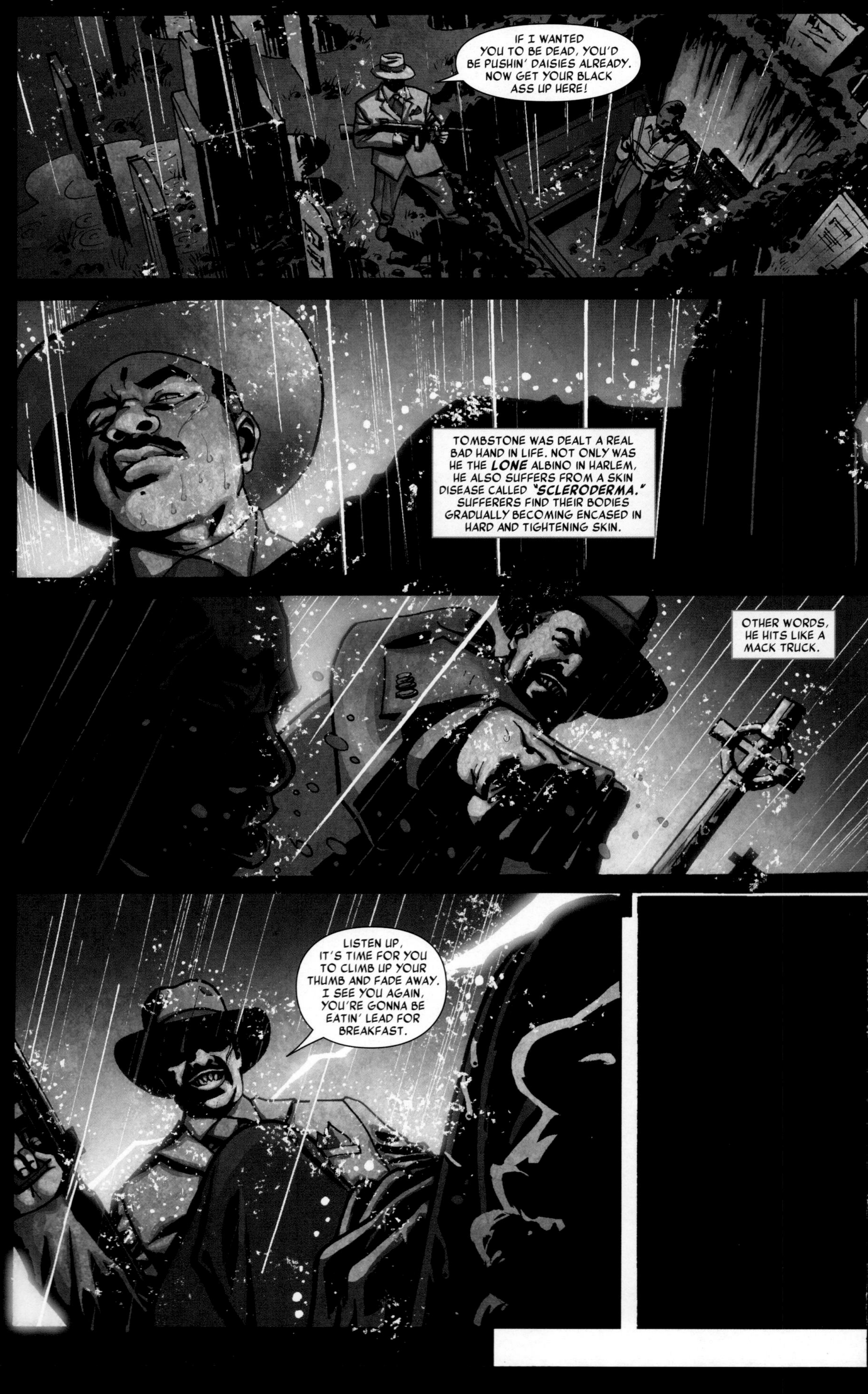
IF I WANTED YOU TO BE DEAD, YOU'D BE PUSHIN' DAISIES ALREADY. NOW GET YOUR BLACK ASS UP HERE!
TOMBSTONE WAS DEALT A REAL BAD HAND IN LIFE. NOT ONLY WAS HE THE LONE ALBINO IN HARLEM, HE ALSO SUFFERS FROM A SKIN DISEASE CALLED "SCLERODERMA." SUFFERERS FIND THEIR BODIES GRADUALLY BECOMING ENCASED IN HARD AND TIGHTENING SKIN.
OTHER WORDS, HE HITS LIKE A MACK TRUCK.
LISTEN UP, IT'S TIME FOR YOU TO CLIMB UP YOUR THUMB AND FADE AWAY. I SEE YOU AGAIN, YOU'RE GONNA BE EATIN' LEAD FOR BREAKFAST.

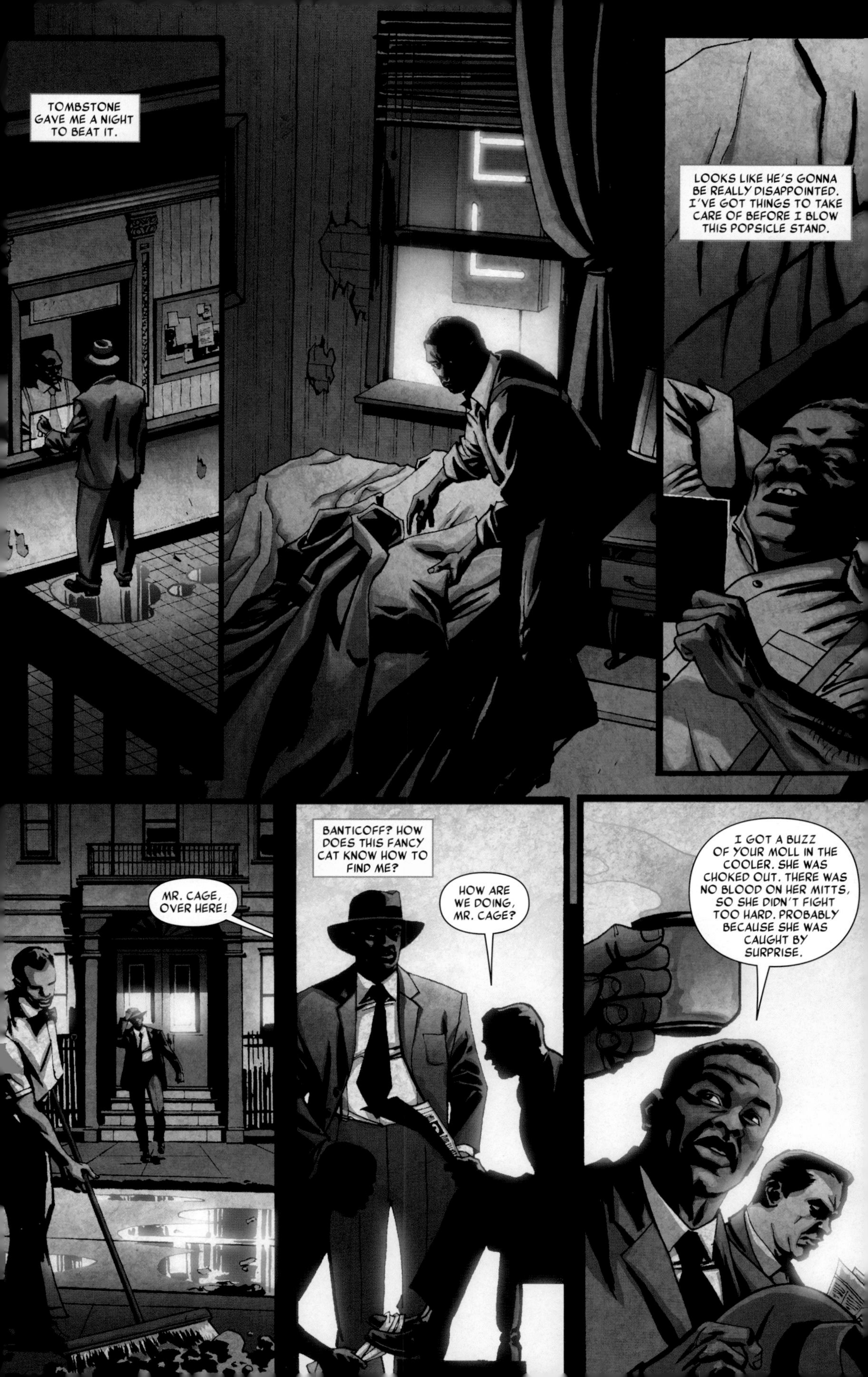
TOMBSTONE GAVE ME A NIGHT TO BEAT IT.
LOOKS LIKE HE'S GONNA BE REALLY DISAPPOINTED. I'VE GOT THINGS TO TAKE CARE OF BEFORE I BLOW THIS POPSICLE STAND.
MR. CAGE, OVER HERE!
BANTICOFF? HOW DOES THIS FANCY CAT KNOW HOW TO FIND ME?
HOW ARE WE DOING, MR. CAGE?
I GOT A BUZZ OF YOUR MOLL IN THE COOLER. SHE WAS CHOKED OUT. THERE WAS NO BLOOD ON HER MITTS, SO SHE DIDN'T FIGHT TOO HARD. PROBABLY BECAUSE SHE WAS CAUGHT BY SURPRISE.

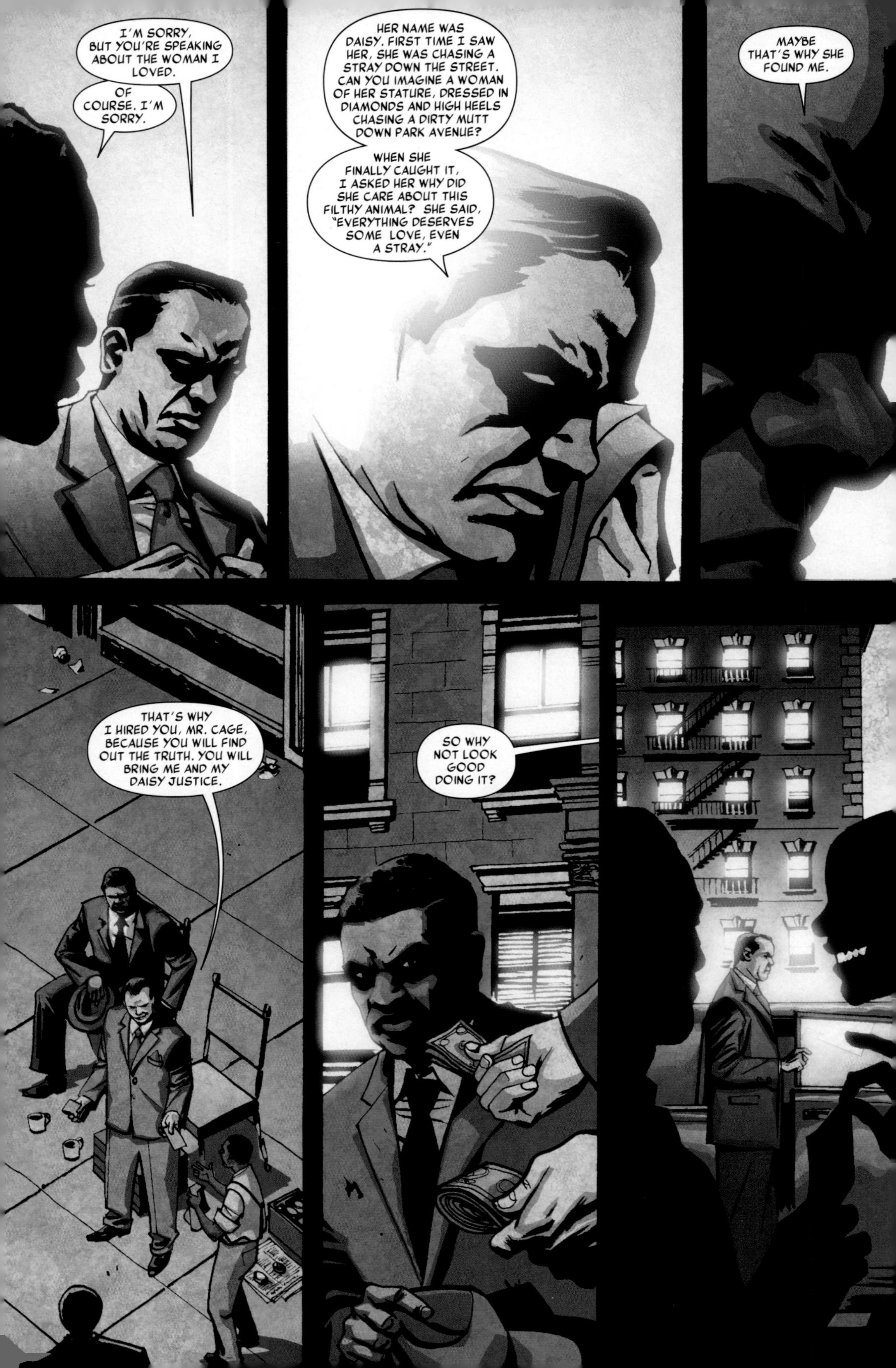

I'M SORRY, BUT YOU'RE SPEAKING ABOUT THE WOMAN I LOVED.
OF COURSE. I'M SORRY.
HER NAME WAS DAISY. FIRST TIME I SAW HER, SHE WAS CHASING A STRAY DOWN THE STREET. CAN YOU IMAGINE A WOMAN OF HER STATURE, DRESSED IN DIAMONDS AND HIGH HEELS CHASING A DIRTY MUTT DOWN PARK AVENUE?
WHEN SHE FINALLY CAUGHT IT, I ASKED HER WHY DID SHE CARE ABOUT THIS FILTHY ANIMAL? SHE SAID, "EVERYTHING DESERVES SOME LOVE, EVEN A STRAY."
MAYBE THAT'S WHY SHE FOUND ME.
THAT'S WHY I HIRED YOU, MR. CAGE, BECAUSE YOU WILL FIND OUT THE TRUTH. YOU WILL BRING ME AND MY DAISY JUSTICE.
SO WHY NOT LOOK GOOD DOING IT?

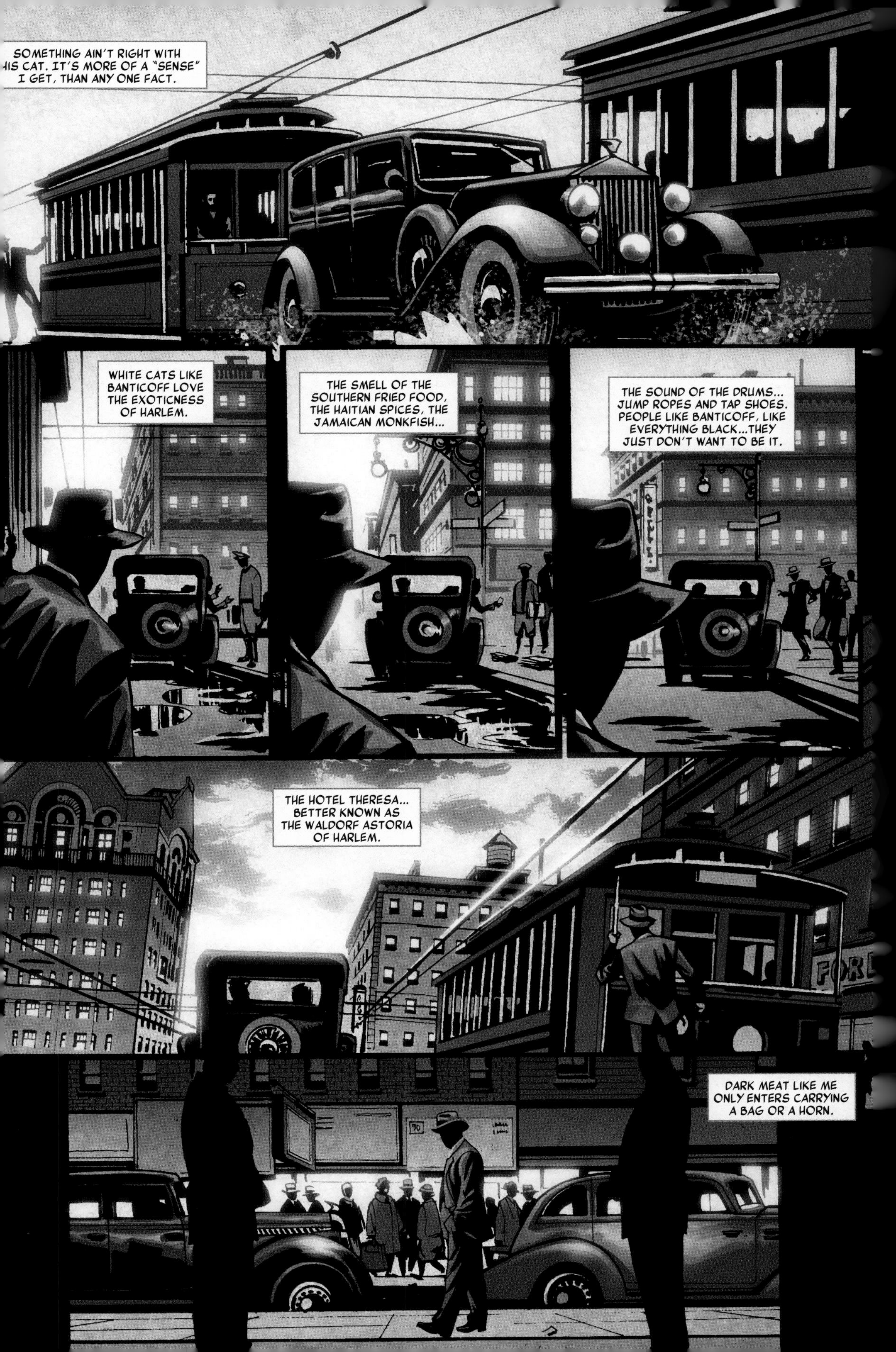
SOMETHING AIN'T RIGHT WITH
HIS CAT. IT'S MORE OF A "SENSE"
I GET, THAN ANY ONE FACT.
WHITE CATS LIKE BANTICOFF LOVE THE EXOTICNESS OF HARLEM.
THE SMELL OF THE SOUTHERN FRIED FOOD, THE HAITIAN SPICES, THE JAMAICAN MONKFISH...
THE SOUND OF THE DRUMS... JUMP ROPES AND TAP SHOES. PEOPLE LIKE BANTICOFF, LIKE EVERYTHING BLACK...THEY JUST DON'T WANT TO BE IT.
THE HOTEL THERESA... BETTER KNOWN AS THE WALDORF ASTORIA OF HARLEM.
DARK MEAT LIKE ME ONLY ENTERS CARRYING A BAG OR A HORN.

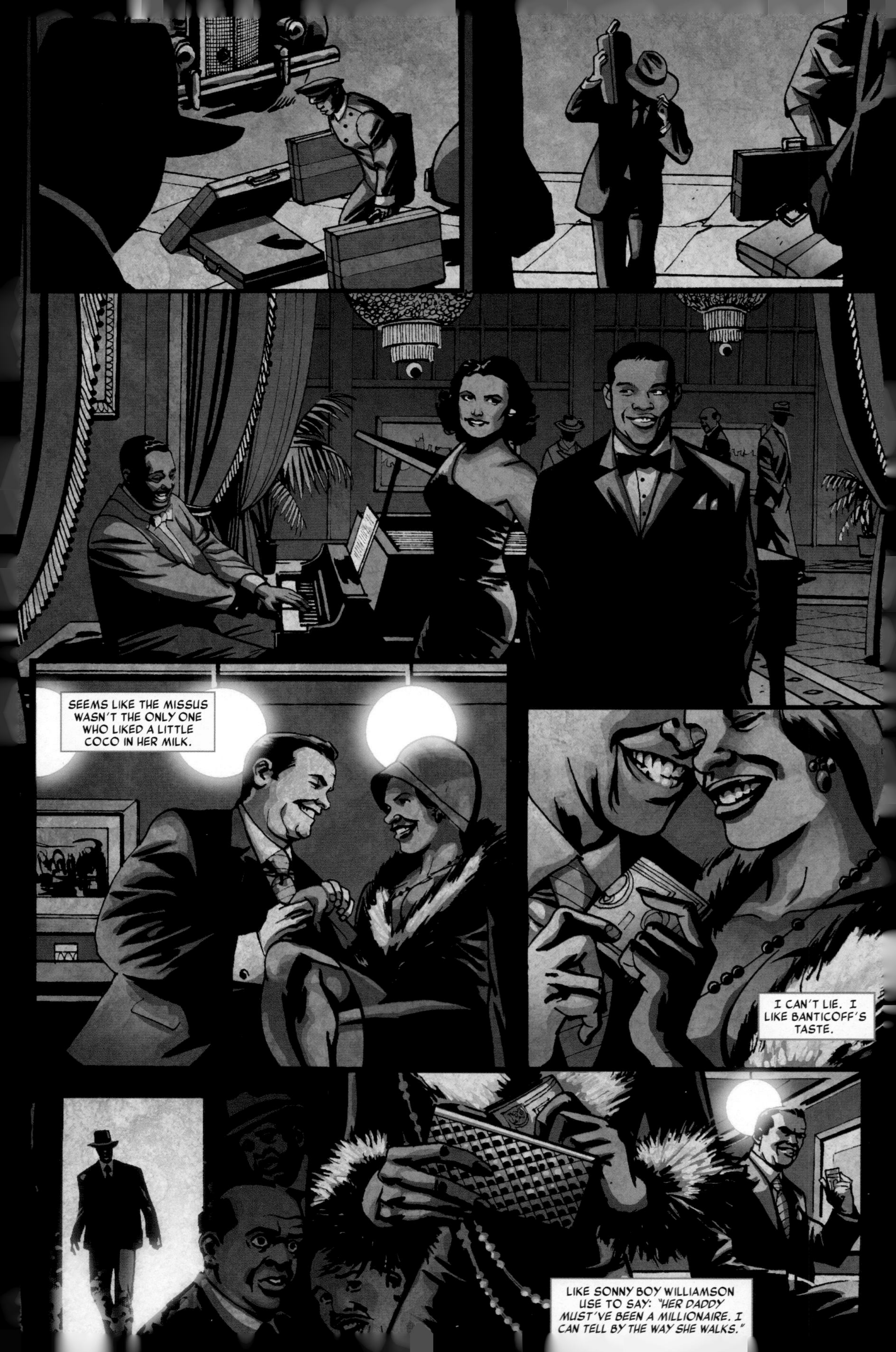
SEEMS LIKE THE MISSUS WASN'T THE ONLY ONE WHO LIKED A LITTLE COCO IN HER MILK.
I CAN'T LIE. I LIKE BANTICOFF'S TASTE.
LIKE SONNY BOY WILLIAMSON USE TO SAY: "HER DADDY MUST'VE BEEN A MILLIONAIRE. I CAN TELL BY THE WAY SHE WALKS."

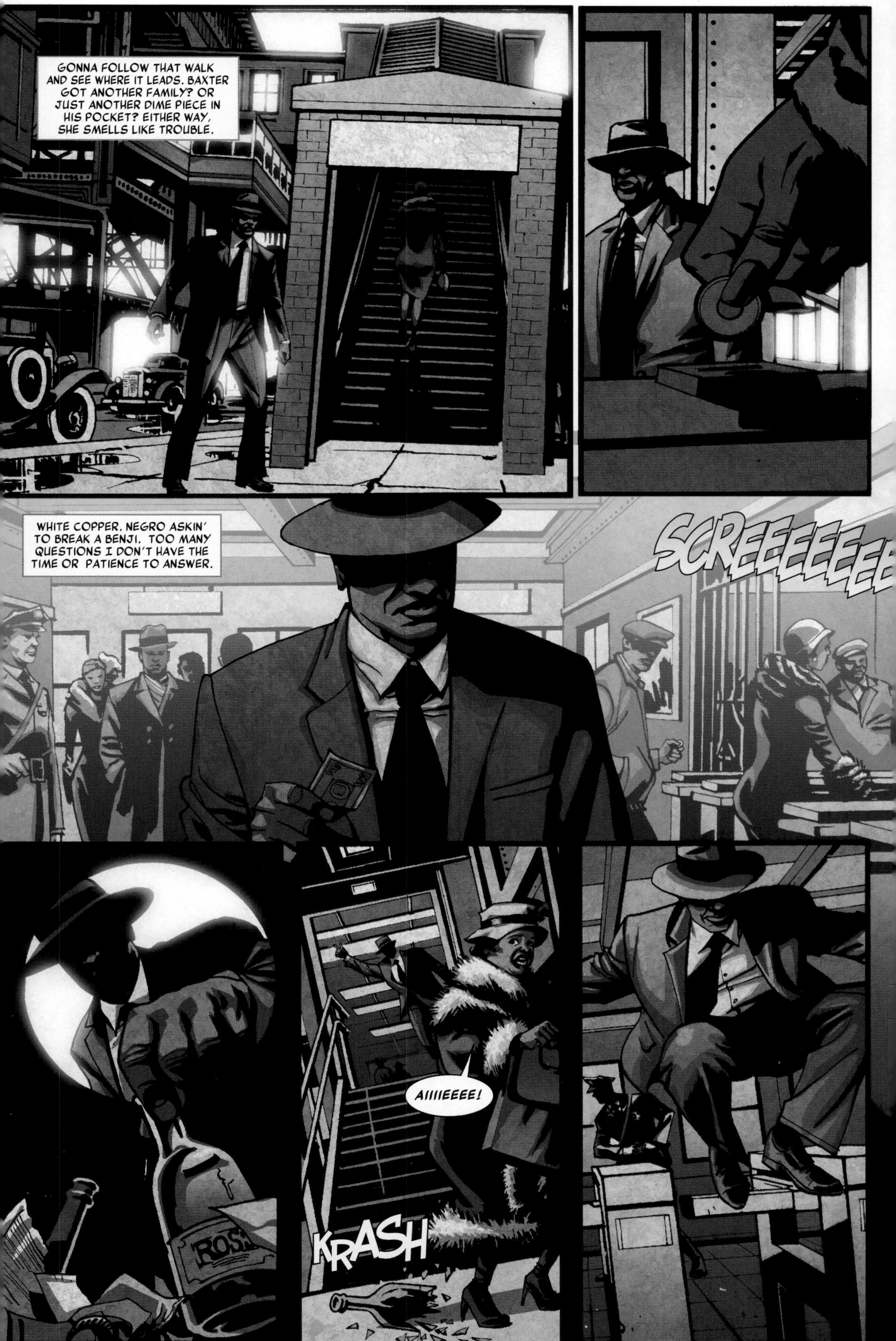
GONNA FOLLOW THAT WALK AND SEE WHERE IT LEADS. BAXTER GOT ANOTHER FAMILY? OR JUST ANOTHER DIME PIECE IN HIS POCKET? EITHER WAY, SHE SMELLS LIKE TROUBLE.
WHITE COPPER. NEGRO ASKIN' TO BREAK A BENJI. TOO MANY QUESTIONS I DON'T HAVE THE TIME OR PATIENCE TO ANSWER.
SCREEEEEEEE
ROSE
KRASH
AIIIIEEEE!

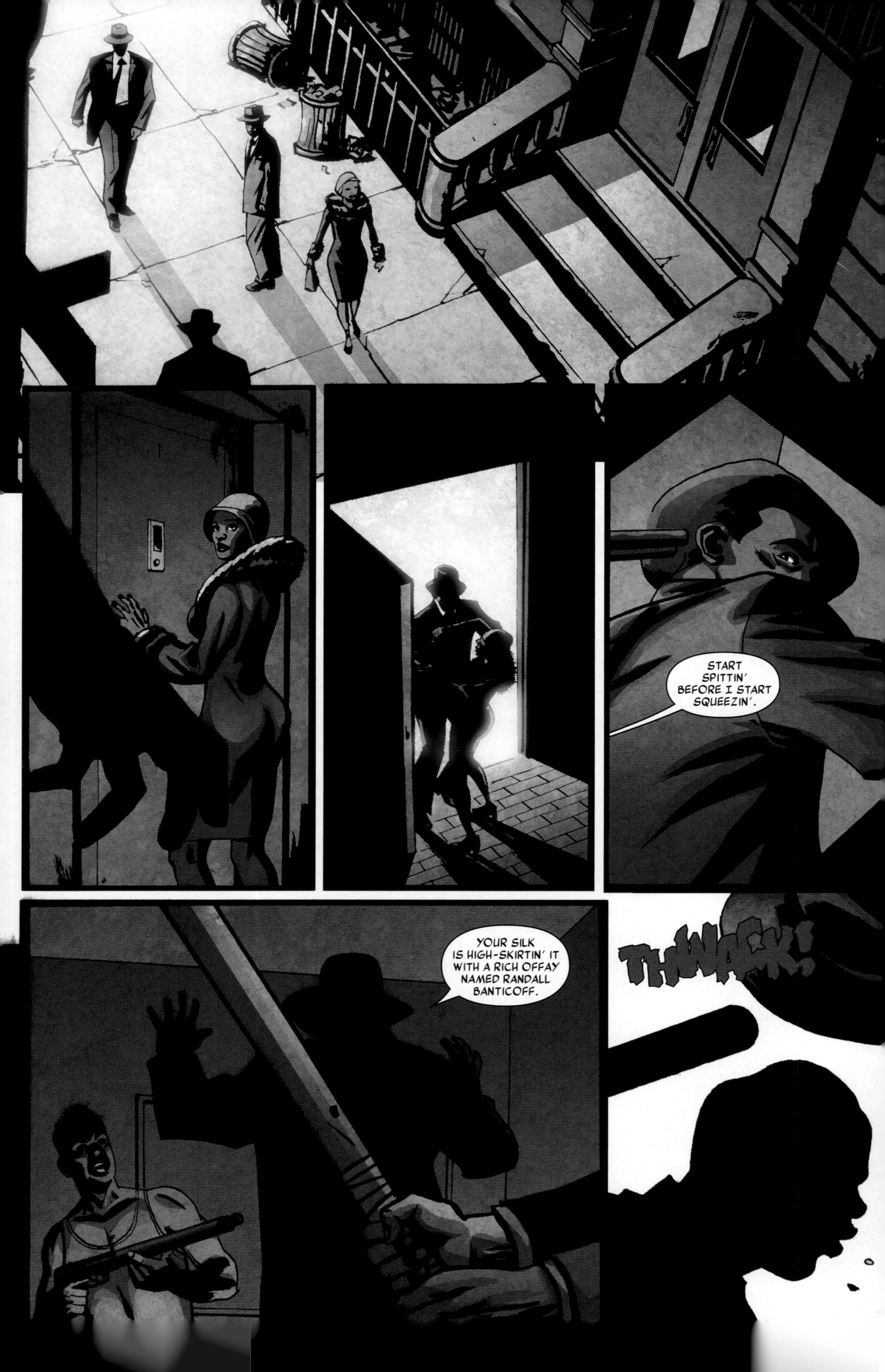
START SPITTIN' BEFORE I START SQUEEZIN'.
YOUR SILK IS HIGH-SKIRTIN' IT WITH A RICH OFFAY NAMED RANDALL BANTICOFF.
THWACK!

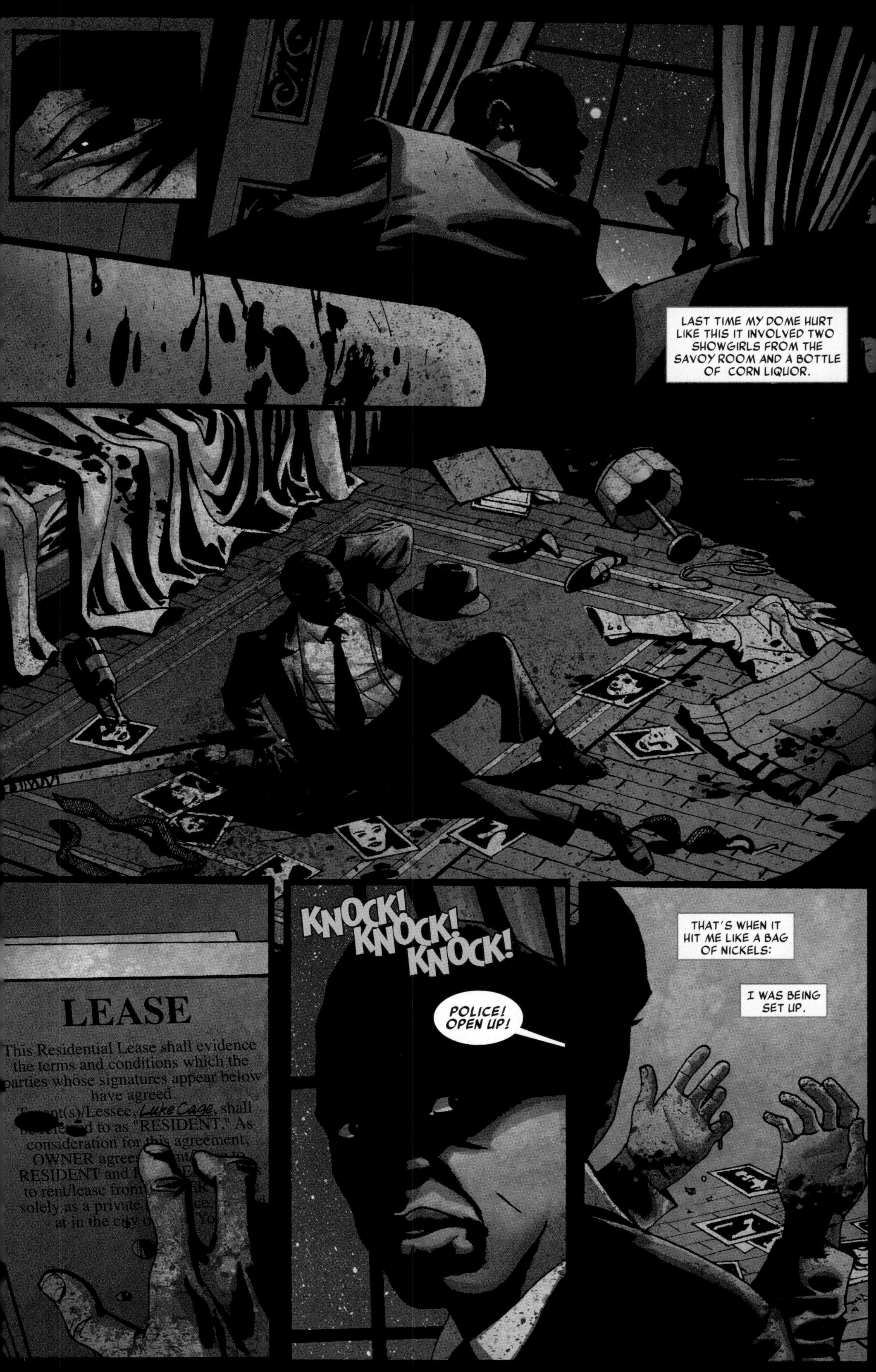

LAST TIME MY DOME HURT LIKE THIS IT INVOLVED TWO SHOWGIRLS FROM THE SAVOY ROOM AND A BOTTLE OF CORN LIQUOR.
LEASE
This Residential Lease shall evidence the terms and conditions which the parties whose signatures appear below have agreed.
KNOCK! KNOCK! KNOCK!
POLICE! OPEN UP!
THAT'S WHEN IT HIT ME LIKE A BAG OF NICKELS:
I WAS BEING SET UP.

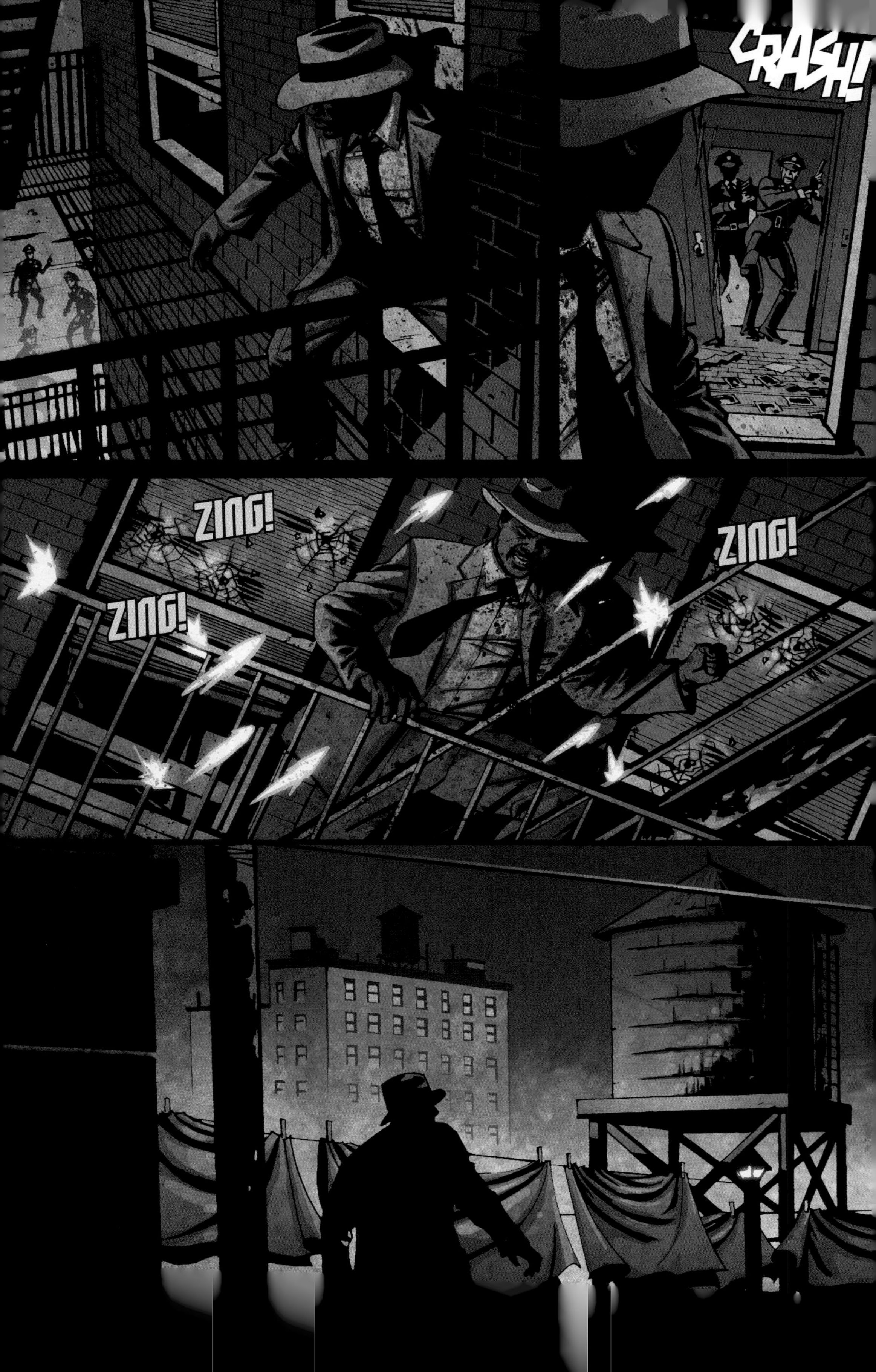
CRASH!
ZING!
ZING!
ZING!

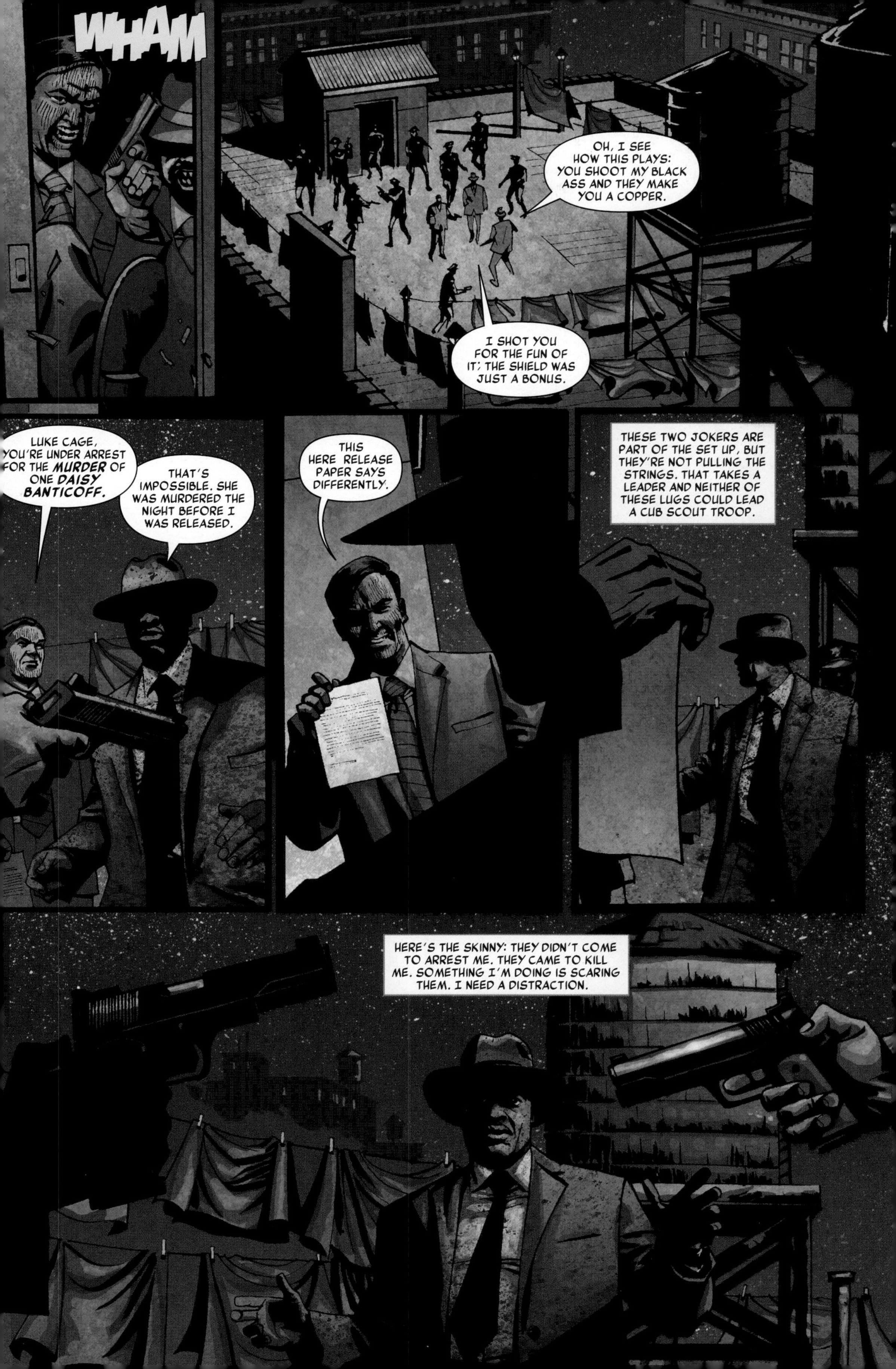
WHAM
OH, I SEE HOW THIS PLAYS: YOU SHOOT MY BLACK ASS AND THEY MAKE YOU A COPPER.
I SHOT YOU FOR THE FUN OF IT; THE SHIELD WAS JUST A BONUS.
LUKE CAGE, YOU'RE UNDER ARREST FOR THE MURDER OF ONE DAISY BANTICOFF.
THAT'S IMPOSSIBLE. SHE WAS MURDERED THE NIGHT BEFORE I WAS RELEASED.
THIS HERE RELEASE PAPER SAYS DIFFERENTLY.
THESE TWO JOKERS ARE PART OF THE SET UP, BUT THEY'RE NOT PULLING THE STRINGS. THAT TAKES A LEADER AND NEITHER OF THESE LUGS COULD LEAD A CUB SCOUT TROOP.
HERE'S THE SKINNY: THEY DIDN'T COME TO ARREST ME. THEY CAME TO KILL ME. SOMETHING I'M DOING IS SCARING THEM. I NEED A DISTRACTION.

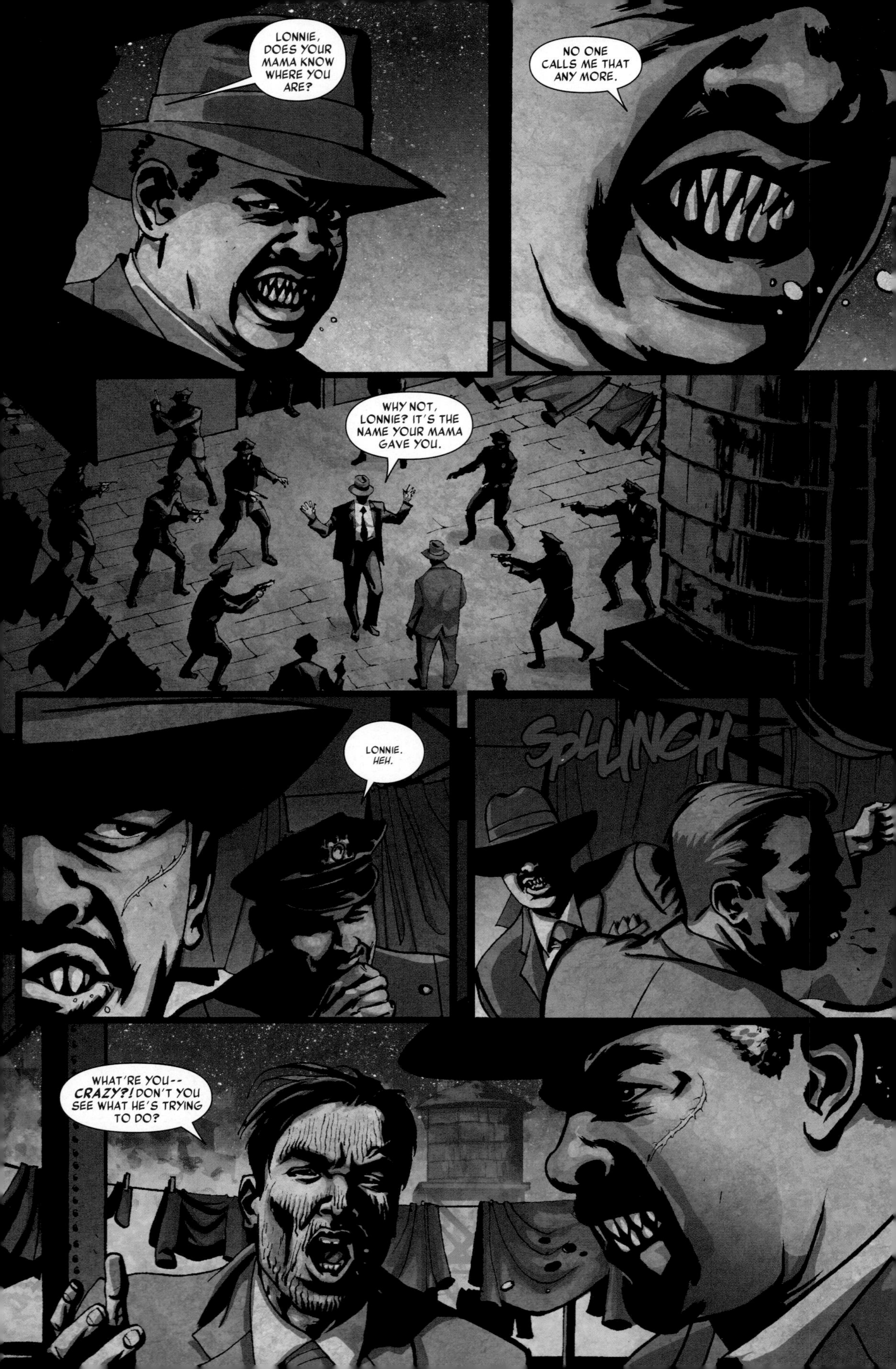
LONNIE, DOES YOUR MAMA KNOW WHERE YOU ARE?
NO ONE CALLS ME THAT ANY MORE.
WHY NOT, LONNIE? IT'S THE NAME YOUR MAMA GAVE YOU.
LONNIE. HEH.
SPLUNCH
WHAT'RE YOU-- *CRAZY?!* DON'T YOU SEE WHAT HE'S TRYING TO DO?

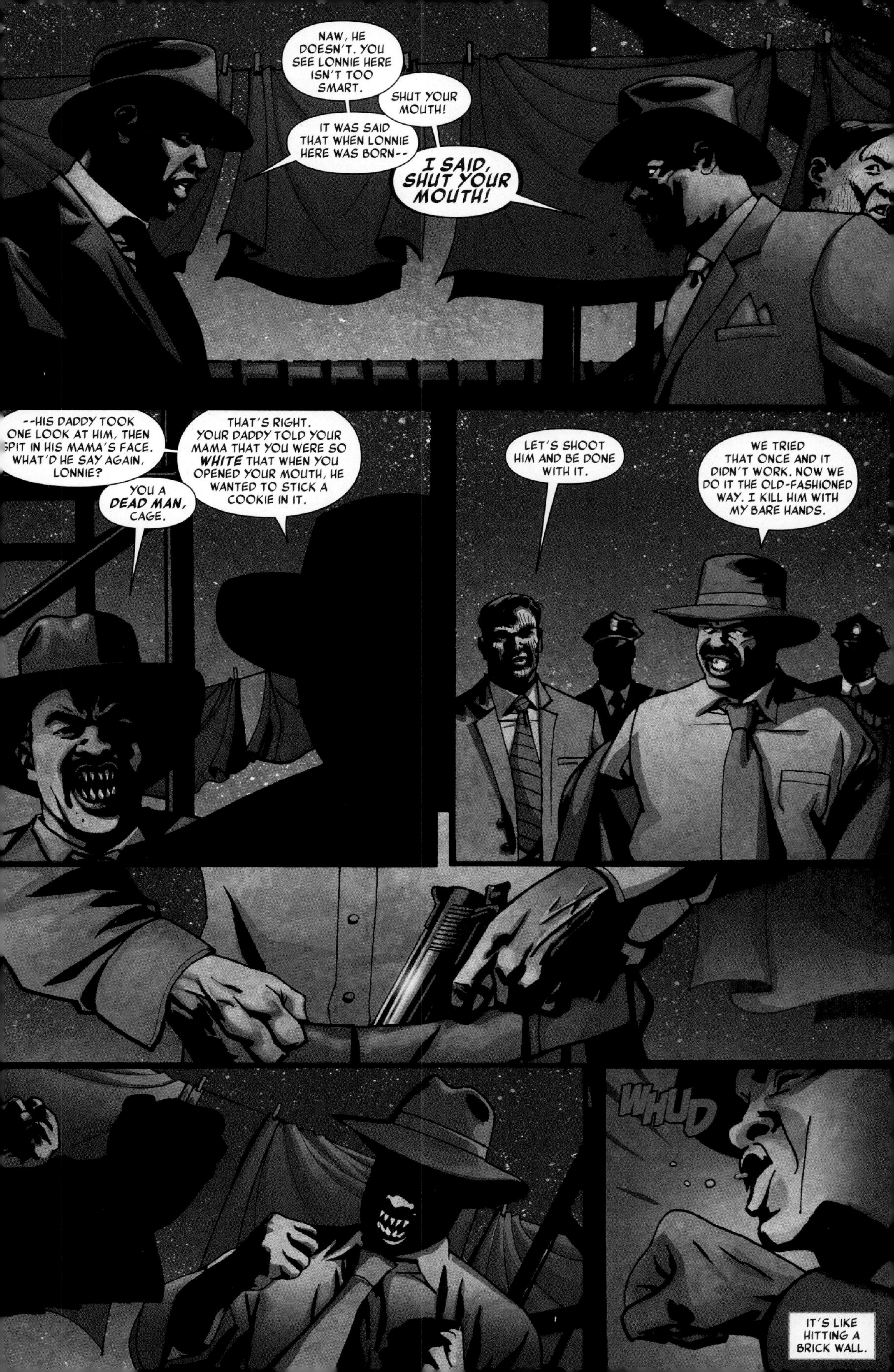
NAW, HE DOESN'T. YOU SEE LONNIE HERE ISN'T TOO SMART.
SHUT YOUR MOUTH!
IT WAS SAID THAT WHEN LONNIE HERE WAS BORN--
I SAID, SHUT YOUR MOUTH!
--HIS DADDY TOOK ONE LOOK AT HIM, THEN SPIT IN HIS MAMA'S FACE. WHAT'D HE SAY AGAIN, LONNIE?
THAT'S RIGHT. YOUR DADDY TOLD YOUR MAMA THAT YOU WERE SO WHITE THAT WHEN YOU OPENED YOUR MOUTH, HE WANTED TO STICK A COOKIE IN IT.
YOU A DEAD MAN, CAGE.
LET'S SHOOT HIM AND BE DONE WITH IT.
WE TRIED THAT ONCE AND IT DIDN'T WORK. NOW WE DO IT THE OLD-FASHIONED WAY. I KILL HIM WITH MY BARE HANDS.
WHUD
IT'S LIKE HITTING A BRICK WALL.

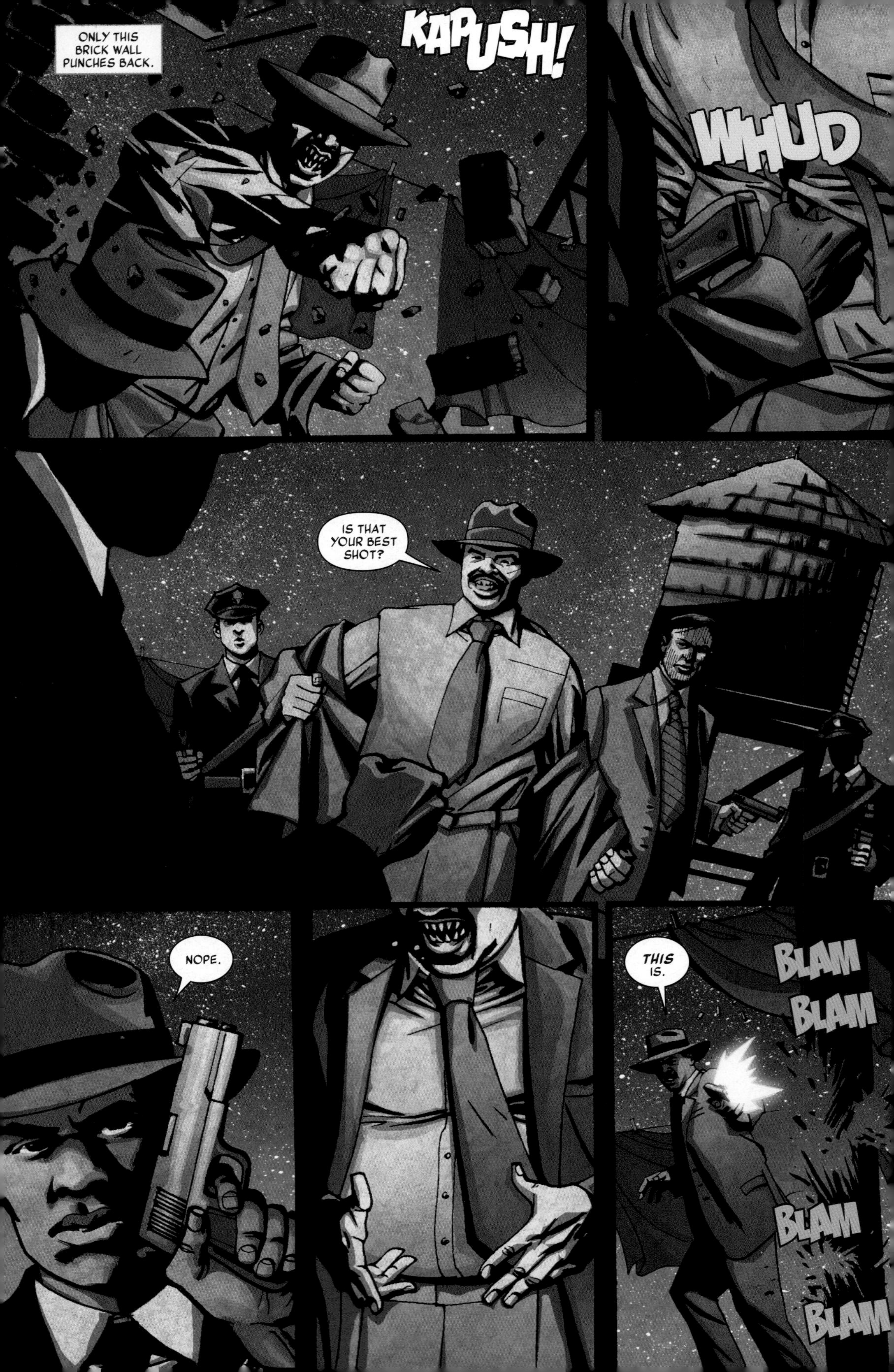
ONLY THIS BRICK WALL PUNCHES BACK.
KAPUSH!
WHUD
IS THAT YOUR BEST SHOT?
NOPE.
THIS IS.
BLAM
BLAM
BLAM
BLAM

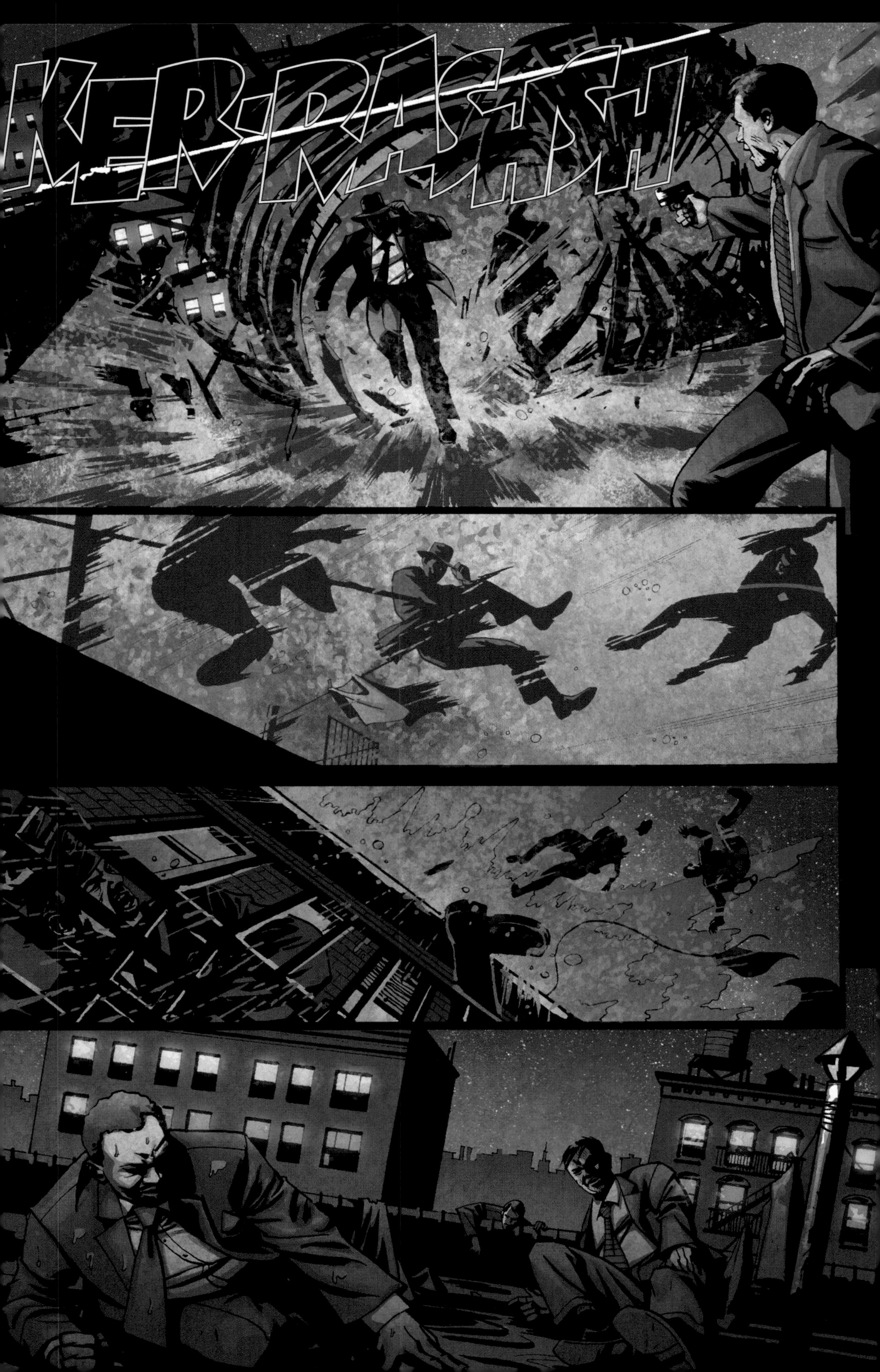
KER-RASSHH

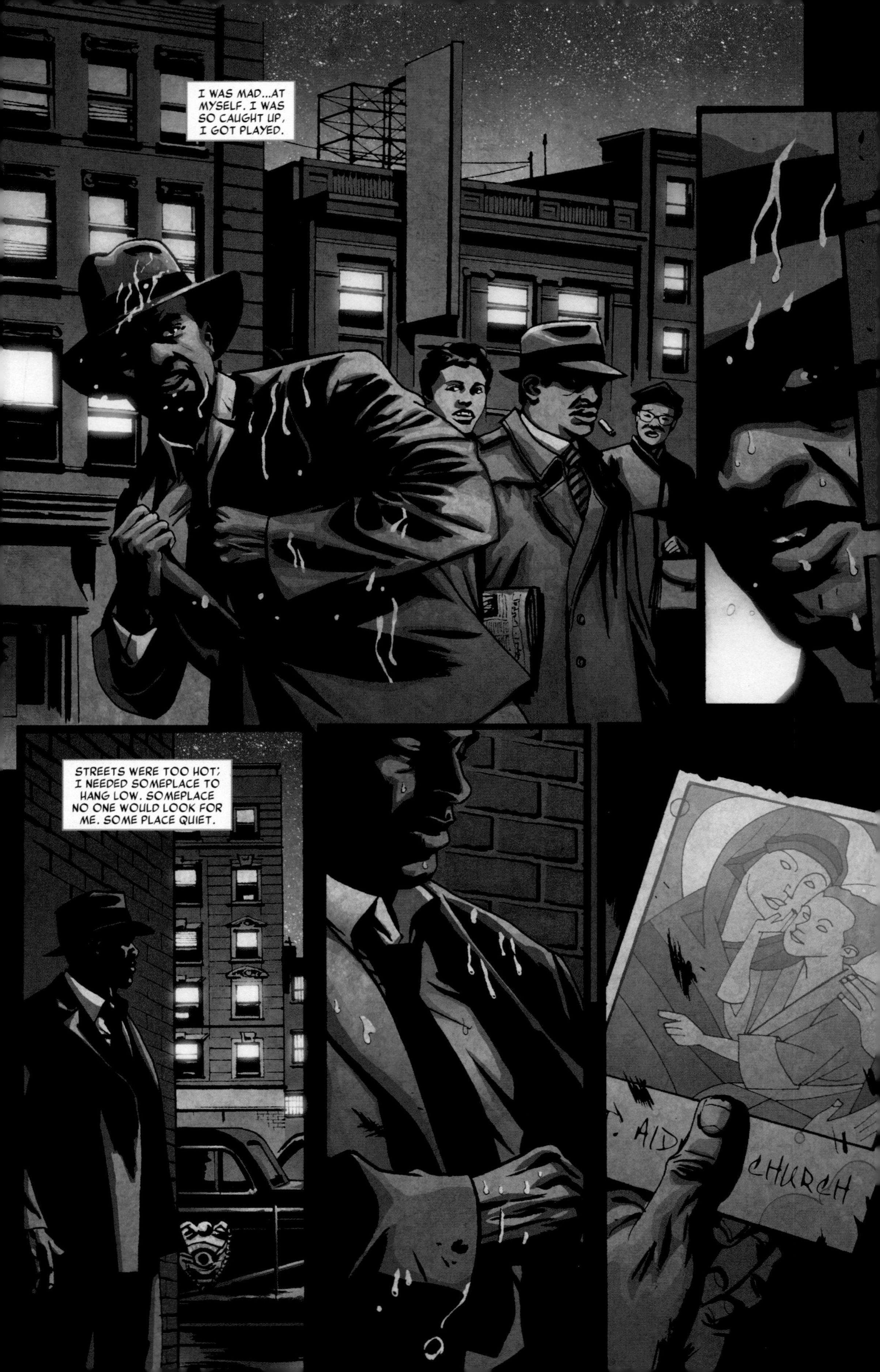
I WAS MAD...AT MYSELF. I WAS SO CAUGHT UP, I GOT PLAYED.
STREETS WERE TOO HOT; I NEEDED SOMEPLACE TO HANG LOW. SOMEPLACE NO ONE WOULD LOOK FOR ME. SOME PLACE QUIET.
AID
CHURCH

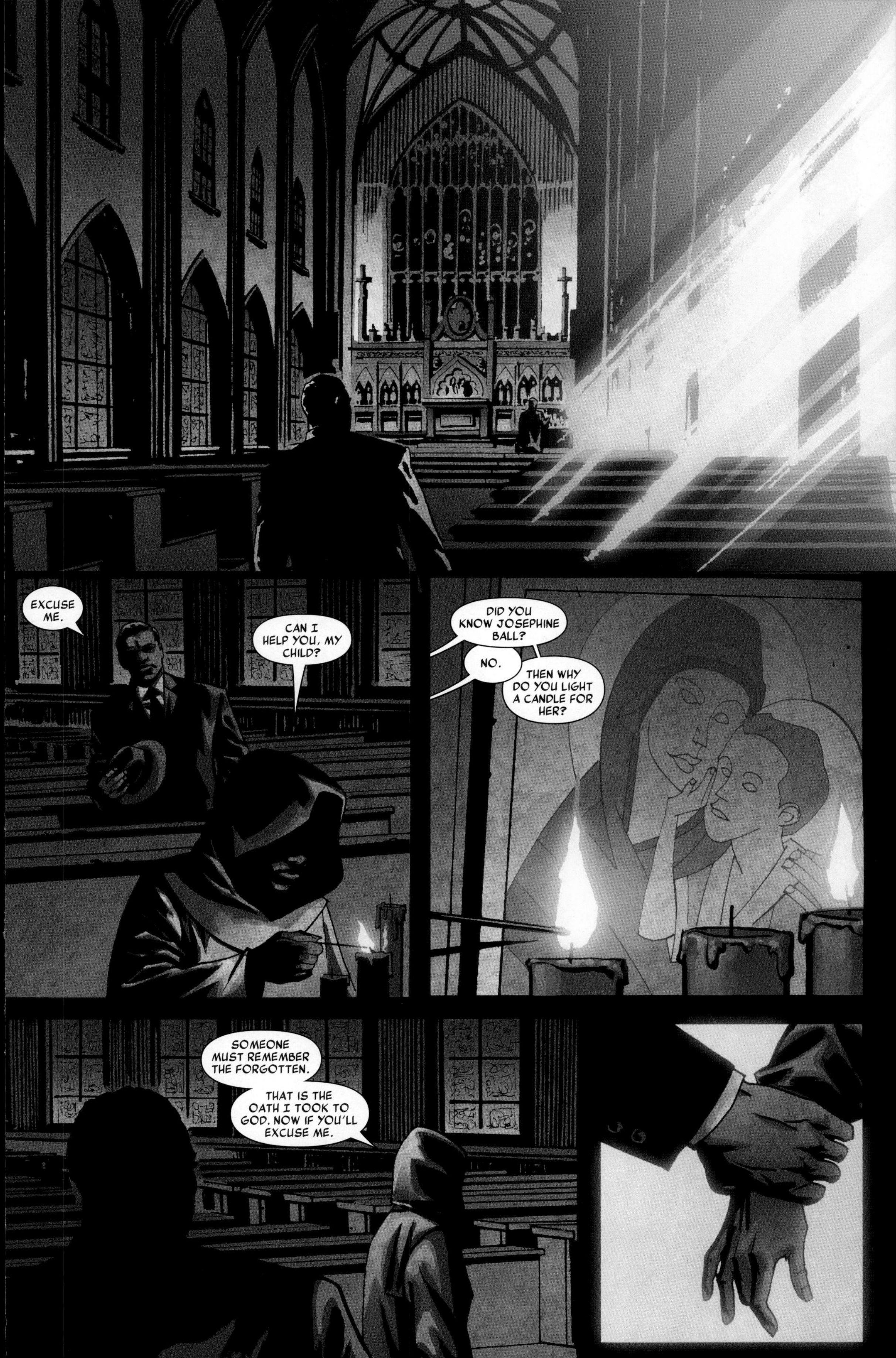
EXCUSE ME.
CAN I HELP YOU, MY CHILD?
DID YOU KNOW JOSEPHINE BALL?
NO.
THEN WHY DO YOU LIGHT A CANDLE FOR HER?
SOMEONE MUST REMEMBER THE FORGOTTEN.
THAT IS THE OATH I TOOK TO GOD. NOW IF YOU'LL EXCUSE ME.

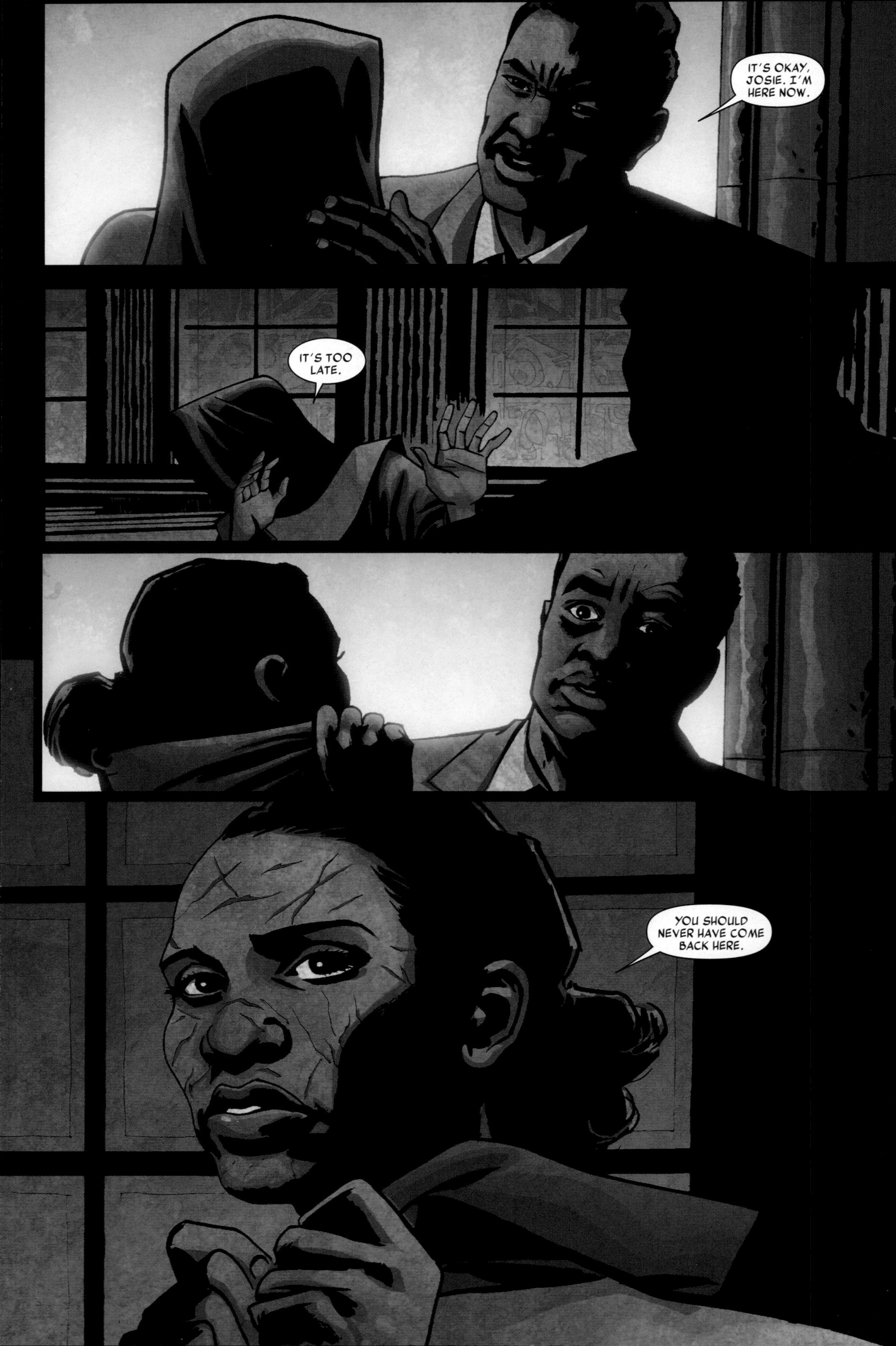
IT'S OKAY, JOSIE. I'M HERE NOW.
IT'S TOO LATE.
YOU SHOULD NEVER HAVE COME BACK HERE.

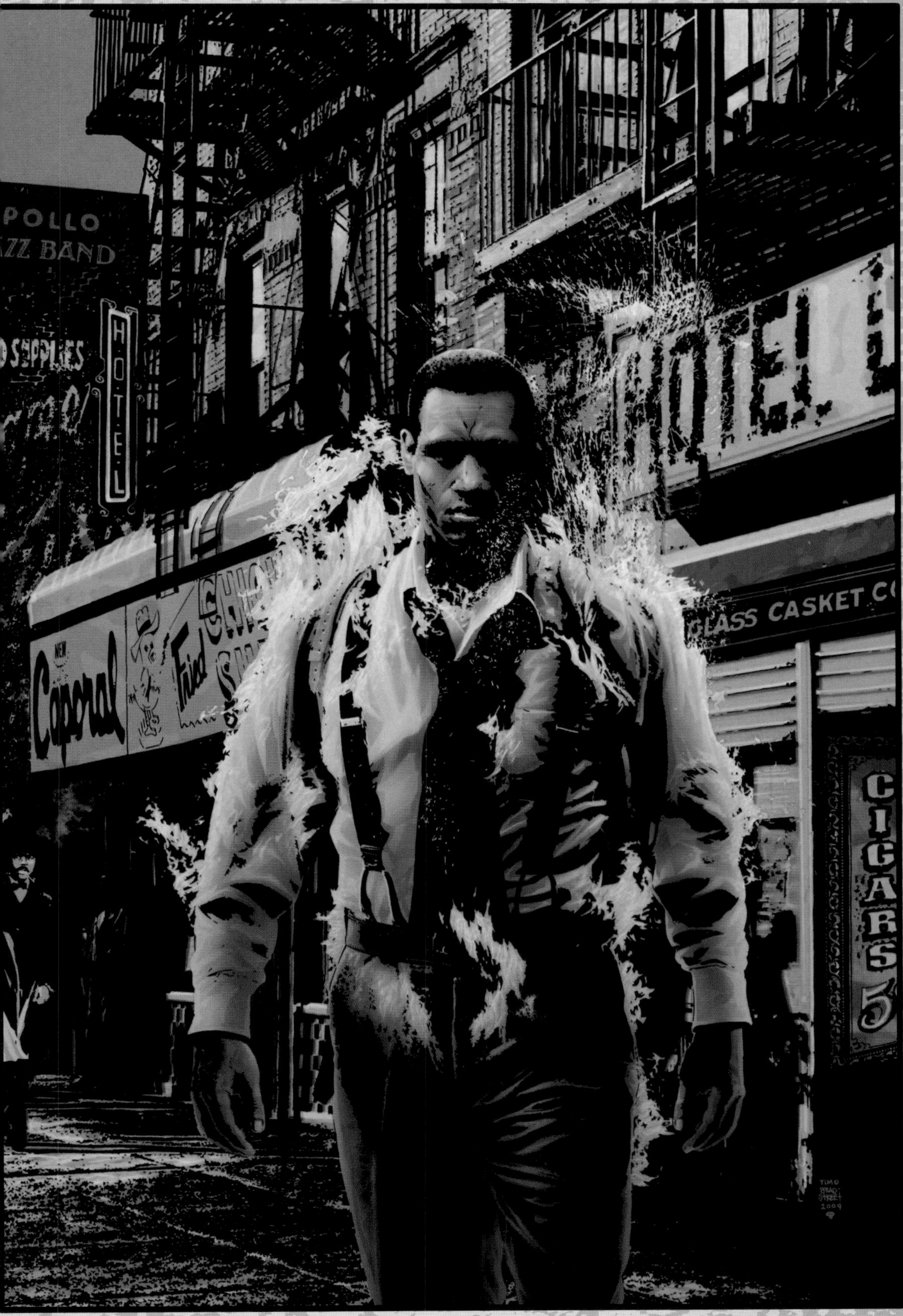
HOTEL
NEW
Caporal
Fried
GLASS CASKET CO
CIGARS

THREE

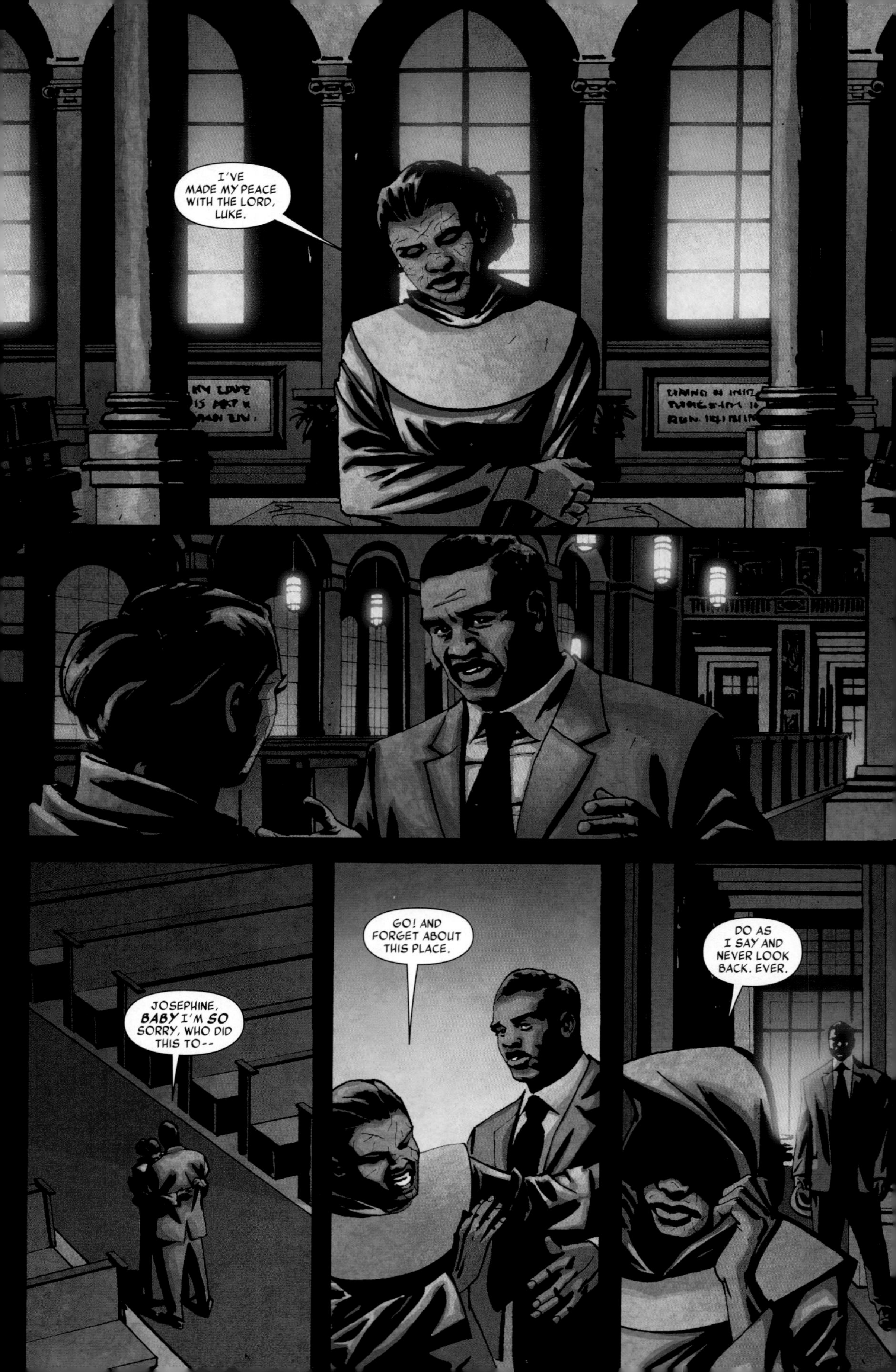
I'VE MADE MY PEACE WITH THE LORD, LUKE.
JOSEPHINE, BABY I'M SO SORRY, WHO DID THIS TO--
GO! AND FORGET ABOUT THIS PLACE.
DO AS I SAY AND NEVER LOOK BACK. EVER.

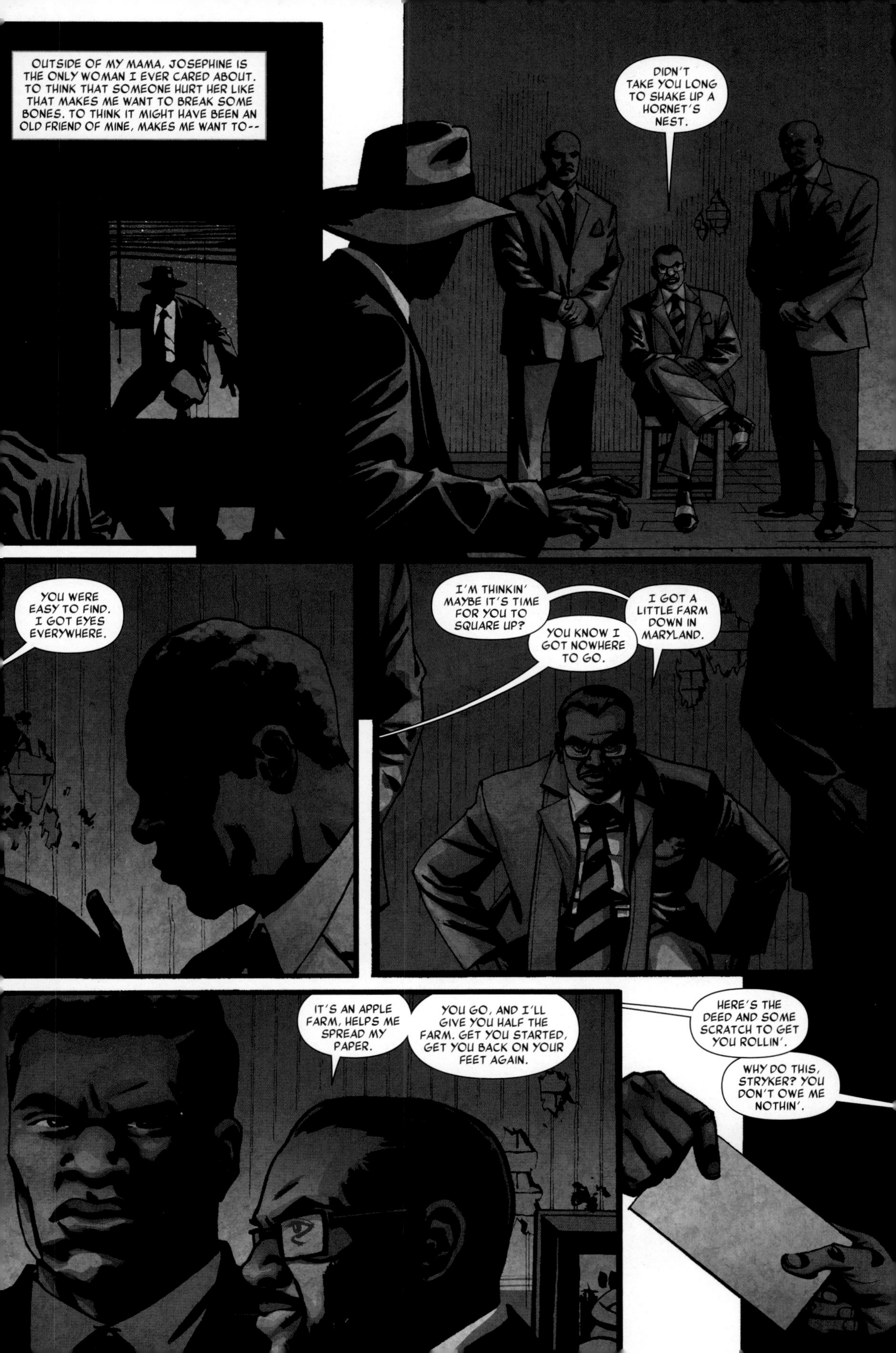
OUTSIDE OF MY MAMA, JOSEPHINE IS THE ONLY WOMAN I EVER CARED ABOUT. TO THINK THAT SOMEONE HURT HER LIKE THAT MAKES ME WANT TO BREAK SOME BONES. TO THINK IT MIGHT HAVE BEEN AN OLD FRIEND OF MINE, MAKES ME WANT TO--
DIDN'T TAKE YOU LONG TO SHAKE UP A HORNET'S NEST.
YOU WERE EASY TO FIND. I GOT EYES EVERYWHERE.
I'M THINKIN' MAYBE IT'S TIME FOR YOU TO SQUARE UP?
YOU KNOW I GOT NOWHERE TO GO.
I GOT A LITTLE FARM DOWN IN MARYLAND.
IT'S AN APPLE FARM, HELPS ME SPREAD MY PAPER.
YOU GO, AND I'LL GIVE YOU HALF THE FARM. GET YOU STARTED, GET YOU BACK ON YOUR FEET AGAIN.
HERE'S THE DEED AND SOME SCRATCH TO GET YOU ROLLIN'.
WHY DO THIS, STRYKER? YOU DON'T OWE ME NOTHIN'.

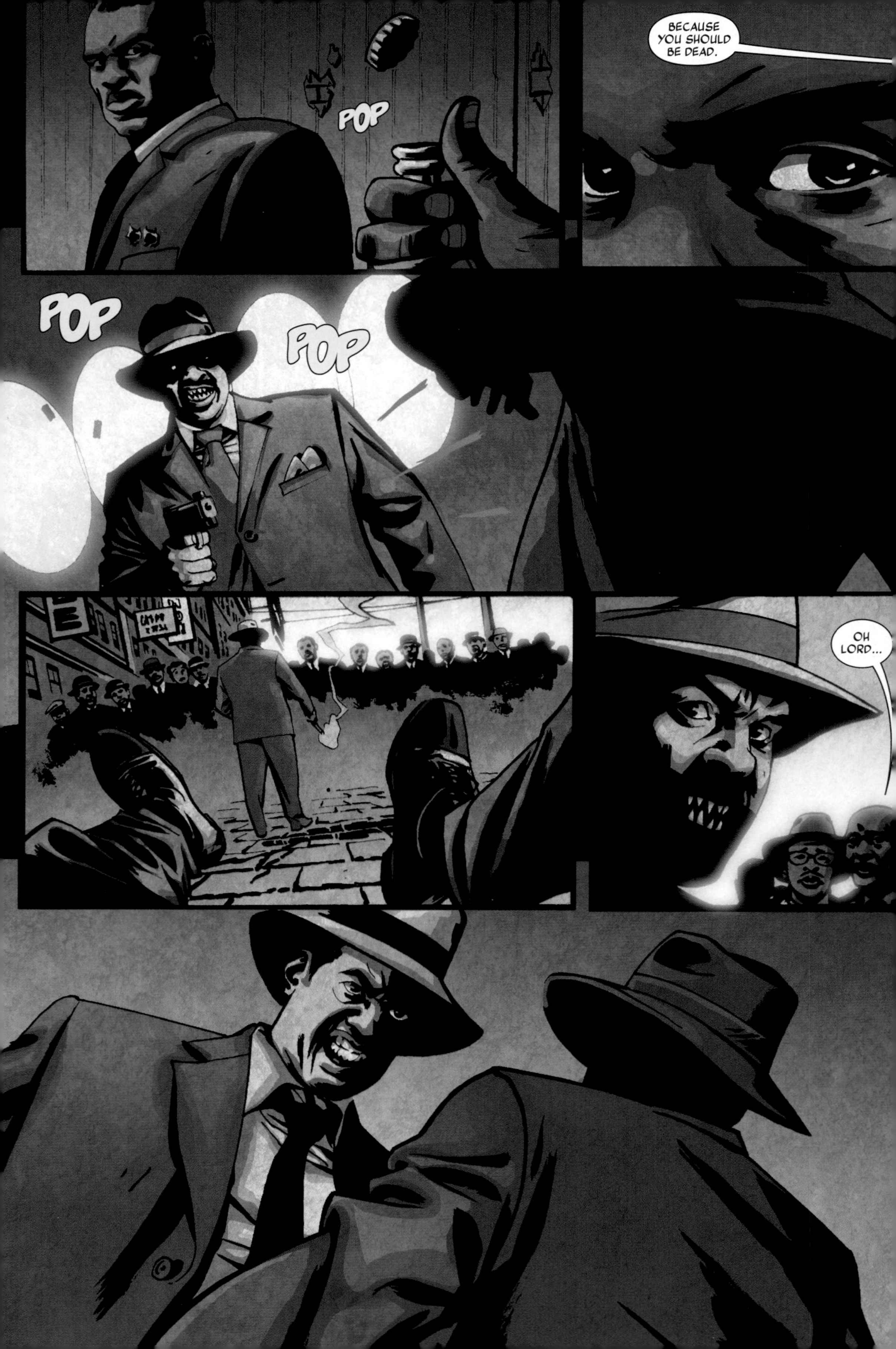
POP
BECAUSE YOU SHOULD BE DEAD.
POP
POP
OH LORD...

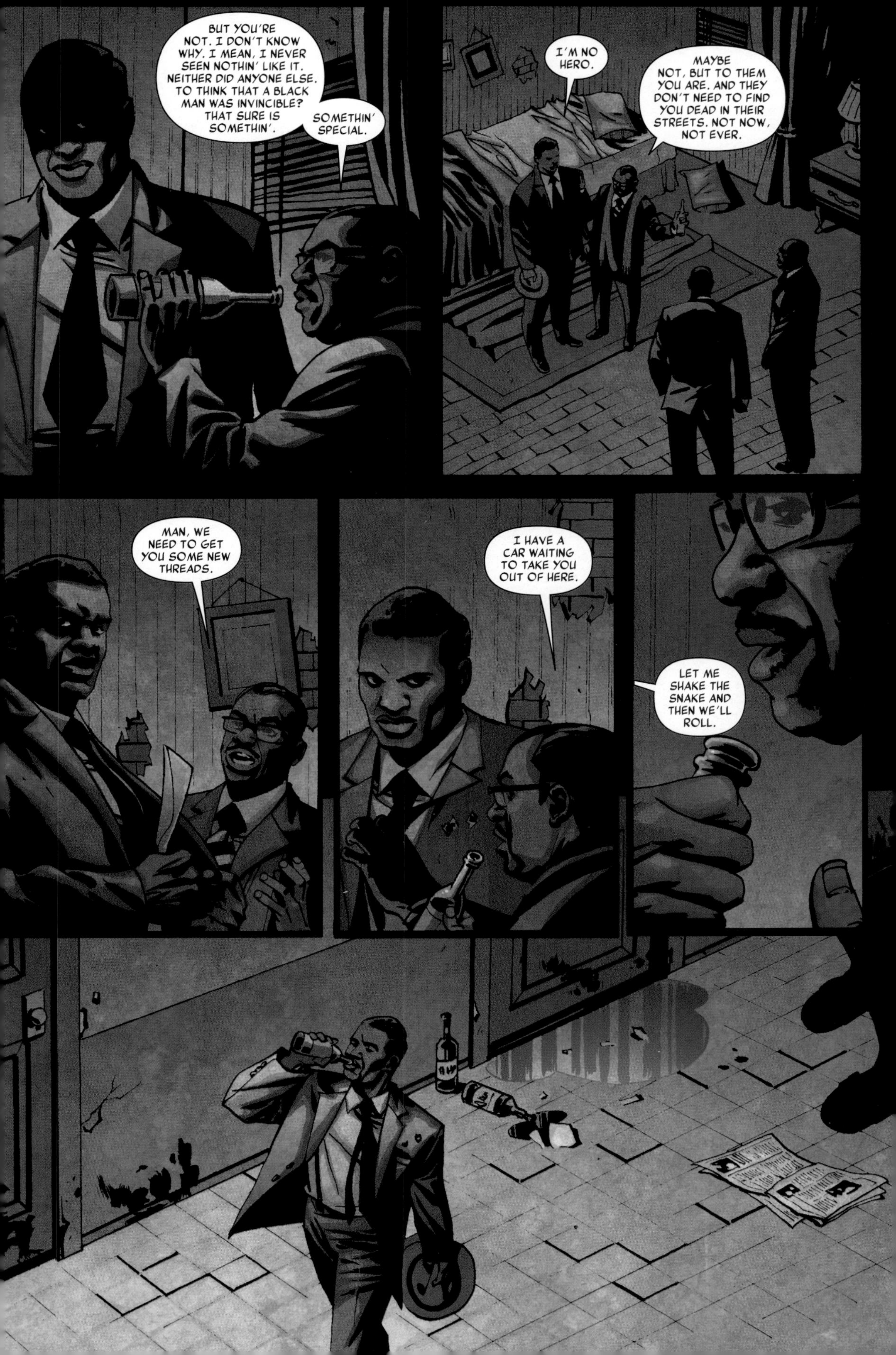
BUT YOU'RE NOT. I DON'T KNOW WHY. I MEAN, I NEVER SEEN NOTHIN' LIKE IT. NEITHER DID ANYONE ELSE. TO THINK THAT A BLACK MAN WAS INVINCIBLE? THAT SURE IS SOMETHIN'.
SOMETHIN' SPECIAL.
I'M NO HERO.
MAYBE NOT, BUT TO THEM YOU ARE. AND THEY DON'T NEED TO FIND YOU DEAD IN THEIR STREETS. NOT NOW, NOT EVER.
MAN, WE NEED TO GET YOU SOME NEW THREADS.
I HAVE A CAR WAITING TO TAKE YOU OUT OF HERE.
LET ME SHAKE THE SNAKE AND THEN WE'LL ROLL.

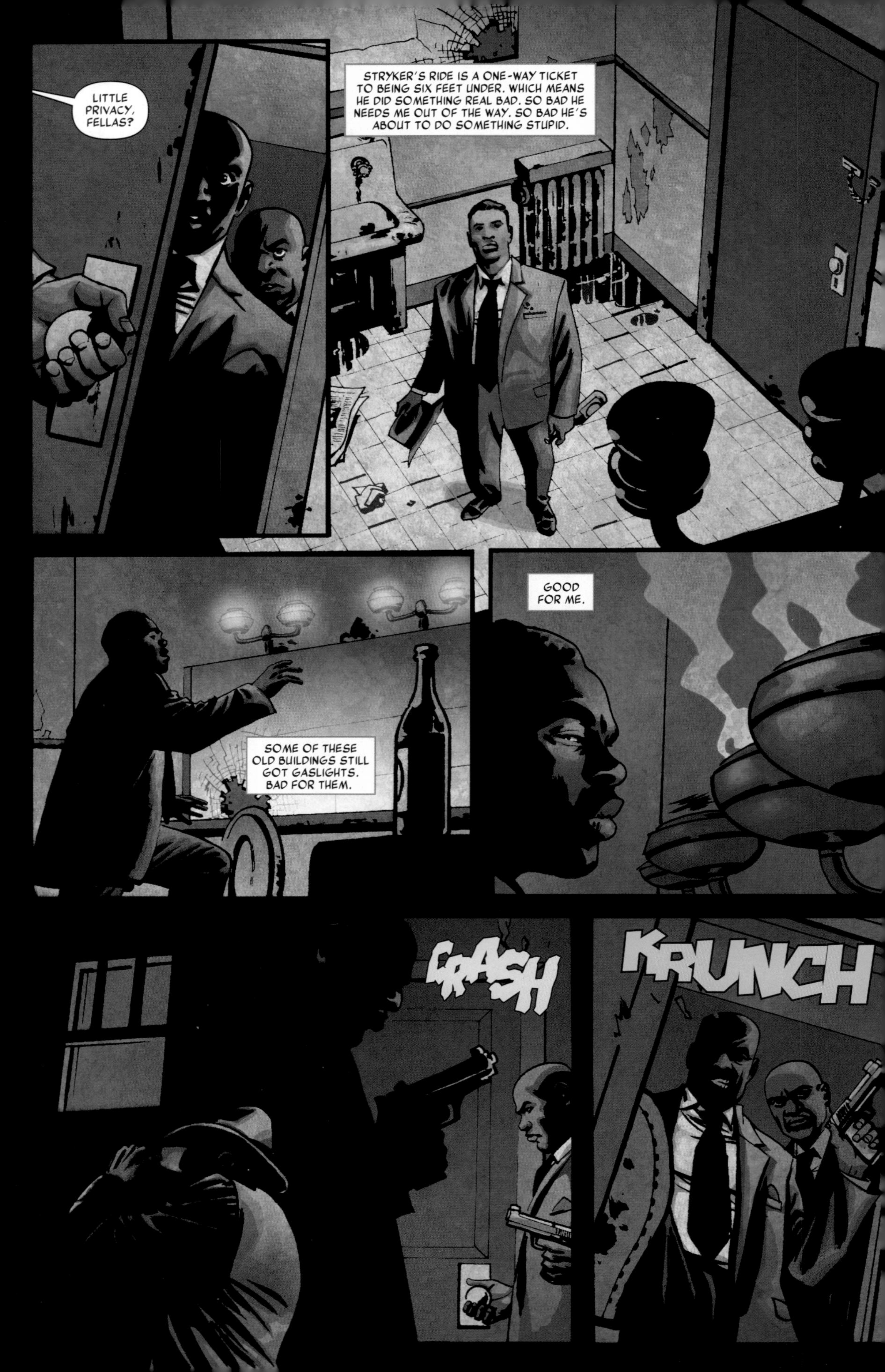
LITTLE PRIVACY, FELLAS?
STRYKER'S RIDE IS A ONE-WAY TICKET TO BEING SIX FEET UNDER. WHICH MEANS HE DID SOMETHING REAL BAD. SO BAD HE NEEDS ME OUT OF THE WAY. SO BAD HE'S ABOUT TO DO SOMETHING STUPID.
SOME OF THESE OLD BUILDINGS STILL GOT GASLIGHTS. BAD FOR THEM.
GOOD FOR ME.
CRASH
KRUNCH

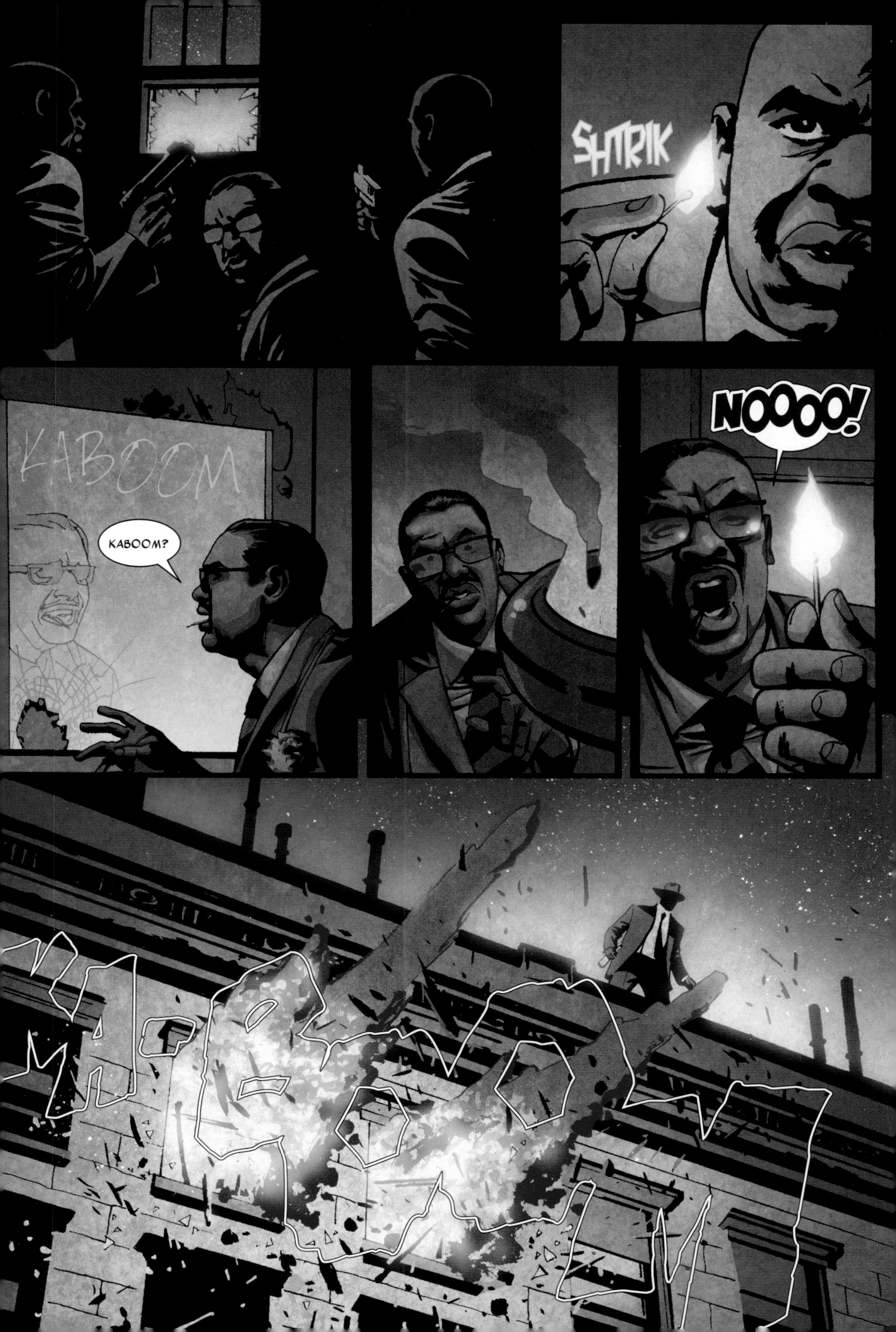
SHTRIK
KABOOM
KABOOM?
NOOOO!
KABOOM

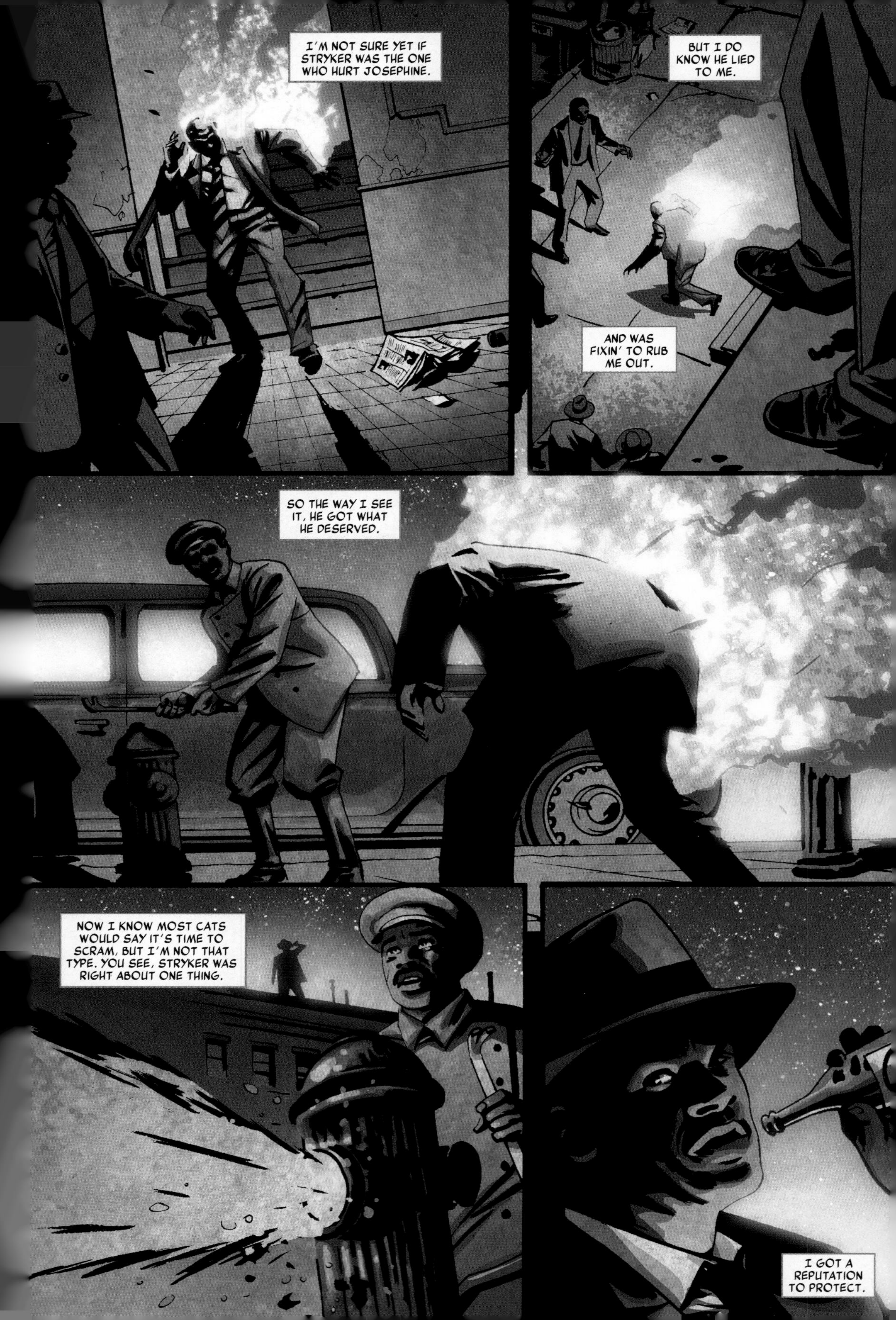
I'M NOT SURE YET IF STRYKER WAS THE ONE WHO HURT JOSEPHINE.
BUT I DO KNOW HE LIED TO ME.
AND WAS FIXIN' TO RUB ME OUT.
SO THE WAY I SEE IT, HE GOT WHAT HE DESERVED.
NOW I KNOW MOST CATS WOULD SAY IT'S TIME TO SCRAM, BUT I'M NOT THAT TYPE. YOU SEE, STRYKER WAS RIGHT ABOUT ONE THING.
I GOT A REPUTATION TO PROTECT.

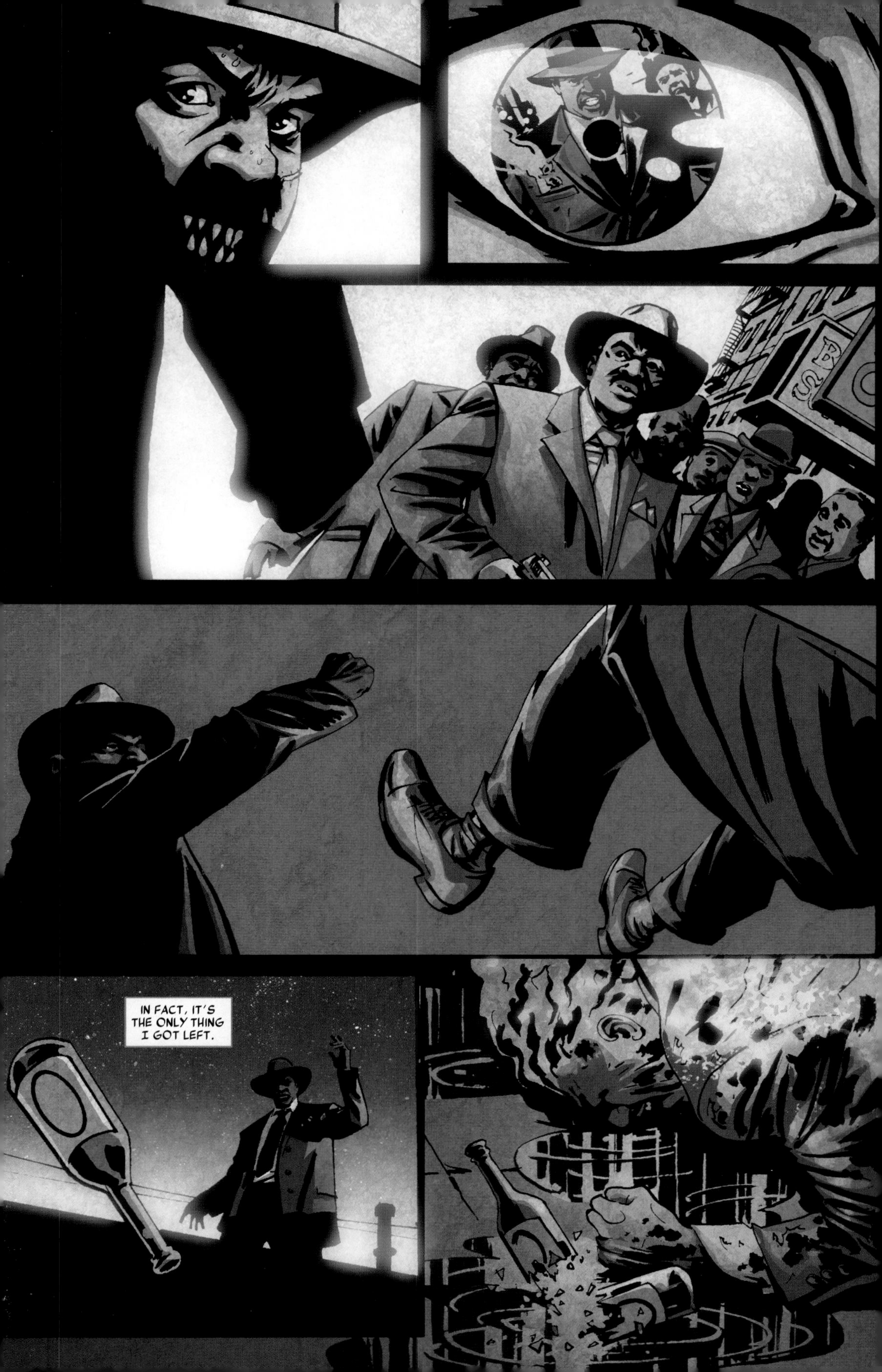
IN FACT, IT'S THE ONLY THING I GOT LEFT.

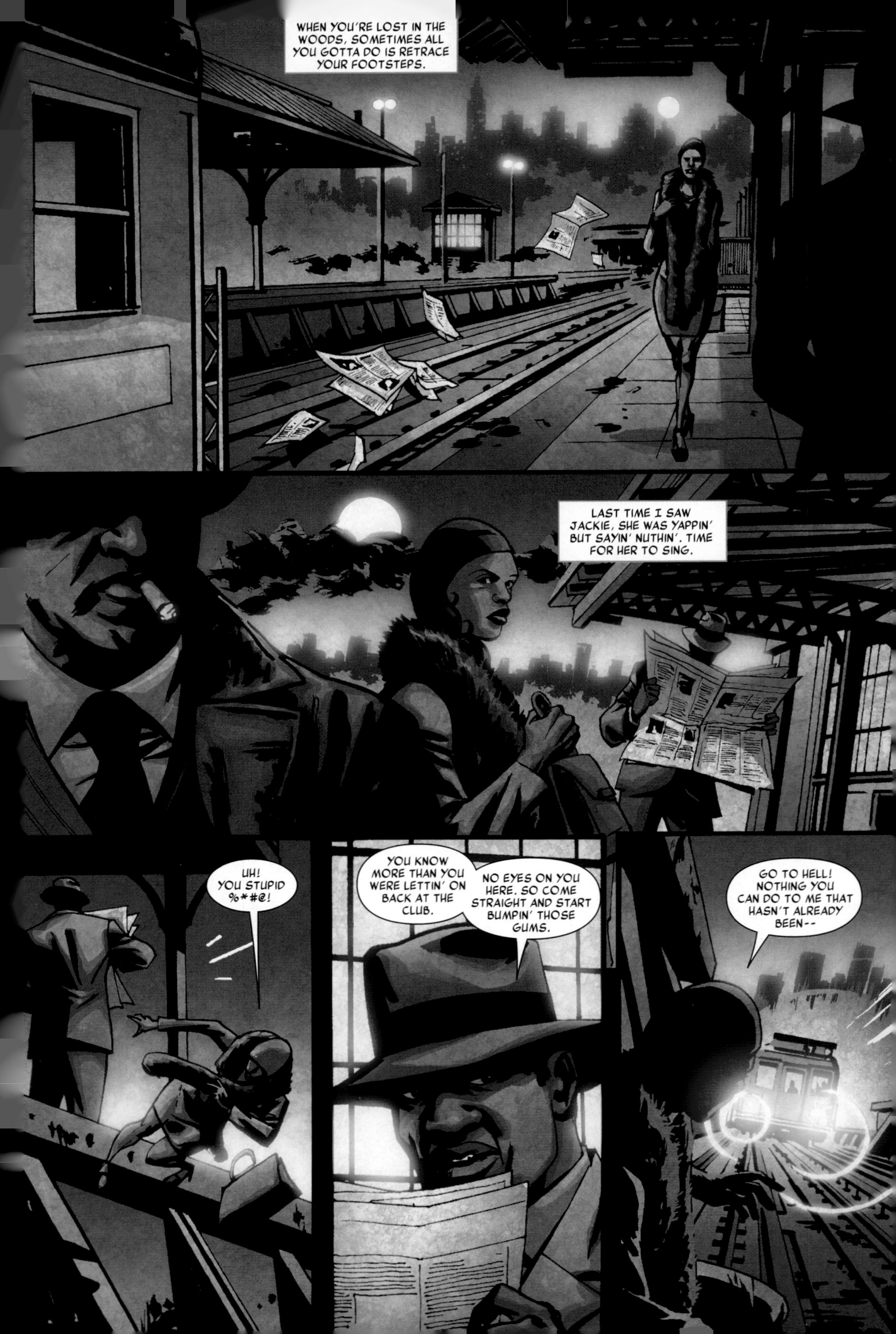
WHEN YOU'RE LOST IN THE WOODS, SOMETIMES ALL YOU GOTTA DO IS RETRACE YOUR FOOTSTEPS.
LAST TIME I SAW JACKIE, SHE WAS YAPPIN' BUT SAYIN' NUTHIN'. TIME FOR HER TO SING.
UH! YOU STUPID %*#@!
YOU KNOW MORE THAN YOU WERE LETTIN' ON BACK AT THE CLUB.
NO EYES ON YOU HERE. SO COME STRAIGHT AND START BUMPIN' THOSE GUMS.
GO TO HELL! NOTHING YOU CAN DO TO ME THAT HASN'T ALREADY BEEN--

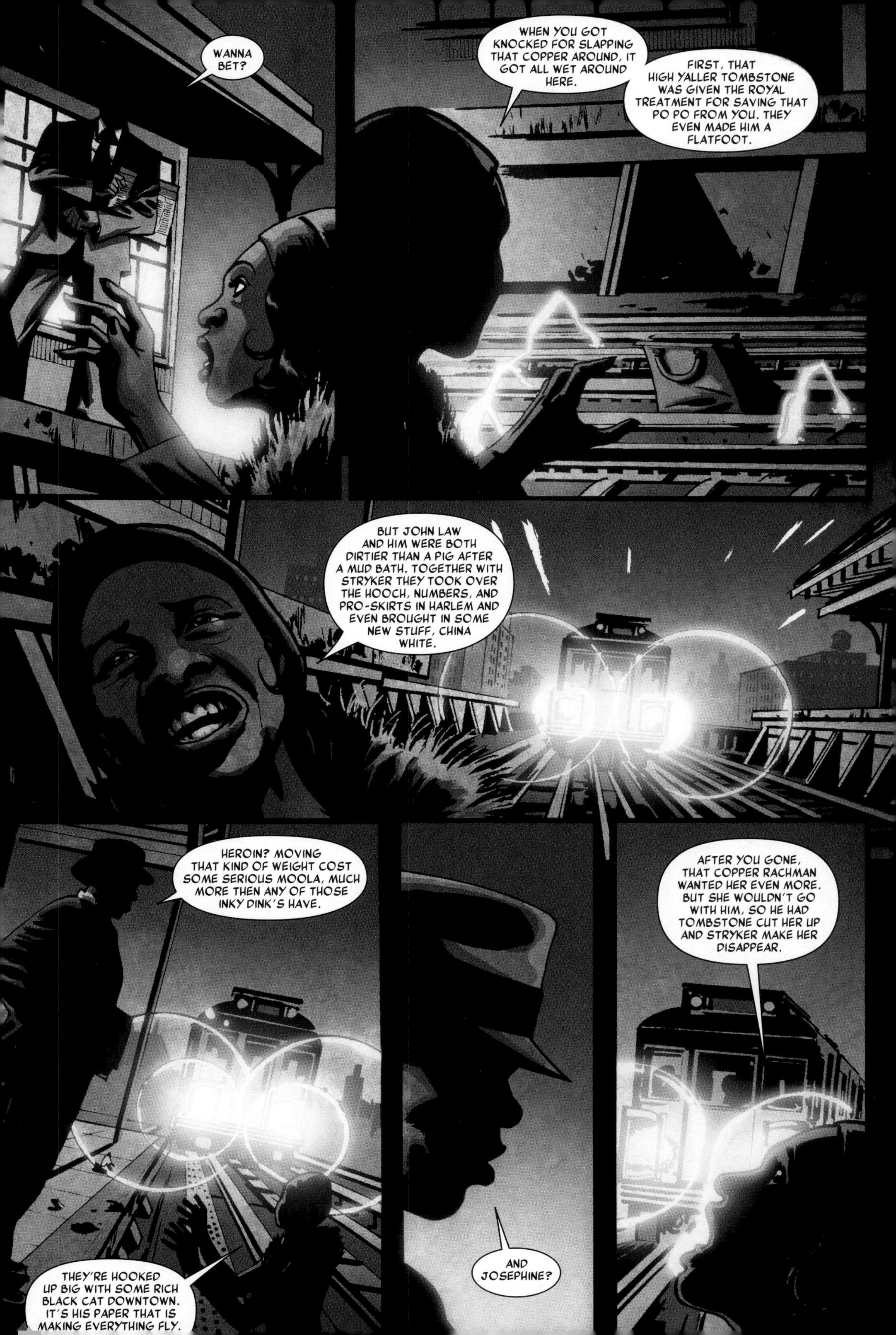
WANNA BET?
WHEN YOU GOT KNOCKED FOR SLAPPING THAT COPPER AROUND, IT GOT ALL WET AROUND HERE.
FIRST, THAT HIGH YALLER TOMBSTONE WAS GIVEN THE ROYAL TREATMENT FOR SAVING THAT PO PO FROM YOU. THEY EVEN MADE HIM A FLATFOOT.
BUT JOHN LAW AND HIM WERE BOTH DIRTIER THAN A PIG AFTER A MUD BATH. TOGETHER WITH STRYKER THEY TOOK OVER THE HOOCH, NUMBERS, AND PRO-SKIRTS IN HARLEM AND EVEN BROUGHT IN SOME NEW STUFF, CHINA WHITE.
HEROIN? MOVING THAT KIND OF WEIGHT COST SOME SERIOUS MOOLA, MUCH MORE THEN ANY OF THOSE INKY DINK'S HAVE.
THEY'RE HOOKED UP BIG WITH SOME RICH BLACK CAT DOWNTOWN. IT'S HIS PAPER THAT IS MAKING EVERYTHING FLY.
AND JOSEPHINE?
AFTER YOU GONE, THAT COPPER RACHMAN WANTED HER EVEN MORE. BUT SHE WOULDN'T GO WITH HIM, SO HE HAD TOMBSTONE CUT HER UP AND STRYKER MAKE HER DISAPPEAR.

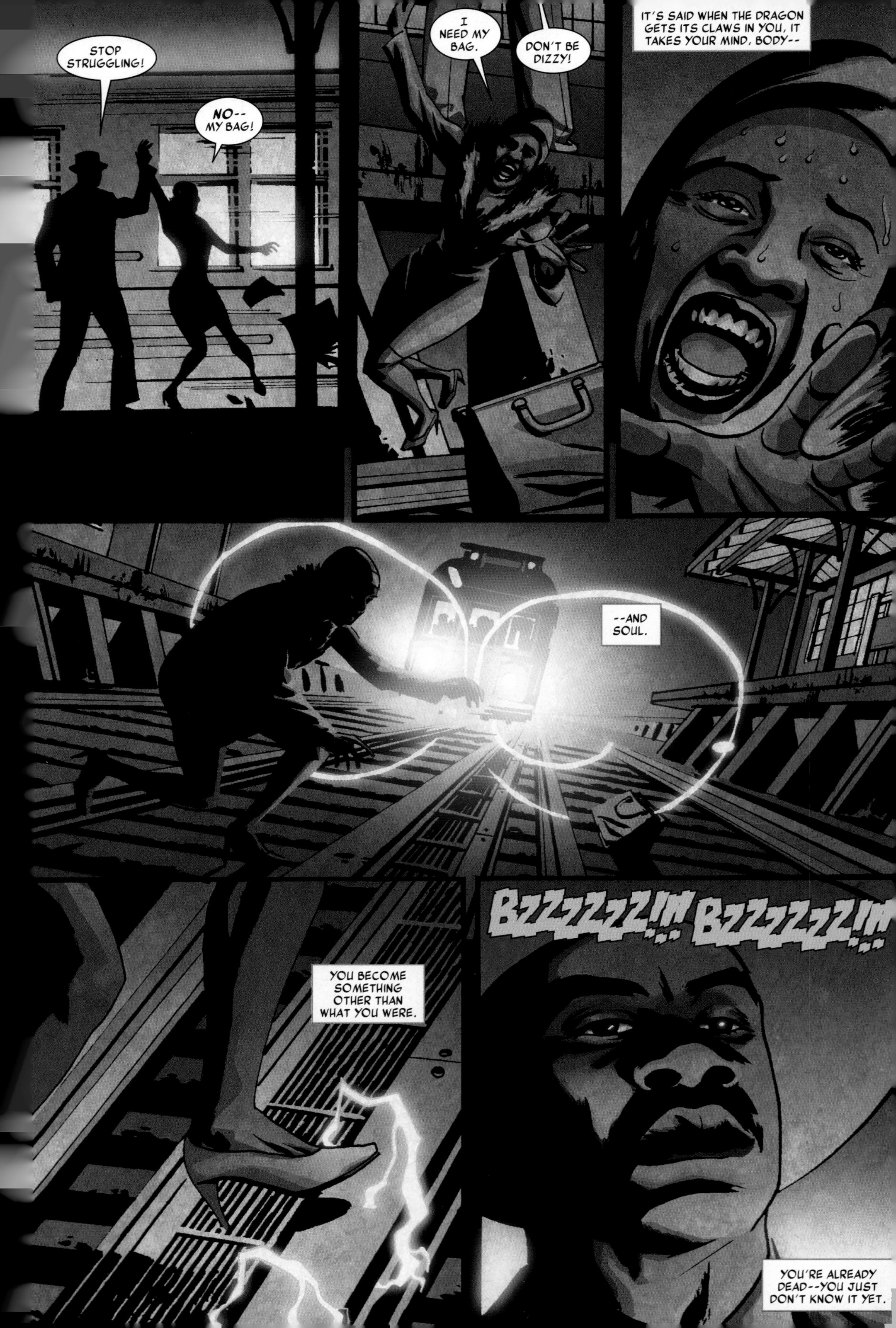
STOP STRUGGLING!
NO-- MY BAG!
I NEED MY BAG.
DON'T BE DIZZY!
IT'S SAID WHEN THE DRAGON GETS ITS CLAWS IN YOU, IT TAKES YOUR MIND, BODY--
--AND SOUL.
YOU BECOME SOMETHING OTHER THAN WHAT YOU WERE.
BZZZZZZ!!! BZZZZZZ!!!
YOU'RE ALREADY DEAD--YOU JUST DON'T KNOW IT YET.

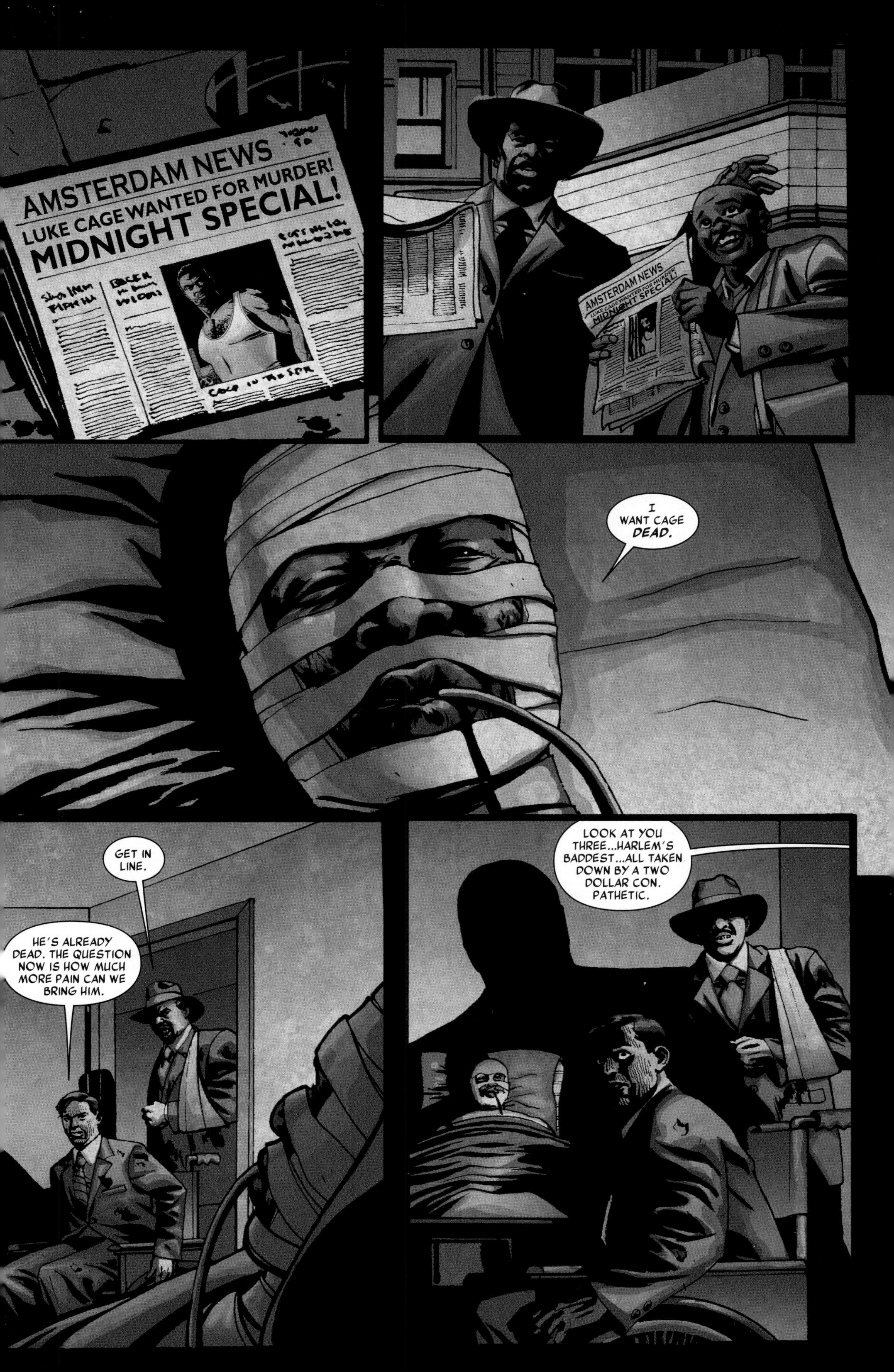

AMSTERDAM NEWS
LUKE CAGE WANTED FOR MURDER!
MIDNIGHT SPECIAL!
AMSTERDAM NEWS
LUKE CAGE WANTED FOR MURDER!
MIDNIGHT SPECIAL!
I WANT CAGE *DEAD.*
GET IN LINE.
HE'S ALREADY DEAD. THE QUESTION NOW IS HOW MUCH MORE PAIN CAN WE BRING HIM.
LOOK AT YOU THREE...HARLEM'S BADDEST...ALL TAKEN DOWN BY A TWO DOLLAR CON. PATHETIC.

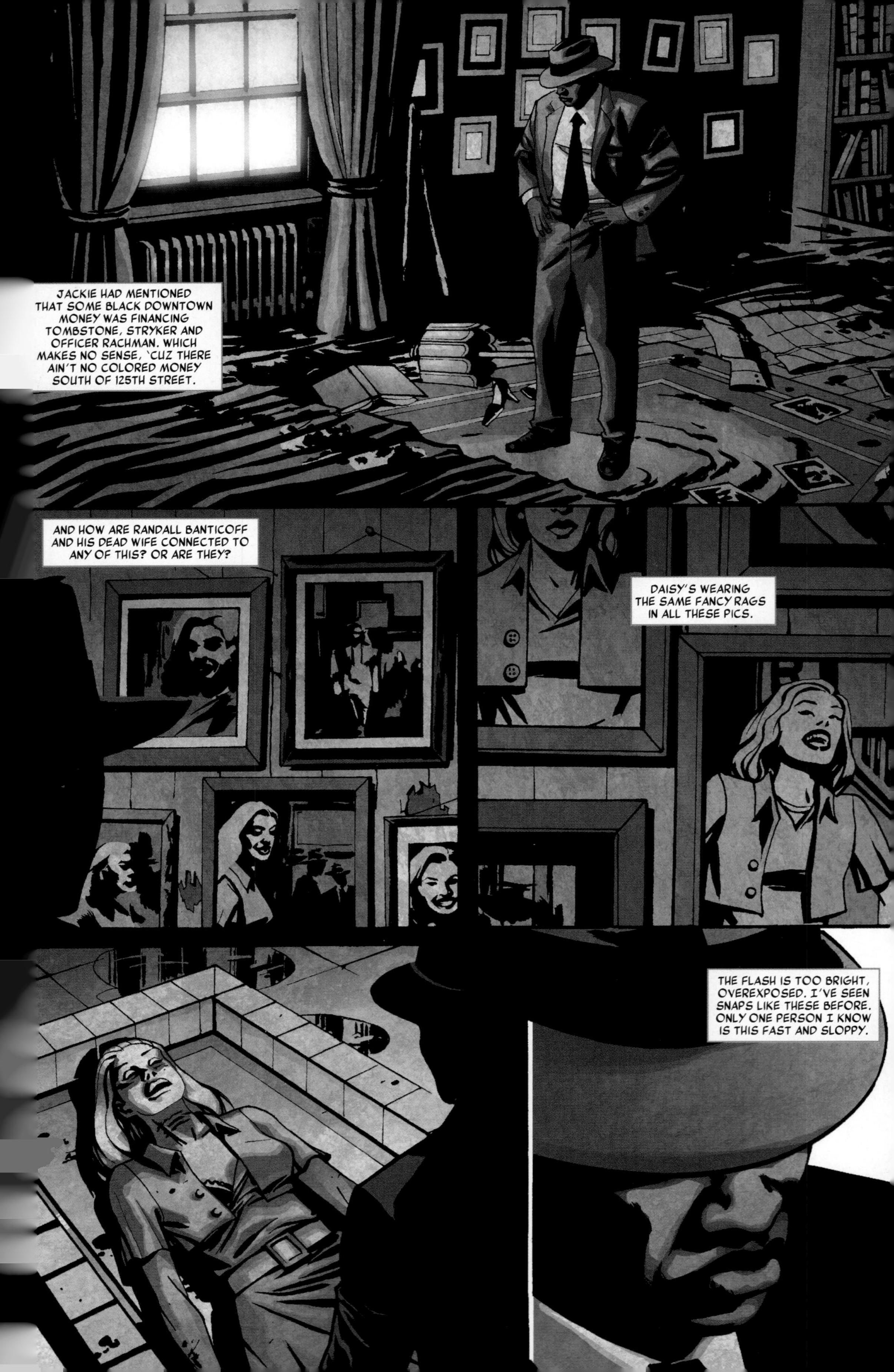
JACKIE HAD MENTIONED THAT SOME BLACK DOWNTOWN MONEY WAS FINANCING TOMBSTONE, STRYKER AND OFFICER RACHMAN. WHICH MAKES NO SENSE, 'CUZ THERE AIN'T NO COLORED MONEY SOUTH OF 125TH STREET.
AND HOW ARE RANDALL BANTICOFF AND HIS DEAD WIFE CONNECTED TO ANY OF THIS? OR ARE THEY?
DAISY'S WEARING THE SAME FANCY RAGS IN ALL THESE PICS.
THE FLASH IS TOO BRIGHT, OVEREXPOSED. I'VE SEEN SNAPS LIKE THESE BEFORE. ONLY ONE PERSON I KNOW IS THIS FAST AND SLOPPY.

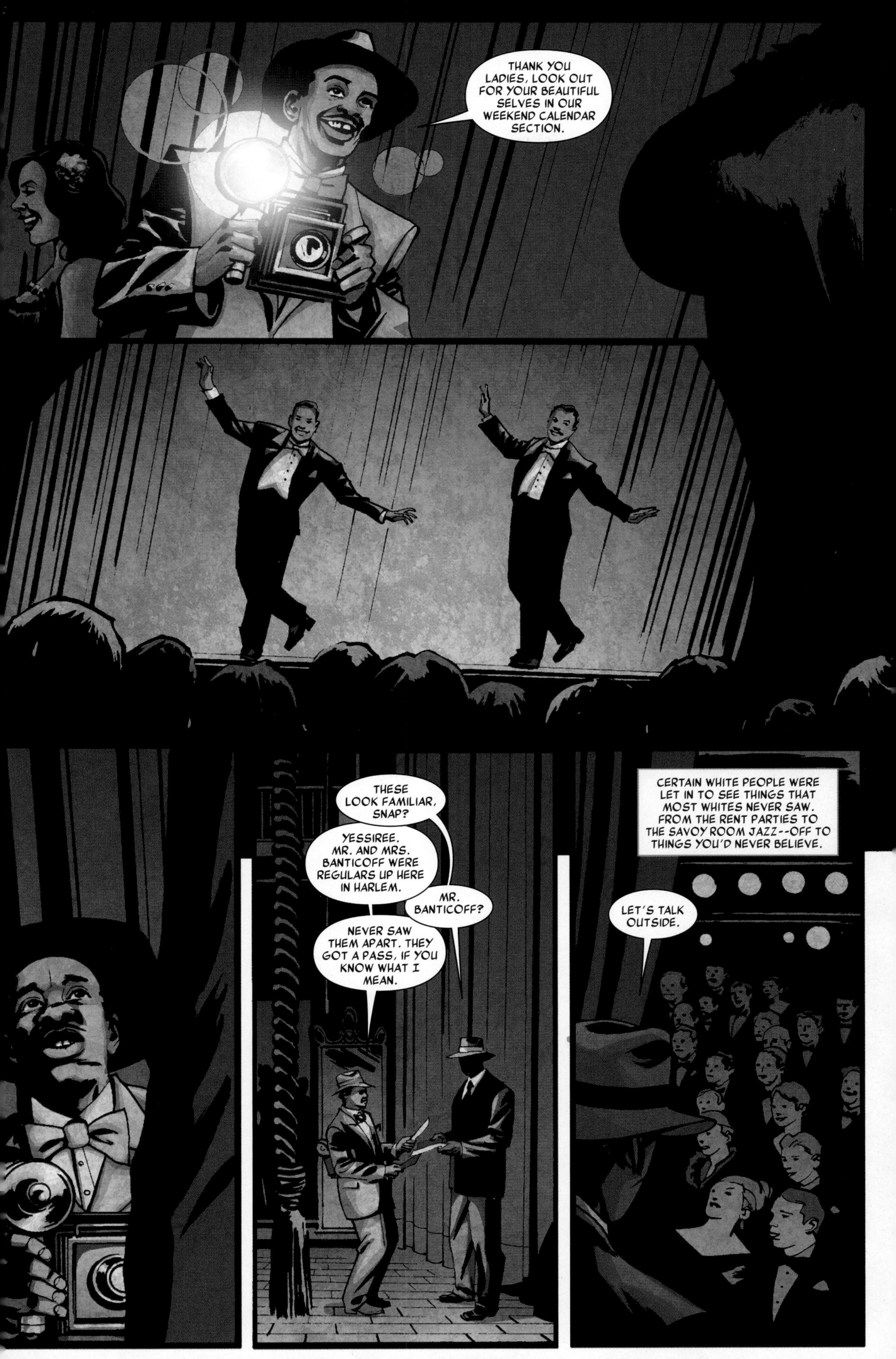
THANK YOU LADIES, LOOK OUT FOR YOUR BEAUTIFUL SELVES IN OUR WEEKEND CALENDAR SECTION.
THESE LOOK FAMILIAR, SNAP?
YESSIREE. MR. AND MRS. BANTICOFF WERE REGULARS UP HERE IN HARLEM.
MR. BANTICOFF?
NEVER SAW THEM APART. THEY GOT A PASS, IF YOU KNOW WHAT I MEAN.
CERTAIN WHITE PEOPLE WERE LET IN TO SEE THINGS THAT MOST WHITES NEVER SAW. FROM THE RENT PARTIES TO THE SAVOY ROOM JAZZ--OFF TO THINGS YOU'D NEVER BELIEVE.
LET'S TALK OUTSIDE.

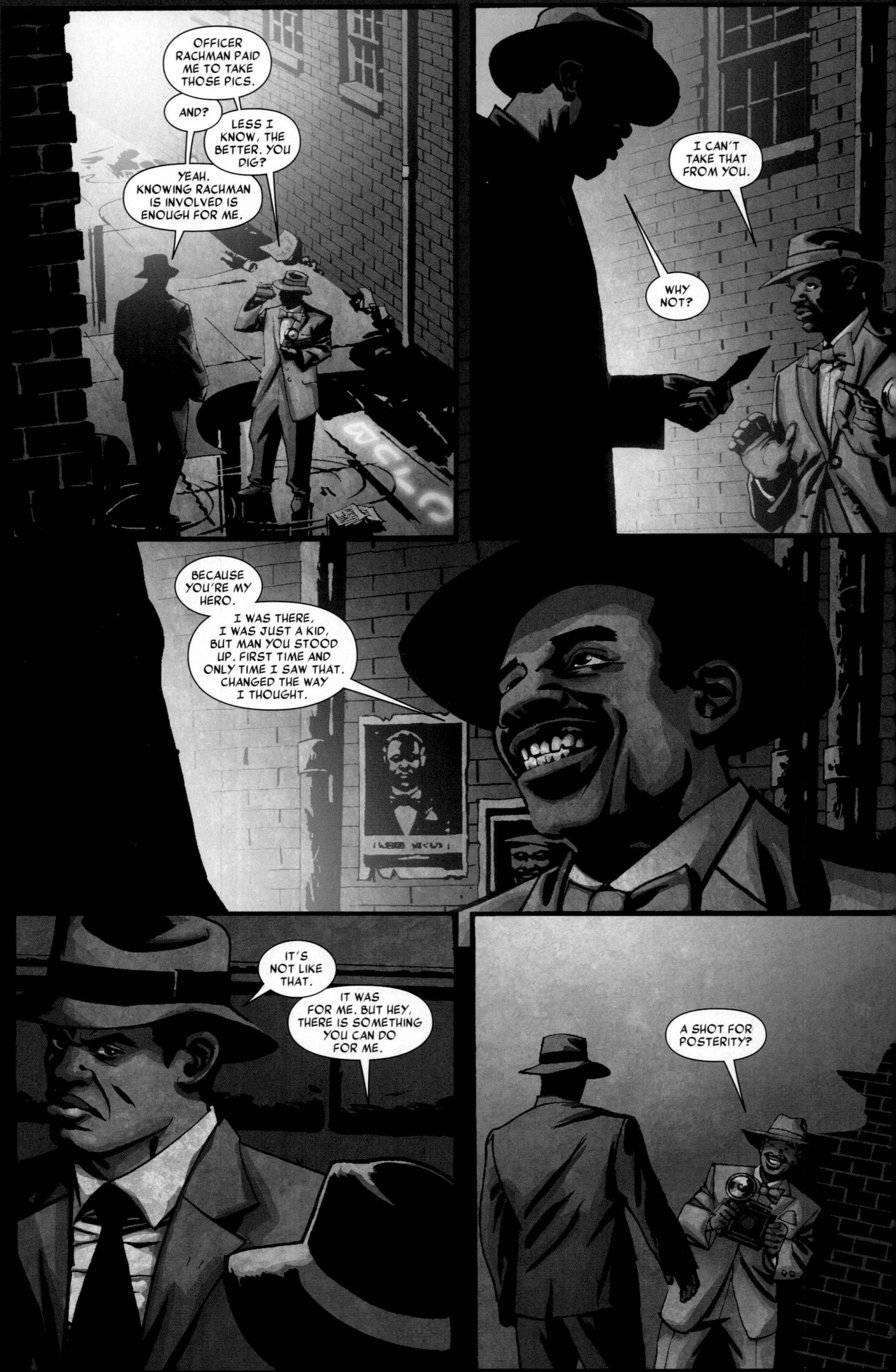
OFFICER RACHMAN PAID ME TO TAKE THOSE PICS.
AND?
LESS I KNOW, THE BETTER. YOU DIG?
YEAH. KNOWING RACHMAN IS INVOLVED IS ENOUGH FOR ME.
I CAN'T TAKE THAT FROM YOU.
WHY NOT?
BECAUSE YOU'RE MY HERO.
I WAS THERE, I WAS JUST A KID, BUT MAN YOU STOOD UP. FIRST TIME AND ONLY TIME I SAW THAT. CHANGED THE WAY I THOUGHT.
IT'S NOT LIKE THAT.
IT WAS FOR ME. BUT HEY, THERE IS SOMETHING YOU CAN DO FOR ME.
A SHOT FOR POSTERITY?

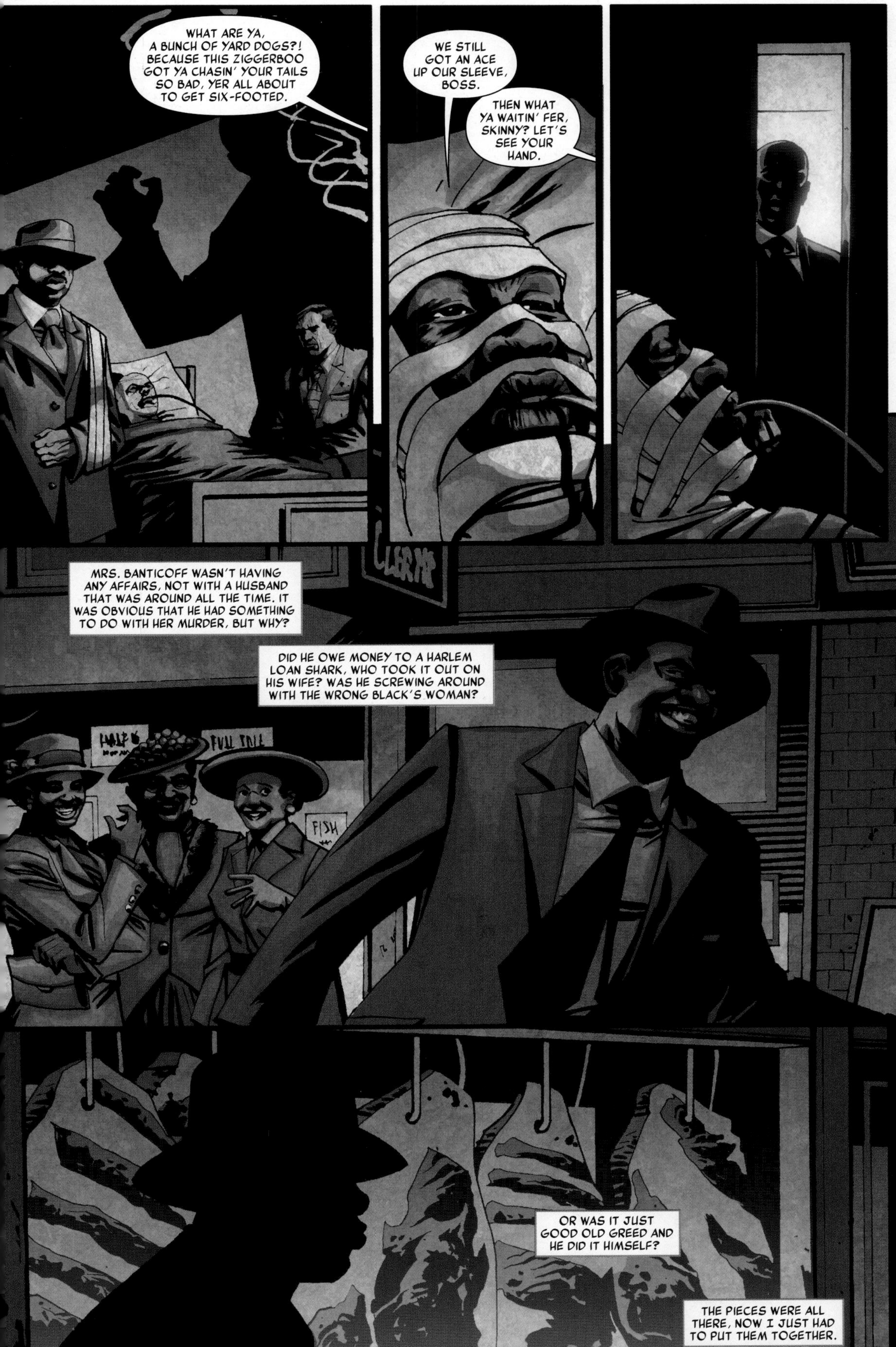

WHAT ARE YA, A BUNCH OF YARD DOGS?! BECAUSE THIS ZIGGERBOO GOT YA CHASIN' YOUR TAILS SO BAD, YER ALL ABOUT TO GET SIX-FOOTED.
WE STILL GOT AN ACE UP OUR SLEEVE, BOSS.
THEN WHAT YA WAITIN' FER, SKINNY? LET'S SEE YOUR HAND.
MRS. BANTICOFF WASN'T HAVING ANY AFFAIRS, NOT WITH A HUSBAND THAT WAS AROUND ALL THE TIME. IT WAS OBVIOUS THAT HE HAD SOMETHING TO DO WITH HER MURDER, BUT WHY?
DID HE OWE MONEY TO A HARLEM LOAN SHARK, WHO TOOK IT OUT ON HIS WIFE? WAS HE SCREWING AROUND WITH THE WRONG BLACK'S WOMAN?
FISH
OR WAS IT JUST GOOD OLD GREED AND HE DID IT HIMSELF?
THE PIECES WERE ALL THERE, NOW I JUST HAD TO PUT THEM TOGETHER.

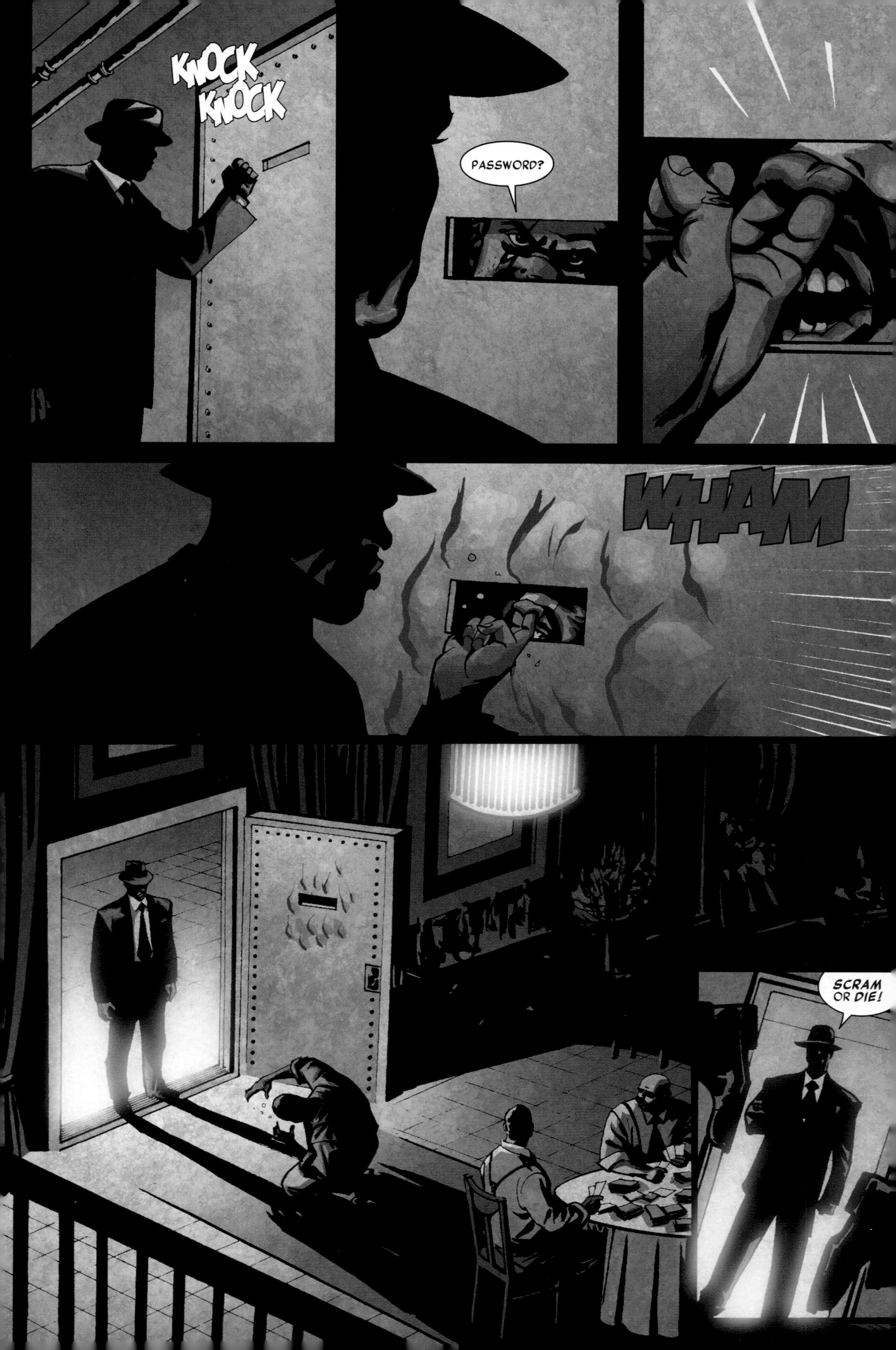
KNOCK KNOCK
PASSWORD?
WHAM
SCRAM OR DIE!

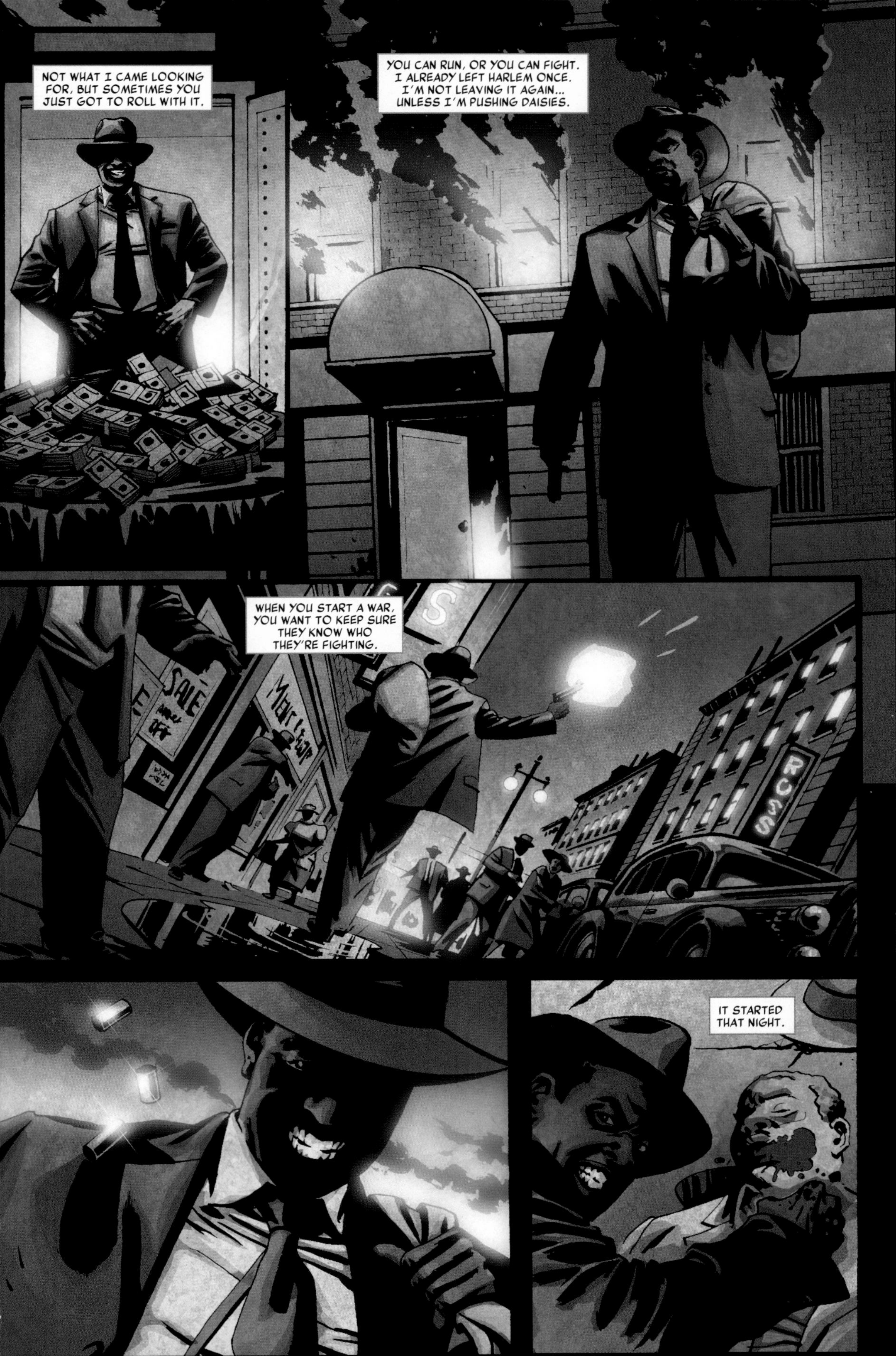
NOT WHAT I CAME LOOKING FOR, BUT SOMETIMES YOU JUST GOT TO ROLL WITH IT.
YOU CAN RUN, OR YOU CAN FIGHT. I ALREADY LEFT HARLEM ONCE. I'M NOT LEAVING IT AGAIN... UNLESS I'M PUSHING DAISIES.
WHEN YOU START A WAR, YOU WANT TO KEEP SURE THEY KNOW WHO THEY'RE FIGHTING.
SALE
IT STARTED THAT NIGHT.

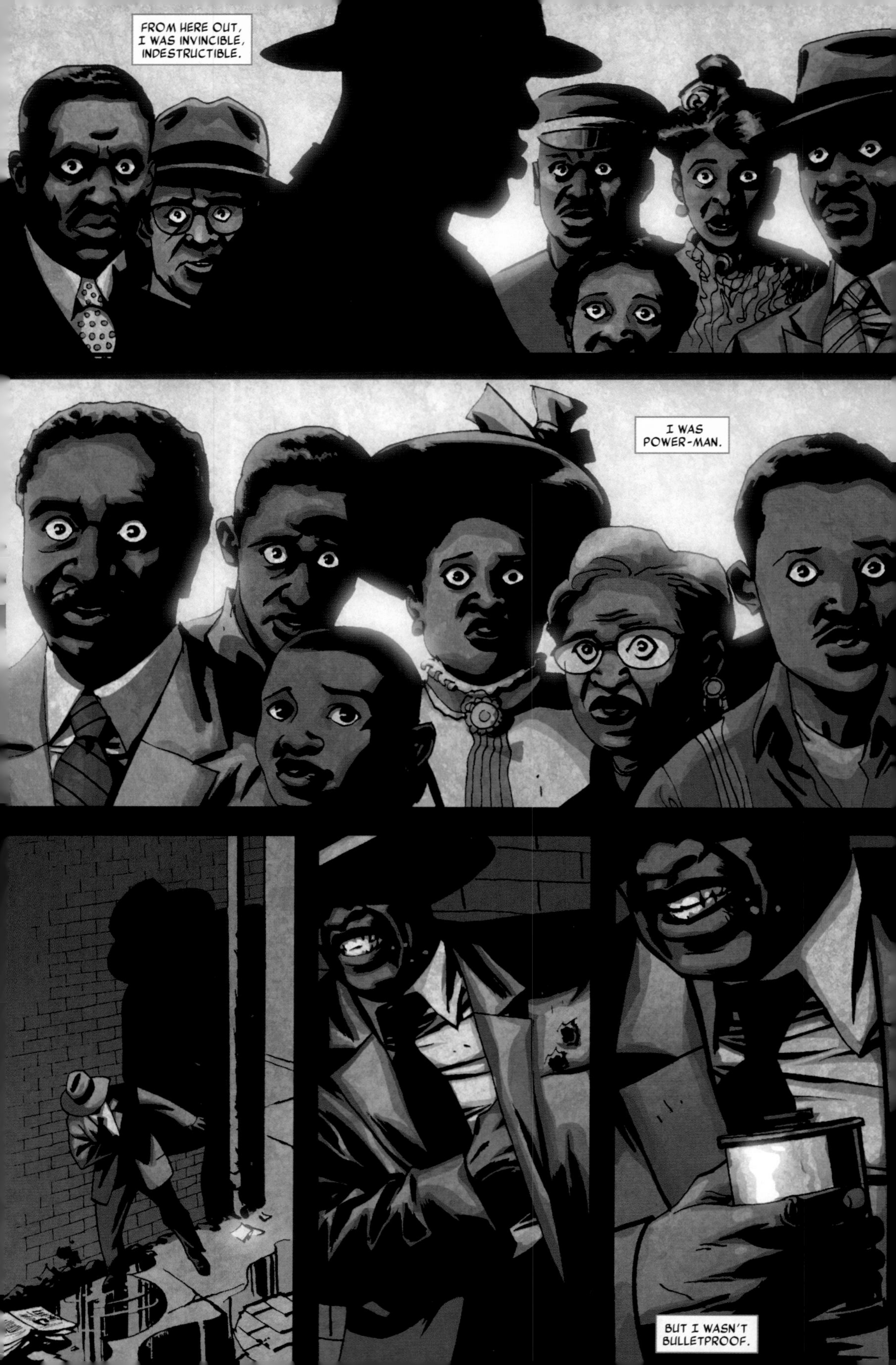
FROM HERE OUT, I WAS INVINCIBLE, INDESTRUCTIBLE.
I WAS POWER-MAN.
BUT I WASN'T BULLETPROOF.

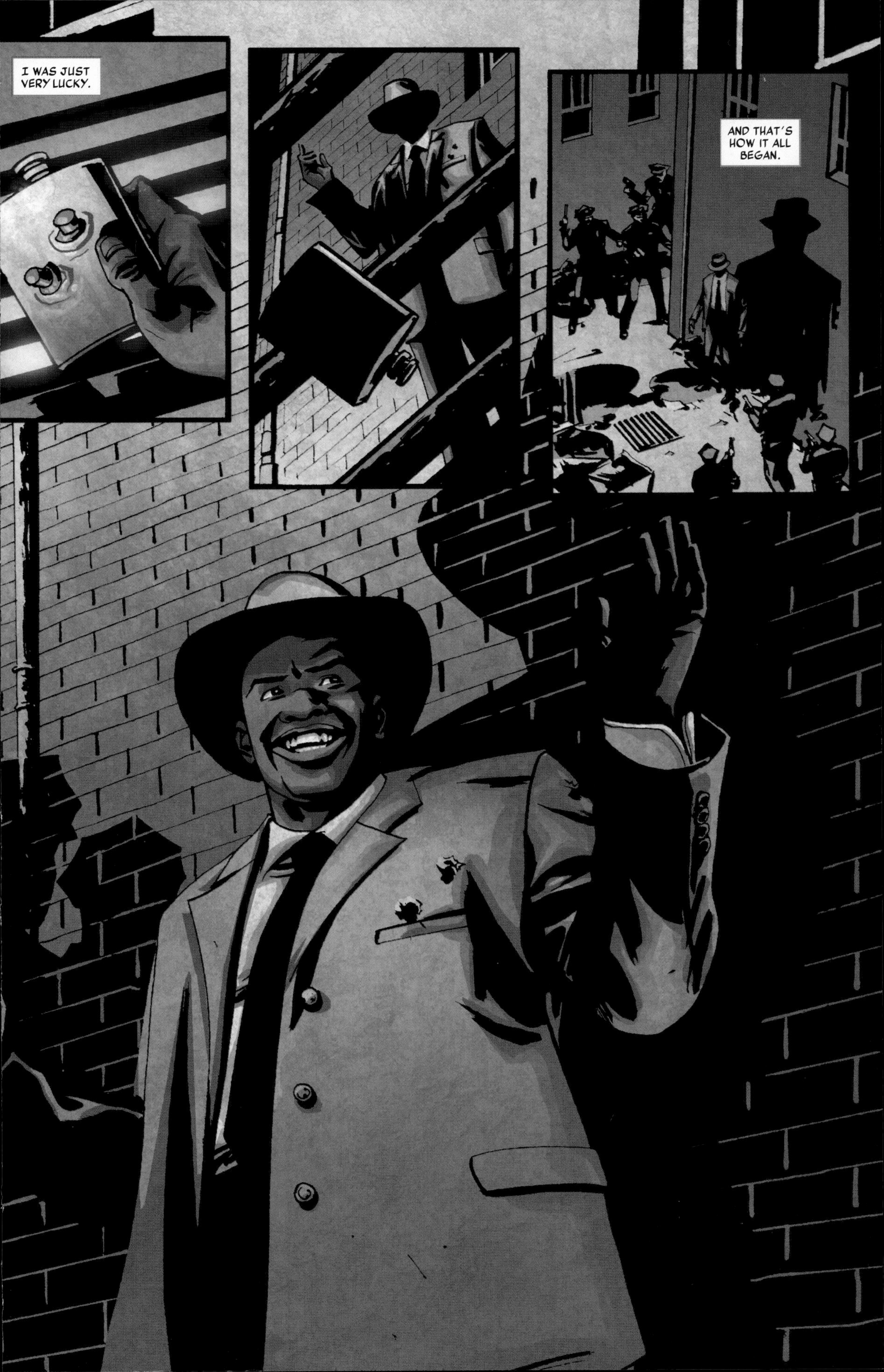
I WAS JUST VERY LUCKY.
AND THAT'S HOW IT ALL BEGAN.

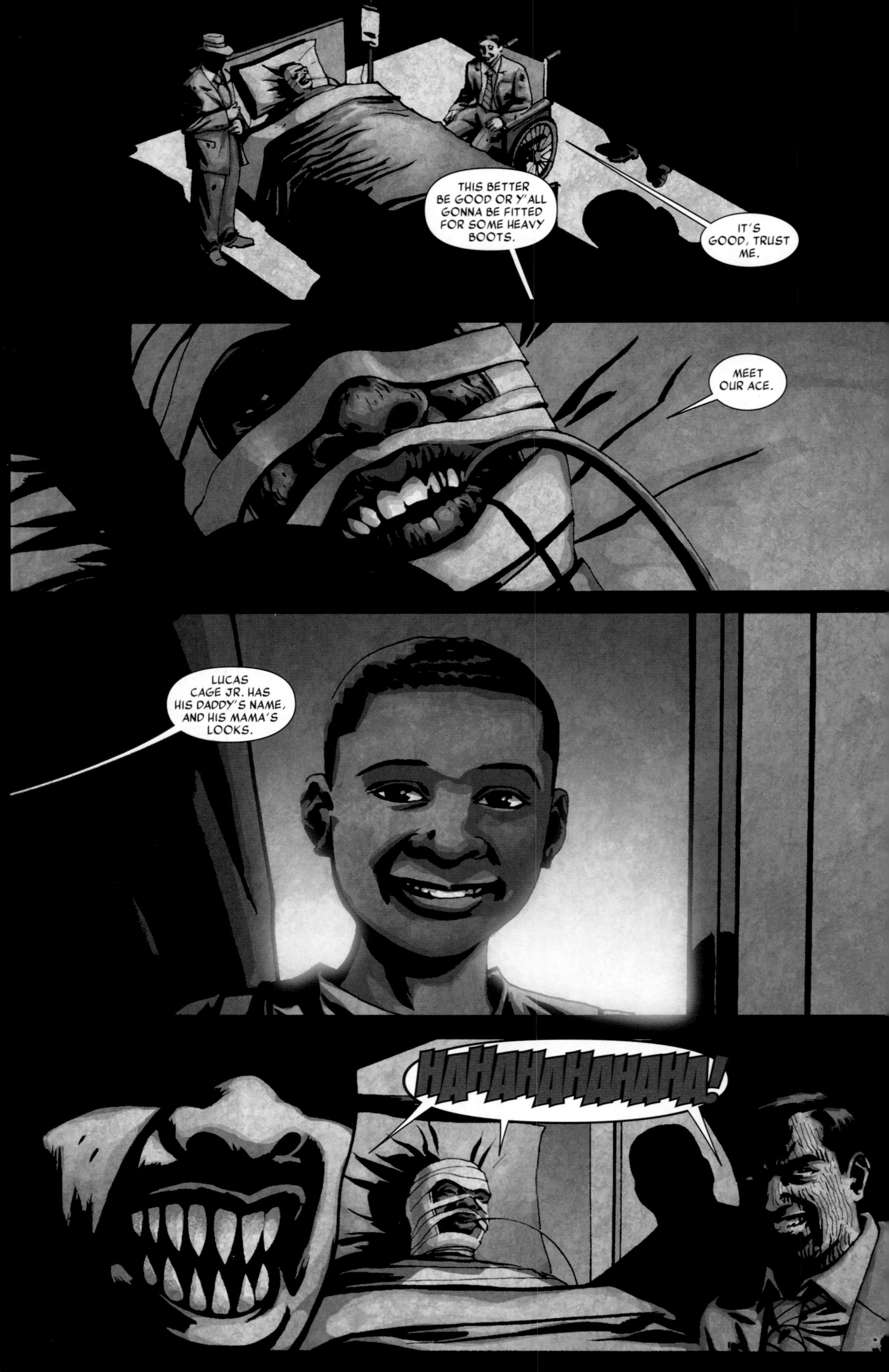
THIS BETTER BE GOOD OR Y'ALL GONNA BE FITTED FOR SOME HEAVY BOOTS.
IT'S GOOD, TRUST ME.
MEET OUR ACE.
LUCAS CAGE JR. HAS HIS DADDY'S NAME, AND HIS MAMA'S LOOKS.
HAHAHAHAHAHA!

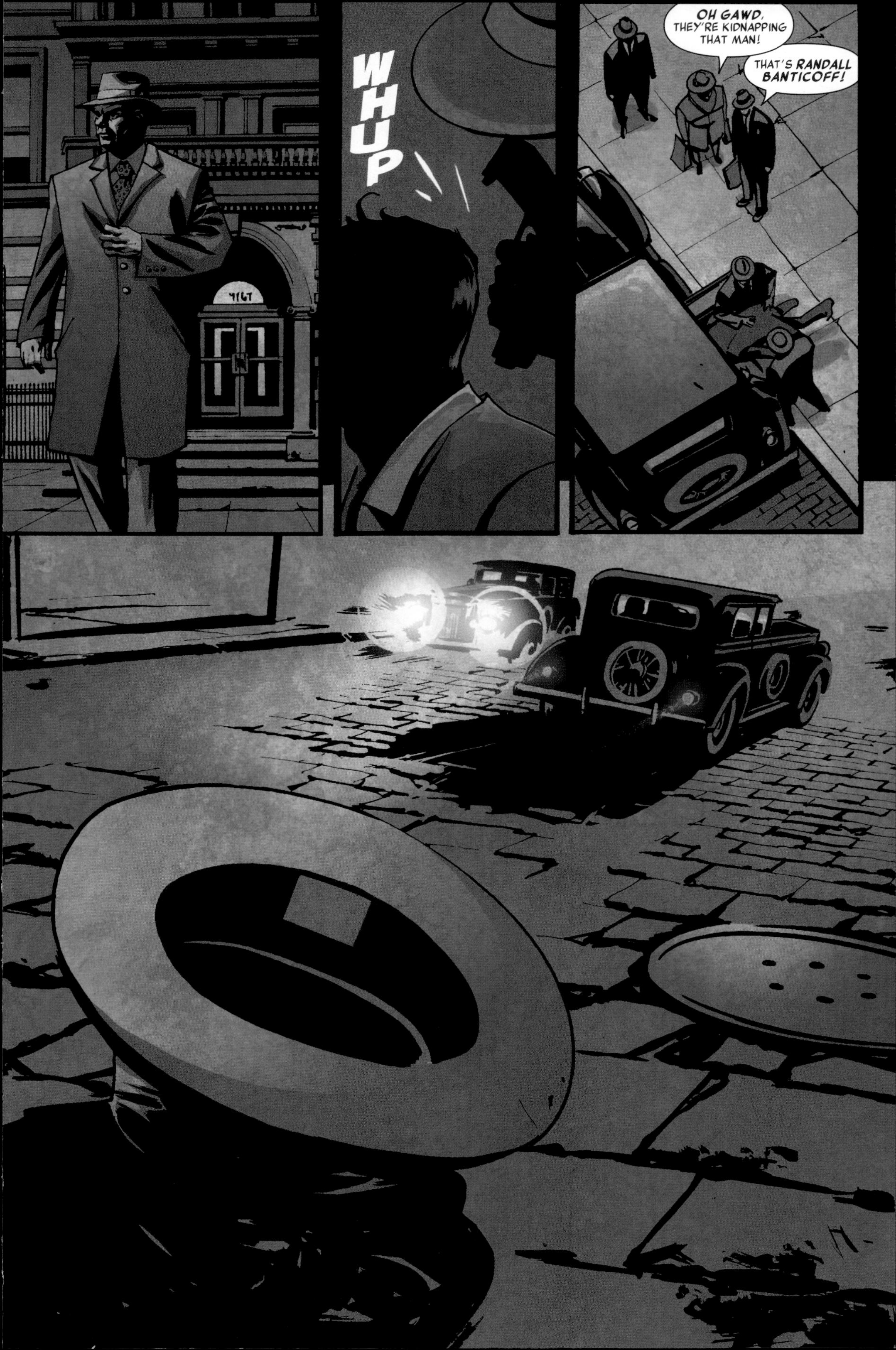
WHUP
OH GAWD, THEY'RE KIDNAPPING THAT MAN!
THAT'S RANDALL BANTICOFF!

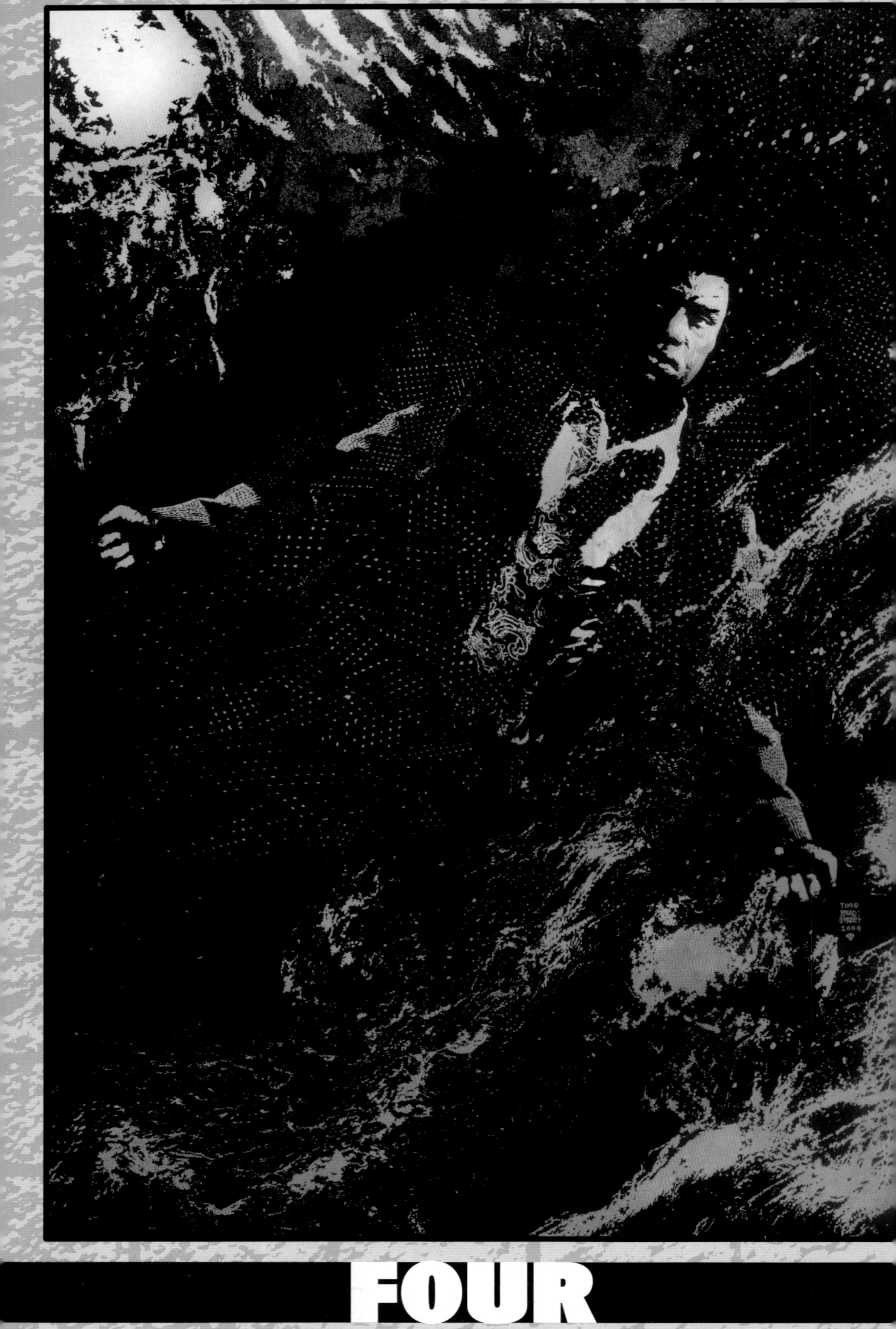

FOUR

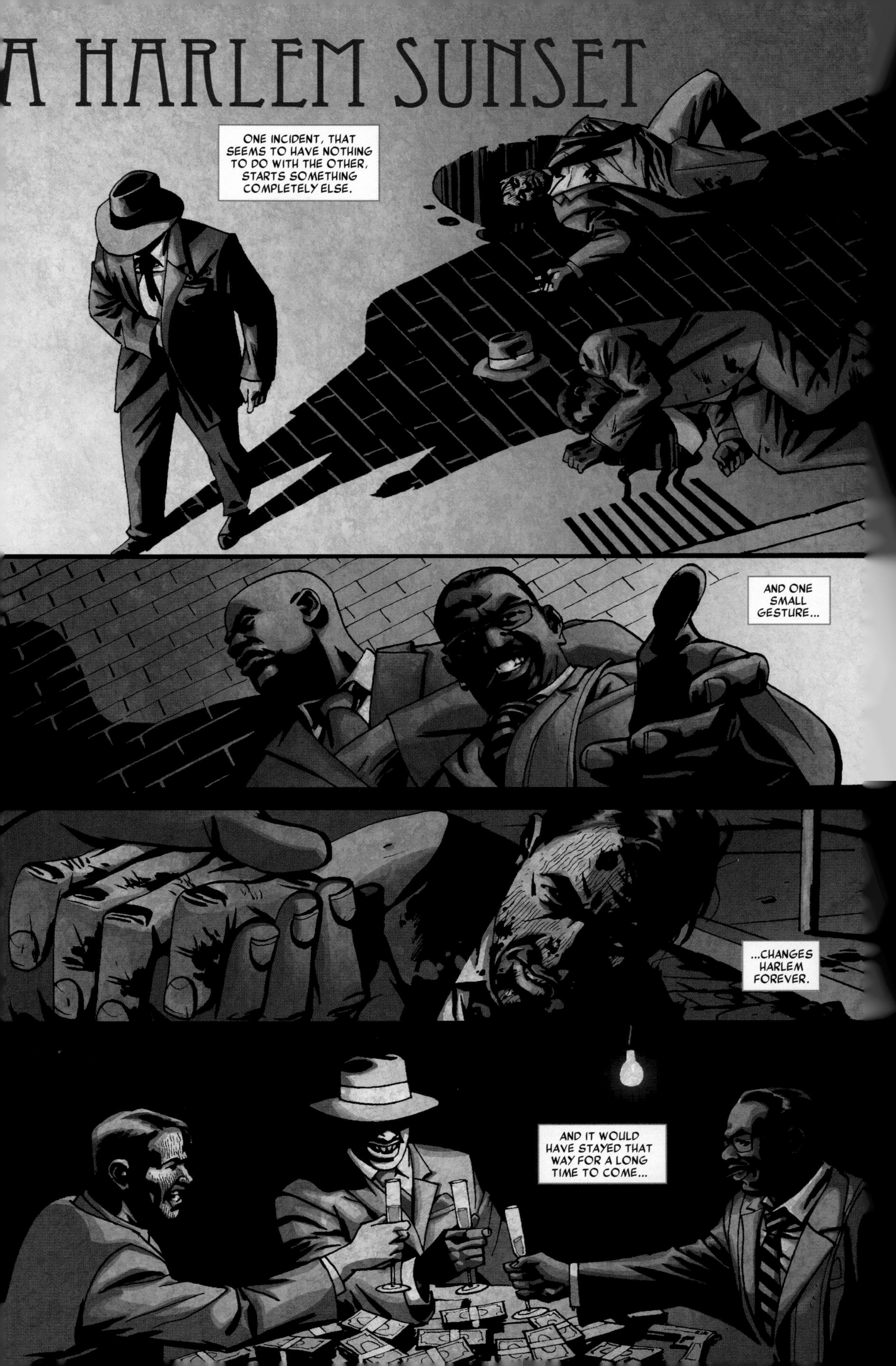
A HARLEM SUNSET
ONE INCIDENT, THAT SEEMS TO HAVE NOTHING TO DO WITH THE OTHER, STARTS SOMETHING COMPLETELY ELSE.
AND ONE SMALL GESTURE...
...CHANGES HARLEM FOREVER.
AND IT WOULD HAVE STAYED THAT WAY FOR A LONG TIME TO COME...

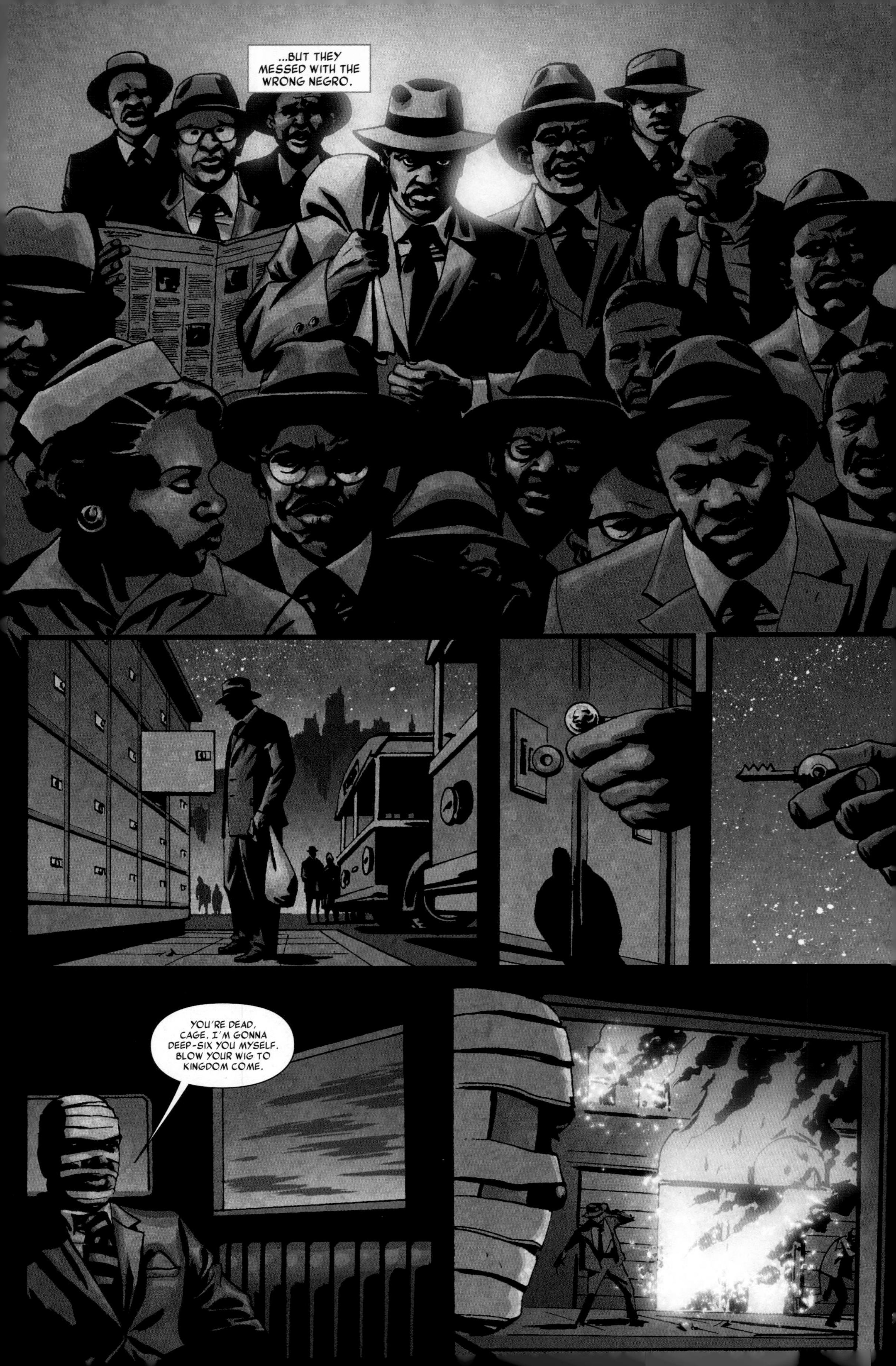

...BUT THEY MESSED WITH THE WRONG NEGRO.
YOU'RE DEAD, CAGE. I'M GONNA DEEP-SIX YOU MYSELF. BLOW YOUR WIG TO KINGDOM COME.

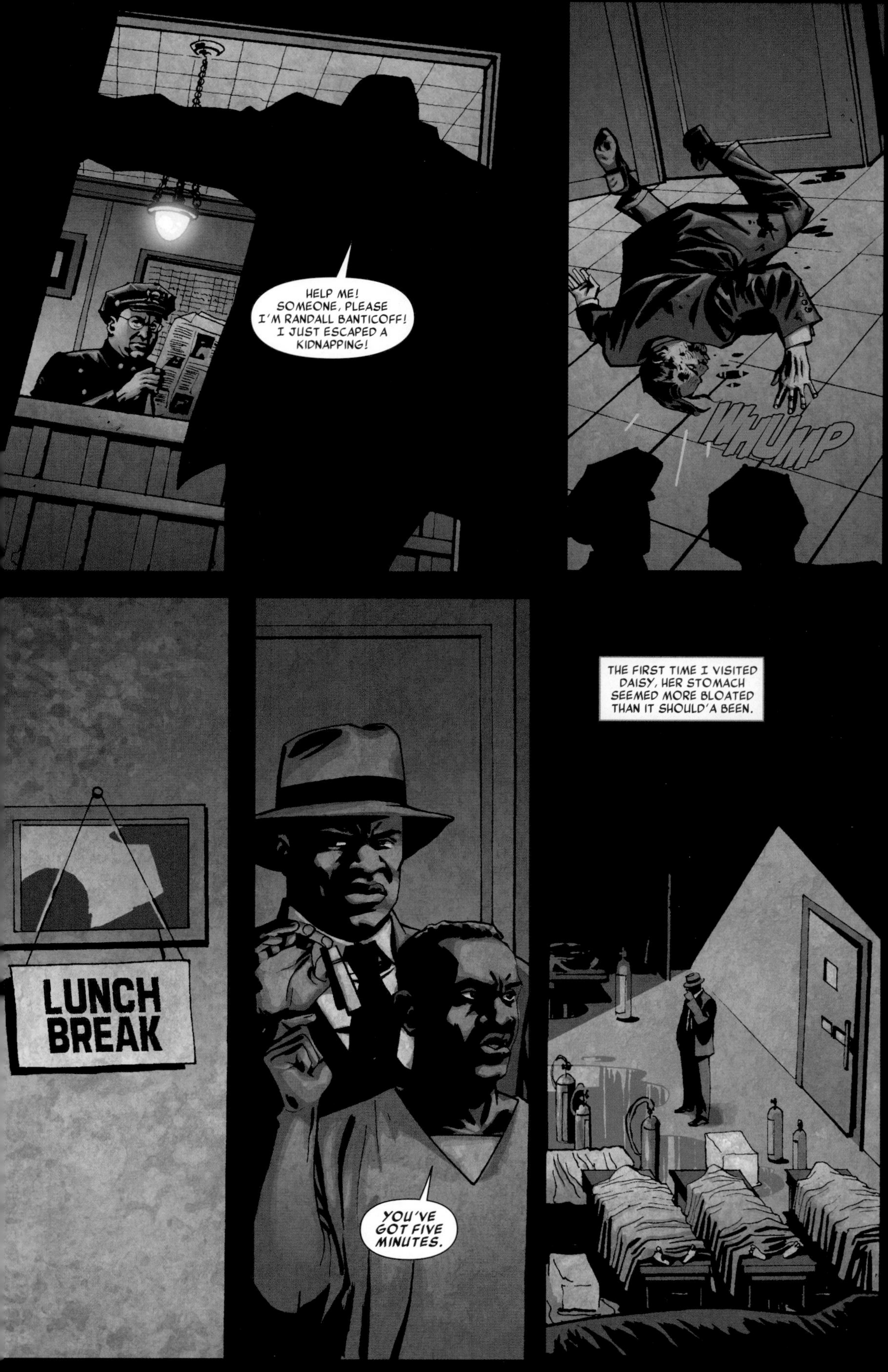
HELP ME! SOMEONE, PLEASE I'M RANDALL BANTICOFF! I JUST ESCAPED A KIDNAPPING!
WHUMP
LUNCH BREAK
YOU'VE GOT FIVE MINUTES.
THE FIRST TIME I VISITED DAISY, HER STOMACH SEEMED MORE BLOATED THAN IT SHOULD'A BEEN.

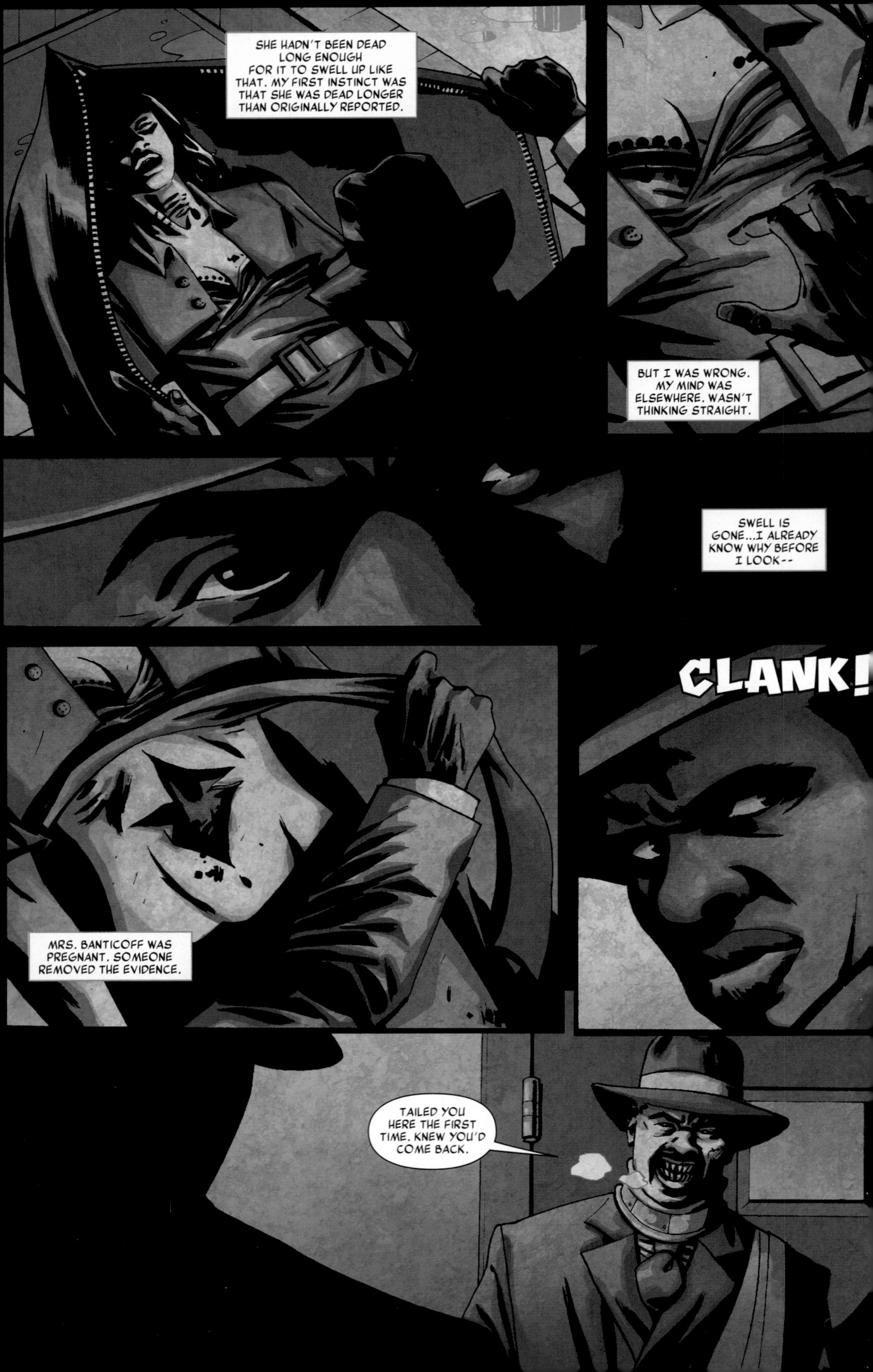
SHE HADN'T BEEN DEAD LONG ENOUGH FOR IT TO SWELL UP LIKE THAT. MY FIRST INSTINCT WAS THAT SHE WAS DEAD LONGER THAN ORIGINALLY REPORTED.
BUT I WAS WRONG. MY MIND WAS ELSEWHERE. WASN'T THINKING STRAIGHT.
SWELL IS GONE...I ALREADY KNOW WHY BEFORE I LOOK--
MRS. BANTICOFF WAS PREGNANT. SOMEONE REMOVED THE EVIDENCE.
CLANK!
TAILED YOU HERE THE FIRST TIME. KNEW YOU'D COME BACK.

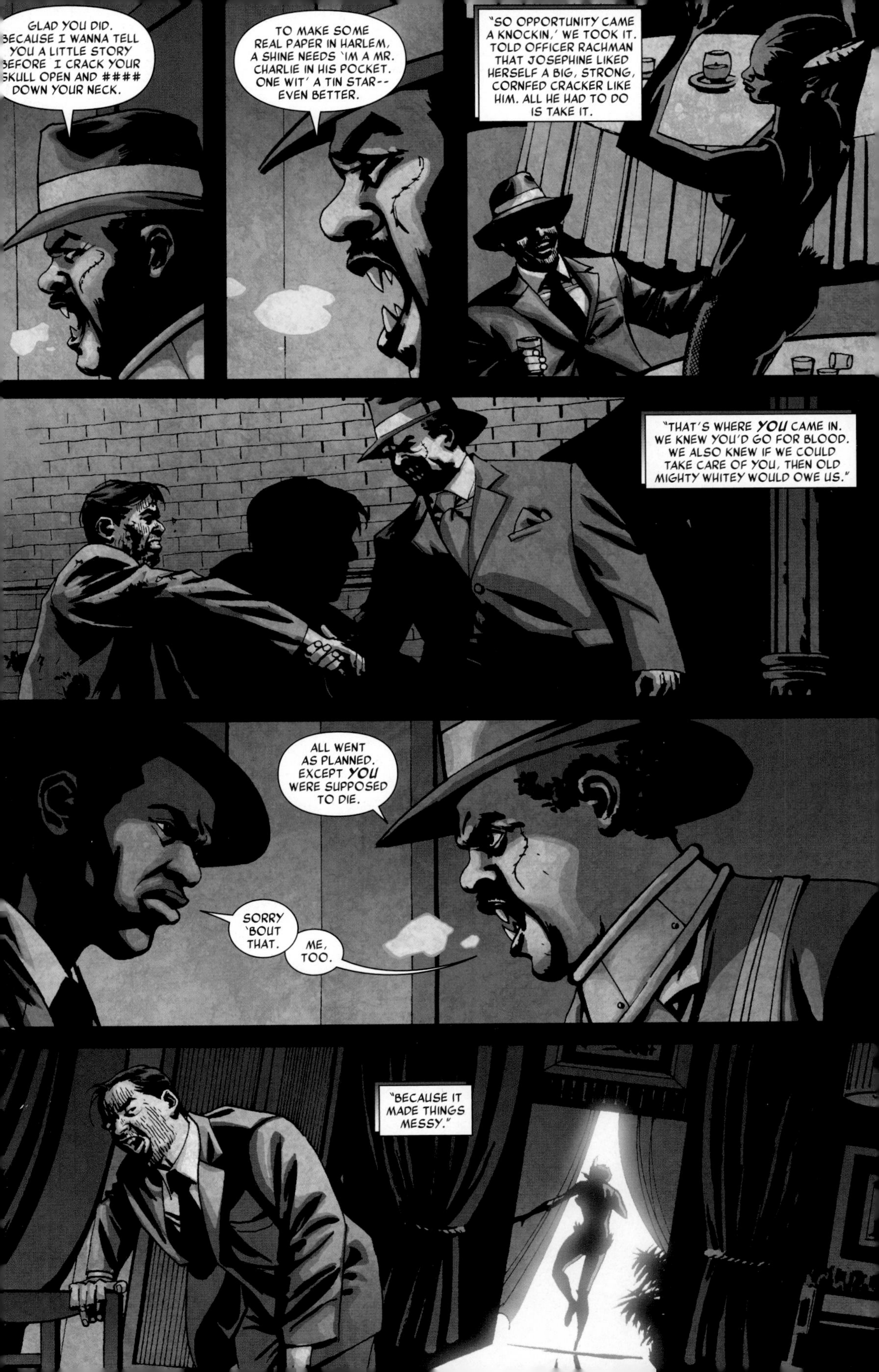
GLAD YOU DID. BECAUSE I WANNA TELL YOU A LITTLE STORY BEFORE I CRACK YOUR SKULL OPEN AND #### DOWN YOUR NECK.
TO MAKE SOME REAL PAPER IN HARLEM, A SHINE NEEDS 'IM A MR. CHARLIE IN HIS POCKET. ONE WIT' A TIN STAR-- EVEN BETTER.
"SO OPPORTUNITY CAME A KNOCKIN,' WE TOOK IT. TOLD OFFICER RACHMAN THAT JOSEPHINE LIKED HERSELF A BIG, STRONG, CORNFED CRACKER LIKE HIM. ALL HE HAD TO DO IS TAKE IT.
"THAT'S WHERE YOU CAME IN. WE KNEW YOU'D GO FOR BLOOD. WE ALSO KNEW IF WE COULD TAKE CARE OF YOU, THEN OLD MIGHTY WHITEY WOULD OWE US."
ALL WENT AS PLANNED. EXCEPT YOU WERE SUPPOSED TO DIE.
SORRY 'BOUT THAT.
ME, TOO.
"BECAUSE IT MADE THINGS MESSY."

AND I HAD TO CLEAN IT UP.

KLIK-KLIK

"I SEE WHAT YOU SAW IN HER--AND I MEAN I *SAW*."

I TOOK MY TIME. AT FIRST, SHE FOUGHT HARD...

...BUT AFTER A WHILE, I THINK SHE STARTED TO ENJOY IT AS MUCH AS I DID.

I DO EXACTLY WHAT TOMBSTONE WANTS ME TO DO--LOSE MY COOL.

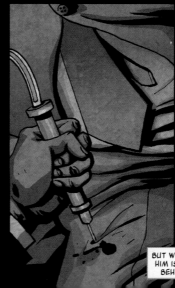

BUT WHAT SURPRISES HIM IS WHAT I HAVE BEHIND MY BACK.

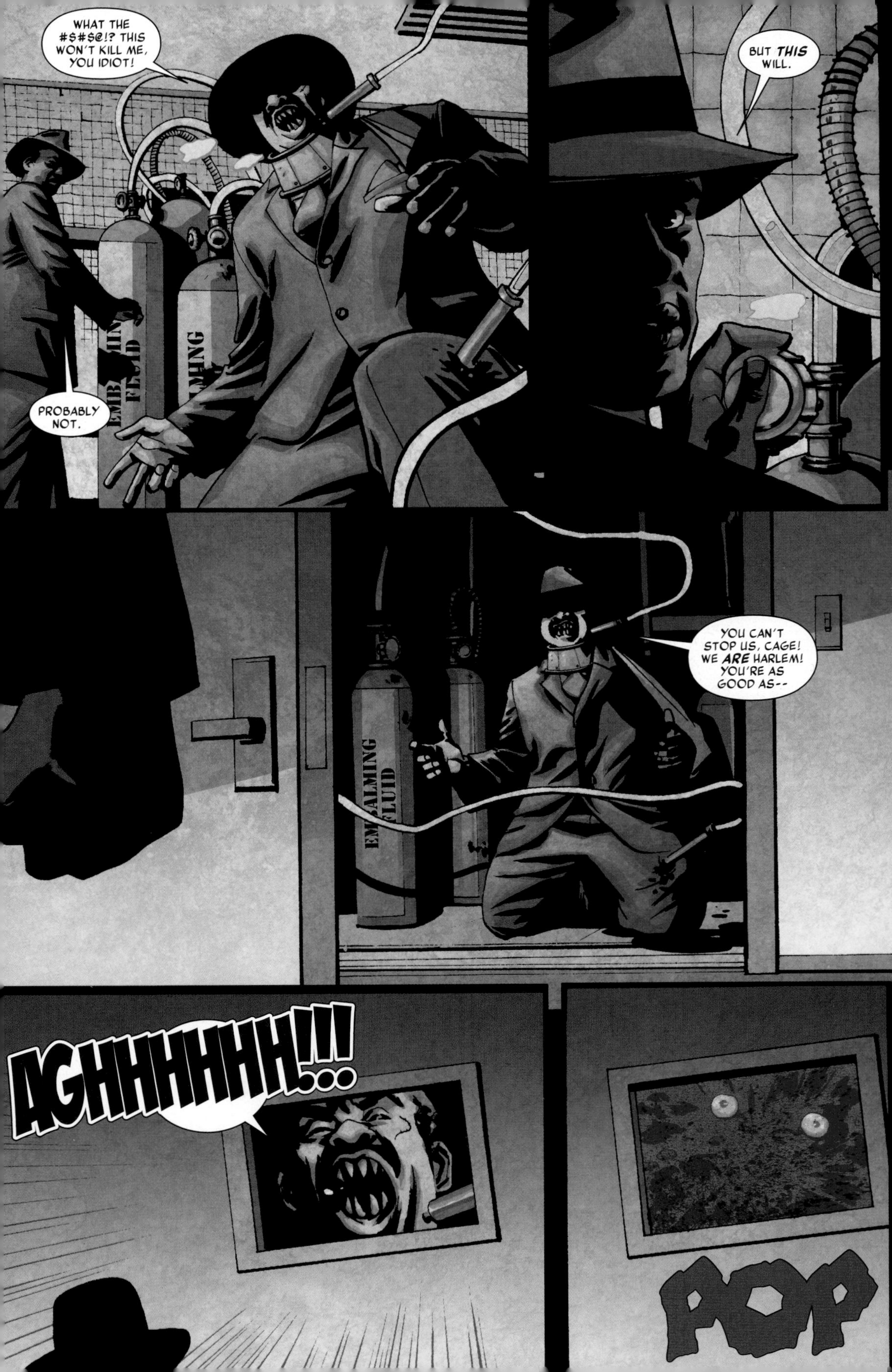
WHAT THE #$#$@!? THIS WON'T KILL ME, YOU IDIOT!
PROBABLY NOT.
EMBALMING FLUID
BUT THIS WILL.
YOU CAN'T STOP US, CAGE! WE ARE HARLEM! YOU'RE AS GOOD AS--
EMBALMING FLUID
AGHHHHHH!!!...
POP

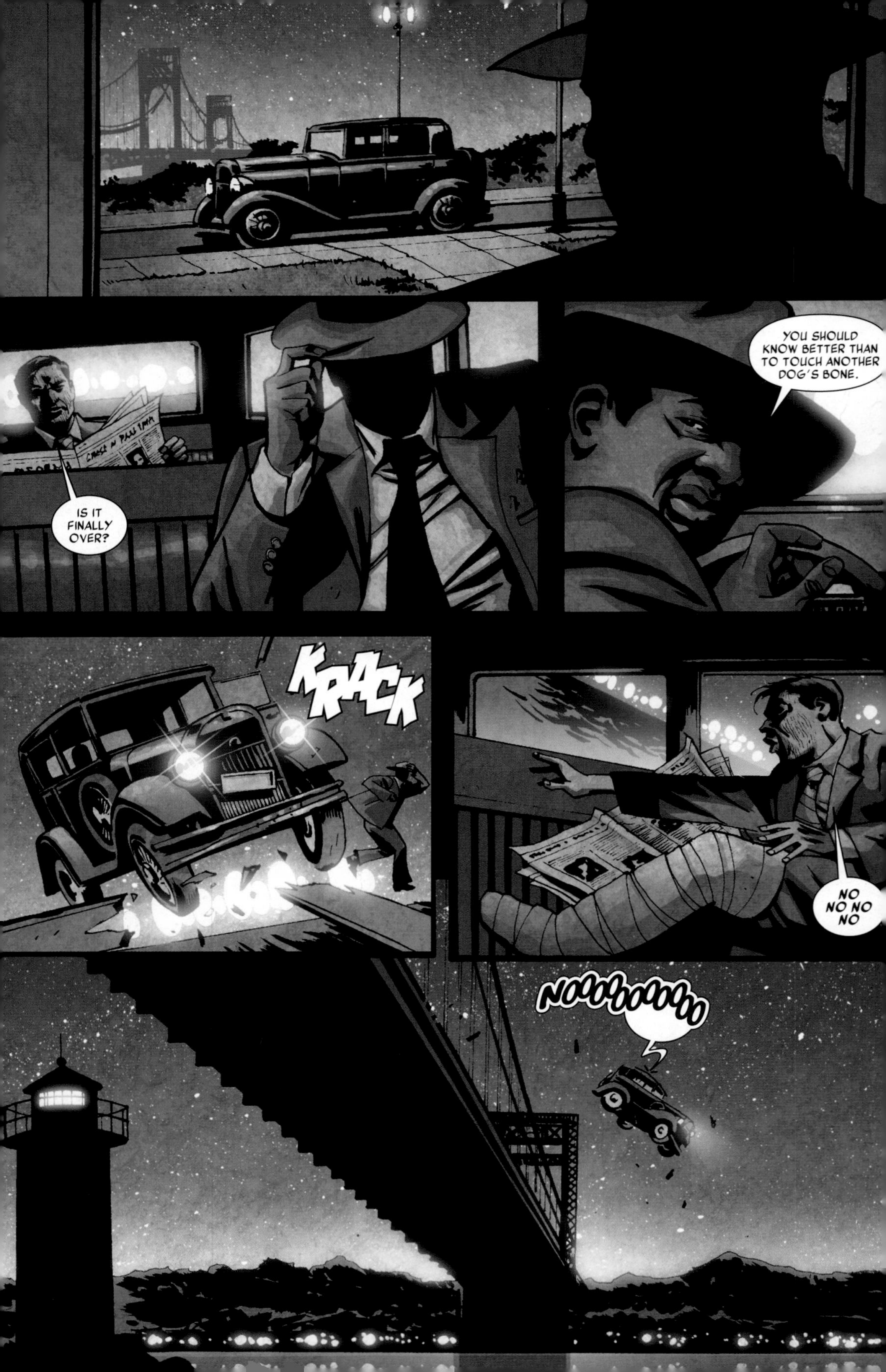
IS IT FINALLY OVER?
YOU SHOULD KNOW BETTER THAN TO TOUCH ANOTHER DOG'S BONE.
KRACK
NO NO NO NO
NOOOOOOOOO

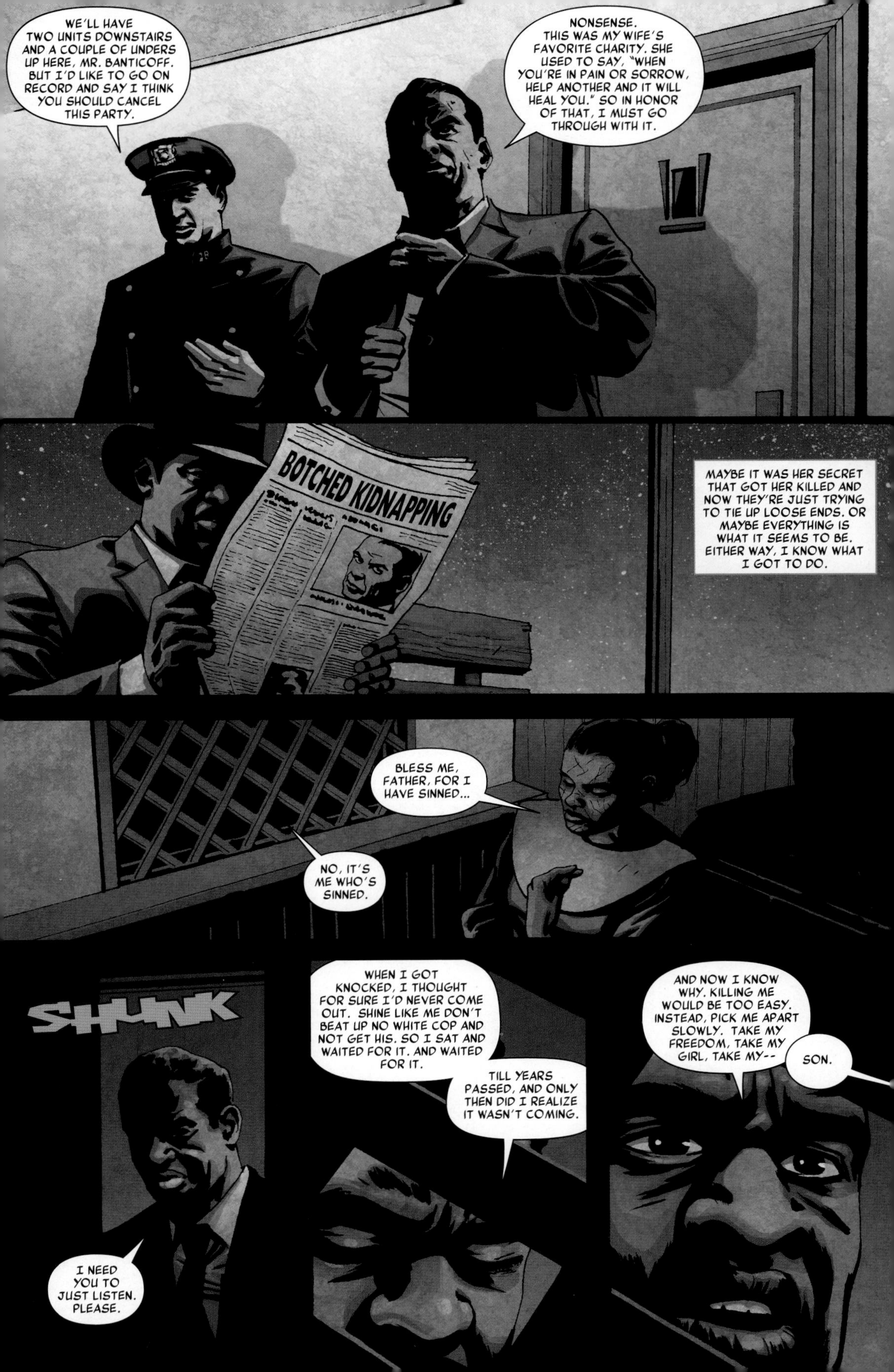
WE'LL HAVE TWO UNITS DOWNSTAIRS AND A COUPLE OF UNDERS UP HERE, MR. BANTICOFF. BUT I'D LIKE TO GO ON RECORD AND SAY I THINK YOU SHOULD CANCEL THIS PARTY.
NONSENSE. THIS WAS MY WIFE'S FAVORITE CHARITY. SHE USED TO SAY, "WHEN YOU'RE IN PAIN OR SORROW, HELP ANOTHER AND IT WILL HEAL YOU." SO IN HONOR OF THAT, I MUST GO THROUGH WITH IT.
BOTCHED KIDNAPPING
MAYBE IT WAS HER SECRET THAT GOT HER KILLED AND NOW THEY'RE JUST TRYING TO TIE UP LOOSE ENDS. OR MAYBE EVERYTHING IS WHAT IT SEEMS TO BE. EITHER WAY, I KNOW WHAT I GOT TO DO.
BLESS ME, FATHER, FOR I HAVE SINNED...
NO, IT'S ME WHO'S SINNED.
SHUNK
I NEED YOU TO JUST LISTEN. PLEASE.
WHEN I GOT KNOCKED, I THOUGHT FOR SURE I'D NEVER COME OUT. SHINE LIKE ME DON'T BEAT UP NO WHITE COP AND NOT GET HIS. SO I SAT AND WAITED FOR IT. AND WAITED FOR IT.
TILL YEARS PASSED, AND ONLY THEN DID I REALIZE IT WASN'T COMING.
AND NOW I KNOW WHY. KILLING ME WOULD BE TOO EASY. INSTEAD, PICK ME APART SLOWLY. TAKE MY FREEDOM, TAKE MY GIRL, TAKE MY--
SON.

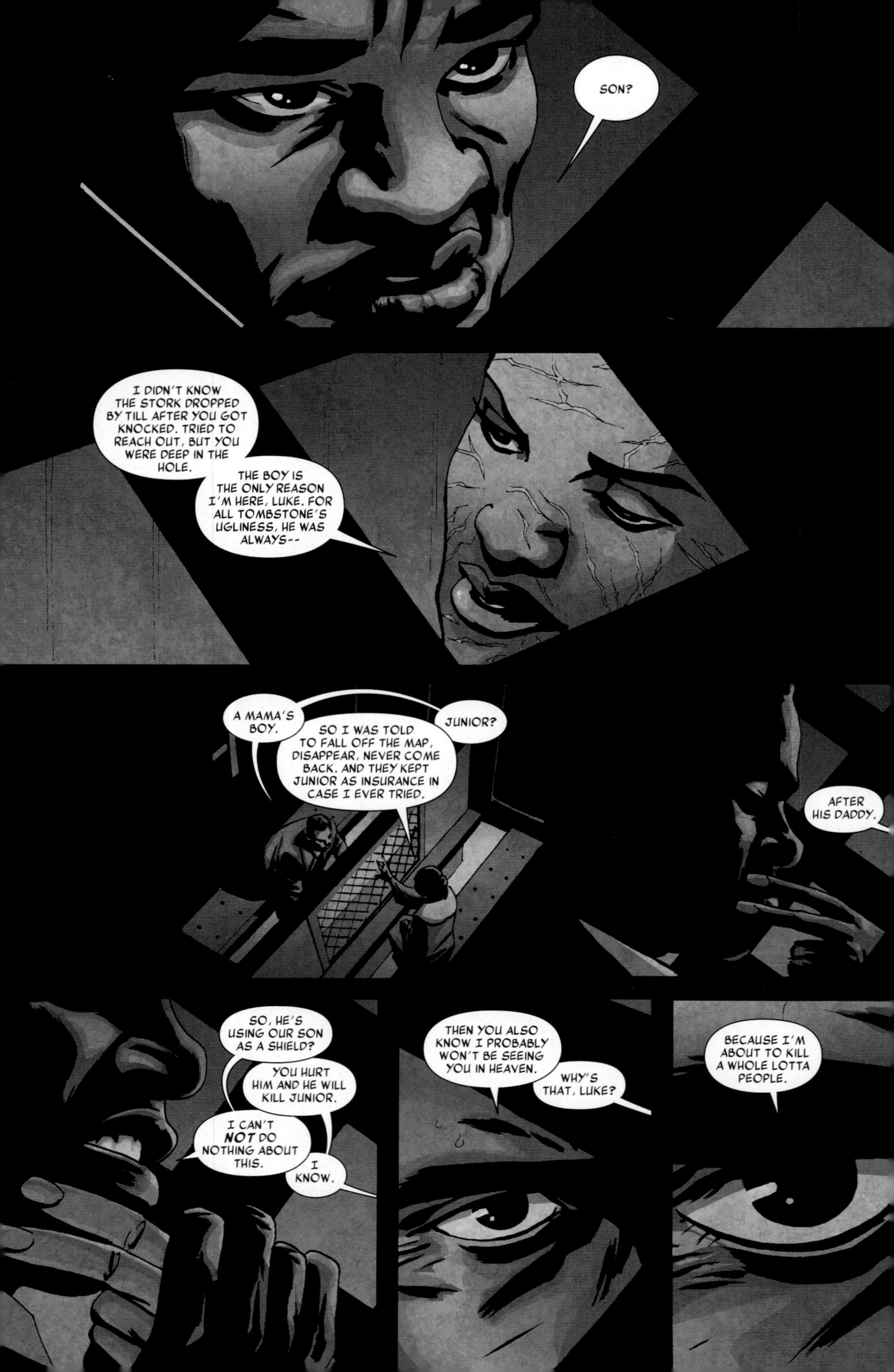
SON?
I DIDN'T KNOW THE STORK DROPPED BY TILL AFTER YOU GOT KNOCKED. TRIED TO REACH OUT, BUT YOU WERE DEEP IN THE HOLE.
THE BOY IS THE ONLY REASON I'M HERE, LUKE. FOR ALL TOMBSTONE'S UGLINESS, HE WAS ALWAYS--
A MAMA'S BOY.
JUNIOR?
SO I WAS TOLD TO FALL OFF THE MAP, DISAPPEAR, NEVER COME BACK. AND THEY KEPT JUNIOR AS INSURANCE IN CASE I EVER TRIED.
AFTER HIS DADDY.
SO, HE'S USING OUR SON AS A SHIELD?
YOU HURT HIM AND HE WILL KILL JUNIOR.
I CAN'T **NOT** DO NOTHING ABOUT THIS.
I KNOW.
THEN YOU ALSO KNOW I PROBABLY WON'T BE SEEING YOU IN HEAVEN.
WHY'S THAT, LUKE?
BECAUSE I'M ABOUT TO KILL A WHOLE LOTTA PEOPLE.

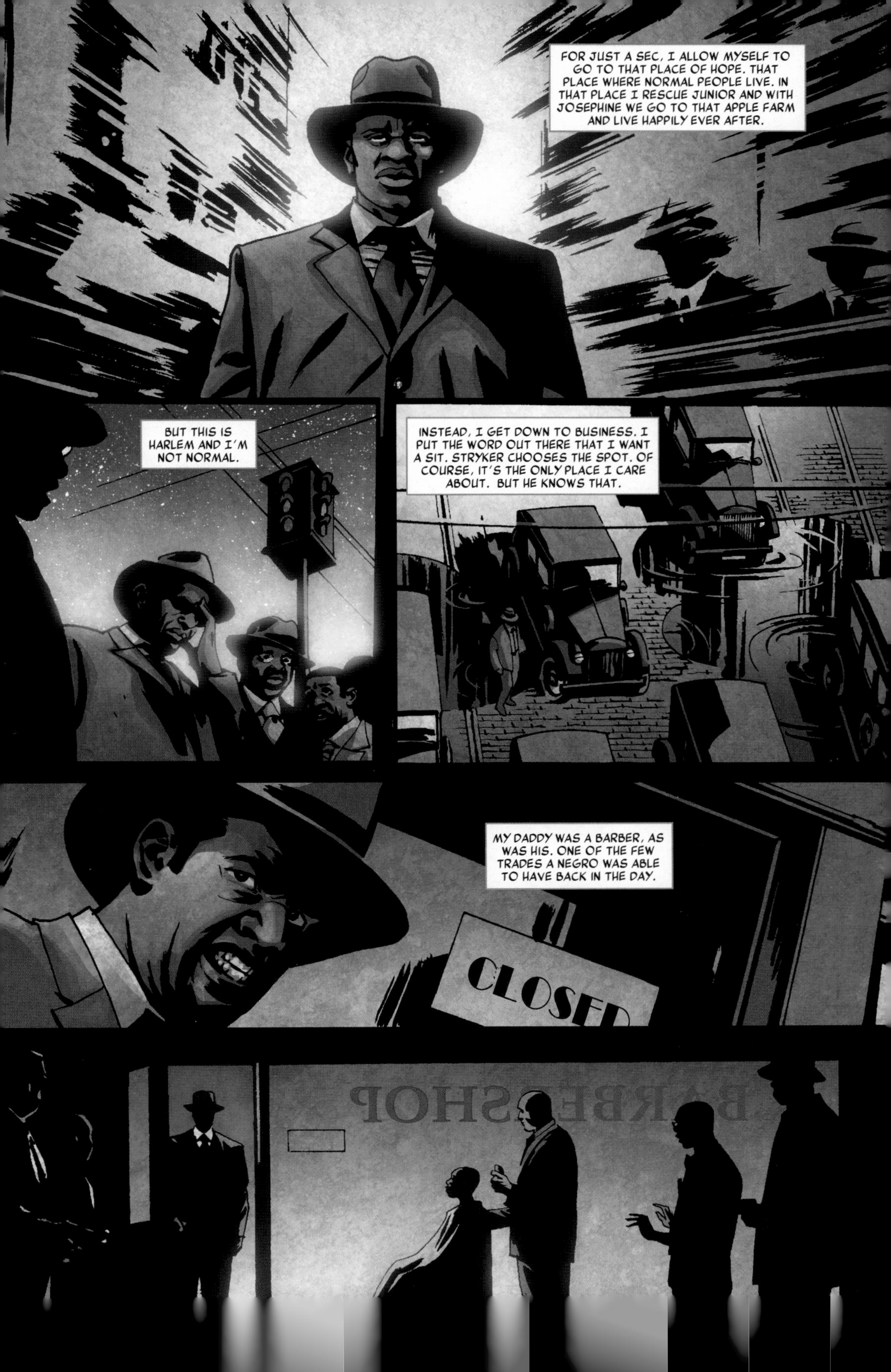
FOR JUST A SEC, I ALLOW MYSELF TO GO TO THAT PLACE OF HOPE. THAT PLACE WHERE NORMAL PEOPLE LIVE. IN THAT PLACE I RESCUE JUNIOR AND WITH JOSEPHINE WE GO TO THAT APPLE FARM AND LIVE HAPPILY EVER AFTER.
BUT THIS IS HARLEM AND I'M NOT NORMAL.
INSTEAD, I GET DOWN TO BUSINESS. I PUT THE WORD OUT THERE THAT I WANT A SIT. STRYKER CHOOSES THE SPOT. OF COURSE, IT'S THE ONLY PLACE I CARE ABOUT. BUT HE KNOWS THAT.
MY DADDY WAS A BARBER, AS WAS HIS. ONE OF THE FEW TRADES A NEGRO WAS ABLE TO HAVE BACK IN THE DAY.
CLOSED
BARBERSHOP

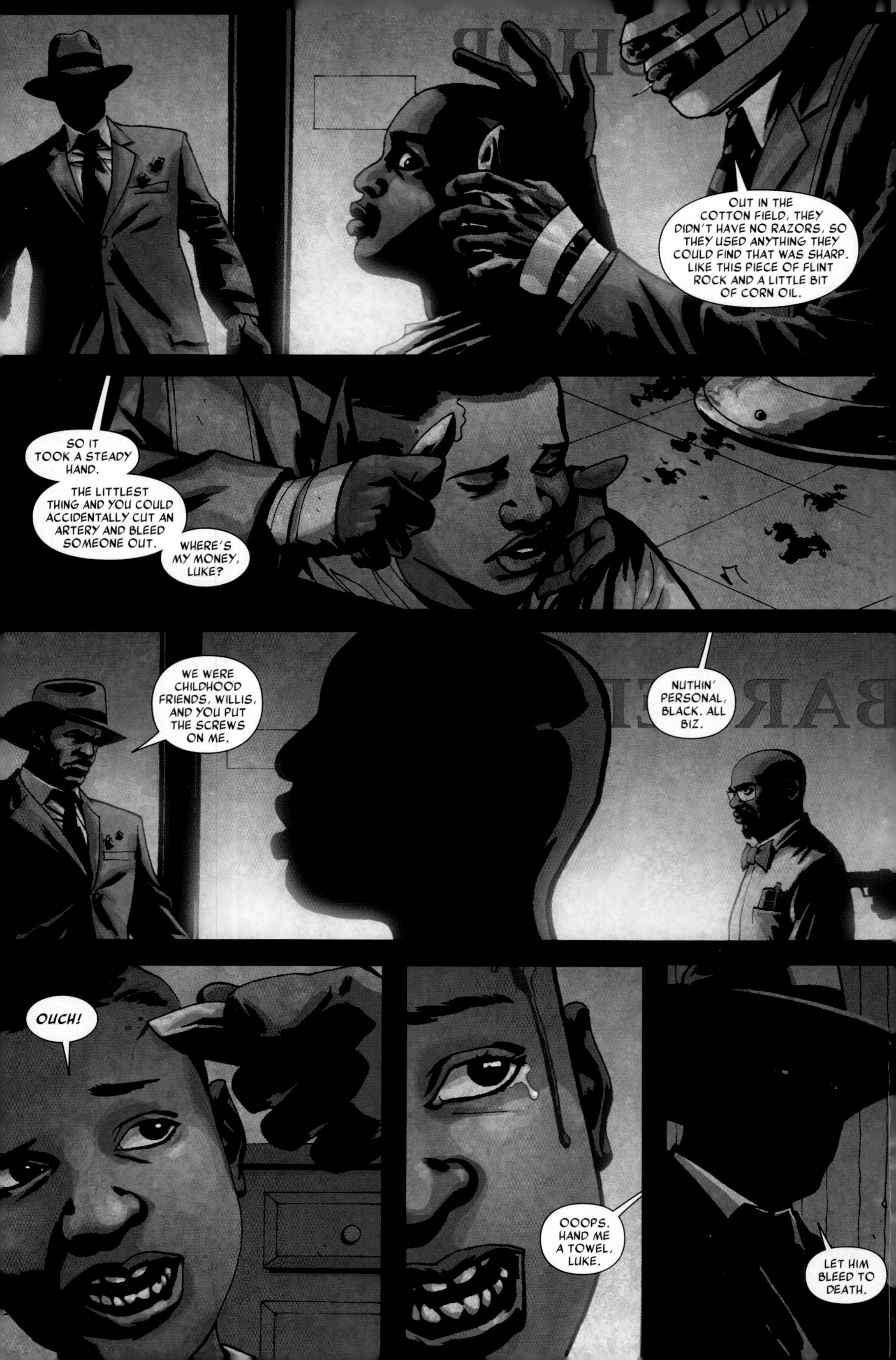
OUT IN THE COTTON FIELD, THEY DIDN'T HAVE NO RAZORS, SO THEY USED ANYTHING THEY COULD FIND THAT WAS SHARP. LIKE THIS PIECE OF FLINT ROCK AND A LITTLE BIT OF CORN OIL.
SO IT TOOK A STEADY HAND.
THE LITTLEST THING AND YOU COULD ACCIDENTALLY CUT AN ARTERY AND BLEED SOMEONE OUT.
WHERE'S MY MONEY, LUKE?
WE WERE CHILDHOOD FRIENDS, WILLIS, AND YOU PUT THE SCREWS ON ME.
NUTHIN' PERSONAL, BLACK. ALL BIZ.
OUCH!
OOOPS. HAND ME A TOWEL, LUKE.
LET HIM BLEED TO DEATH.

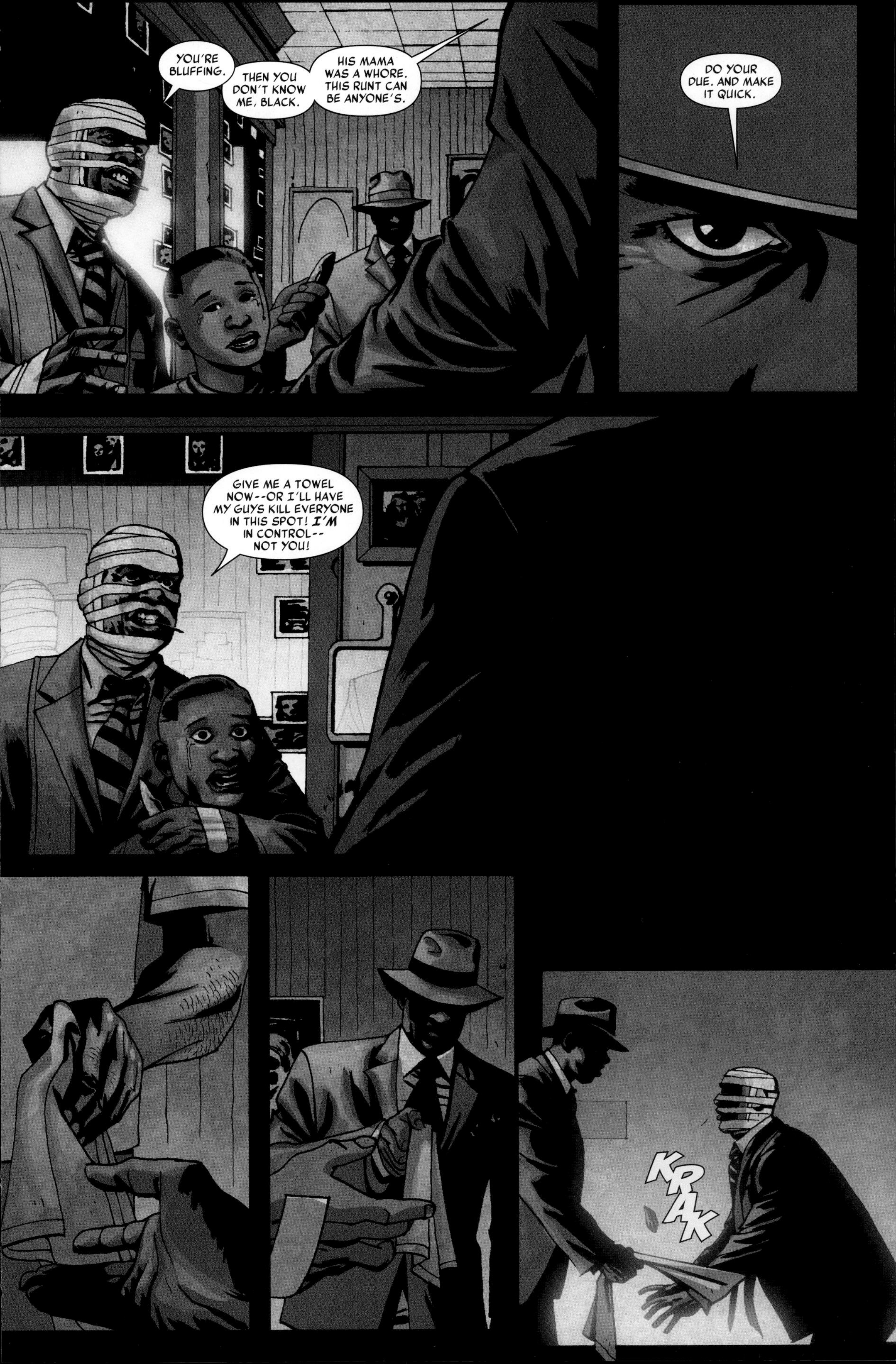
YOU'RE BLUFFING.
THEN YOU DON'T KNOW ME, BLACK.
HIS MAMA WAS A WHORE. THIS RUNT CAN BE ANYONE'S.
DO YOUR DUE. AND MAKE IT QUICK.
GIVE ME A TOWEL NOW--OR I'LL HAVE MY GUYS KILL EVERYONE IN THIS SPOT! *I'M* IN CONTROL--NOT YOU!
KRAK

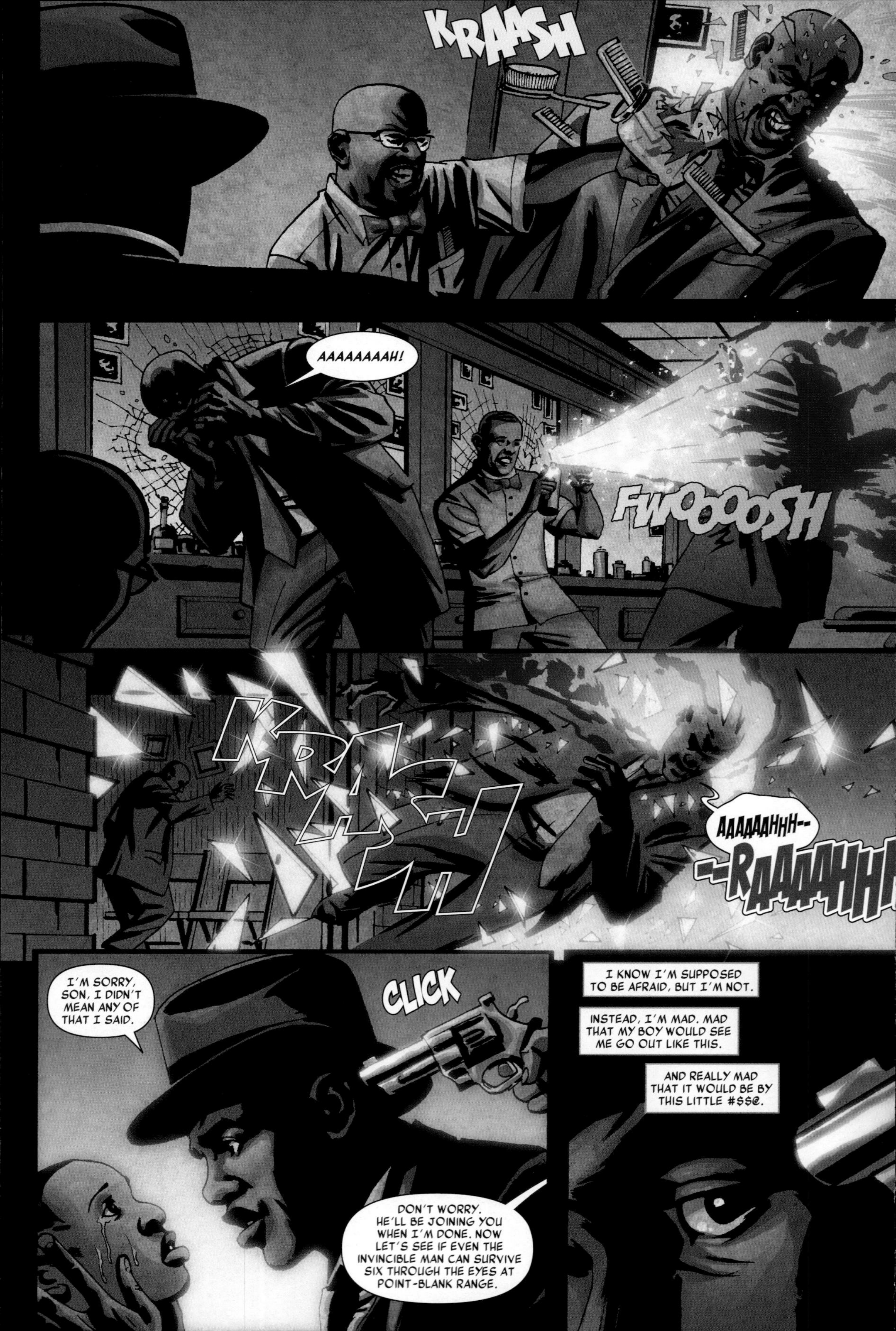
KRAASH
AAAAAAAAH!
FWOOOOSH
KRAASH
AAAAAAHHH--
--RAAAAHHH
I'M SORRY, SON, I DIDN'T MEAN ANY OF THAT I SAID.
CLICK
DON'T WORRY. HE'LL BE JOINING YOU WHEN I'M DONE. NOW LET'S SEE IF EVEN THE INVINCIBLE MAN CAN SURVIVE SIX THROUGH THE EYES AT POINT-BLANK RANGE.
I KNOW I'M SUPPOSED TO BE AFRAID, BUT I'M NOT.
INSTEAD, I'M MAD. MAD THAT MY BOY WOULD SEE ME GO OUT LIKE THIS.
AND REALLY MAD THAT IT WOULD BE BY THIS LITTLE #$$@.

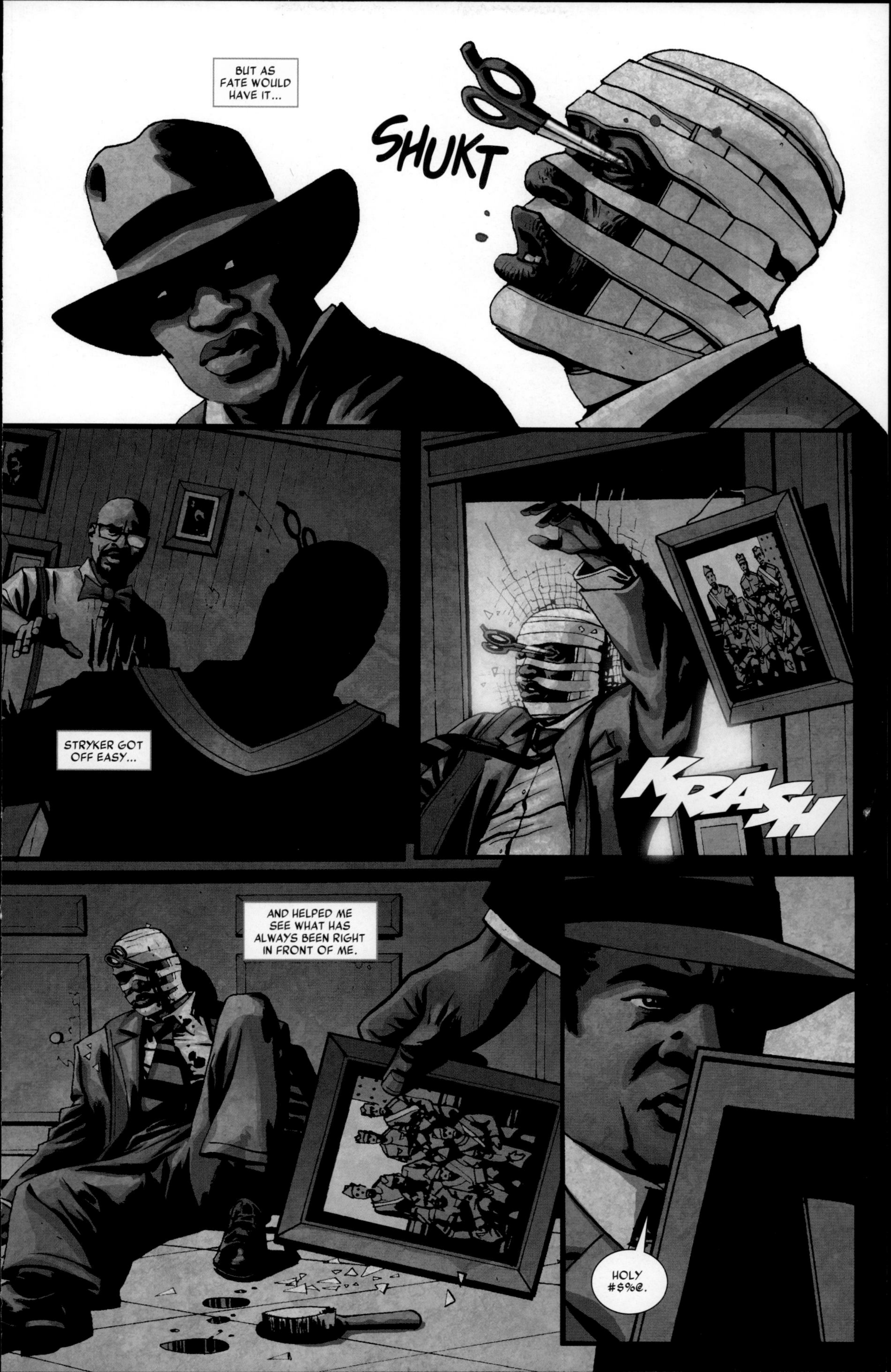

BUT AS FATE WOULD HAVE IT...
SHUKT
STRYKER GOT OFF EASY...
KRASH
AND HELPED ME SEE WHAT HAS ALWAYS BEEN RIGHT IN FRONT OF ME.
HOLY #$%@.

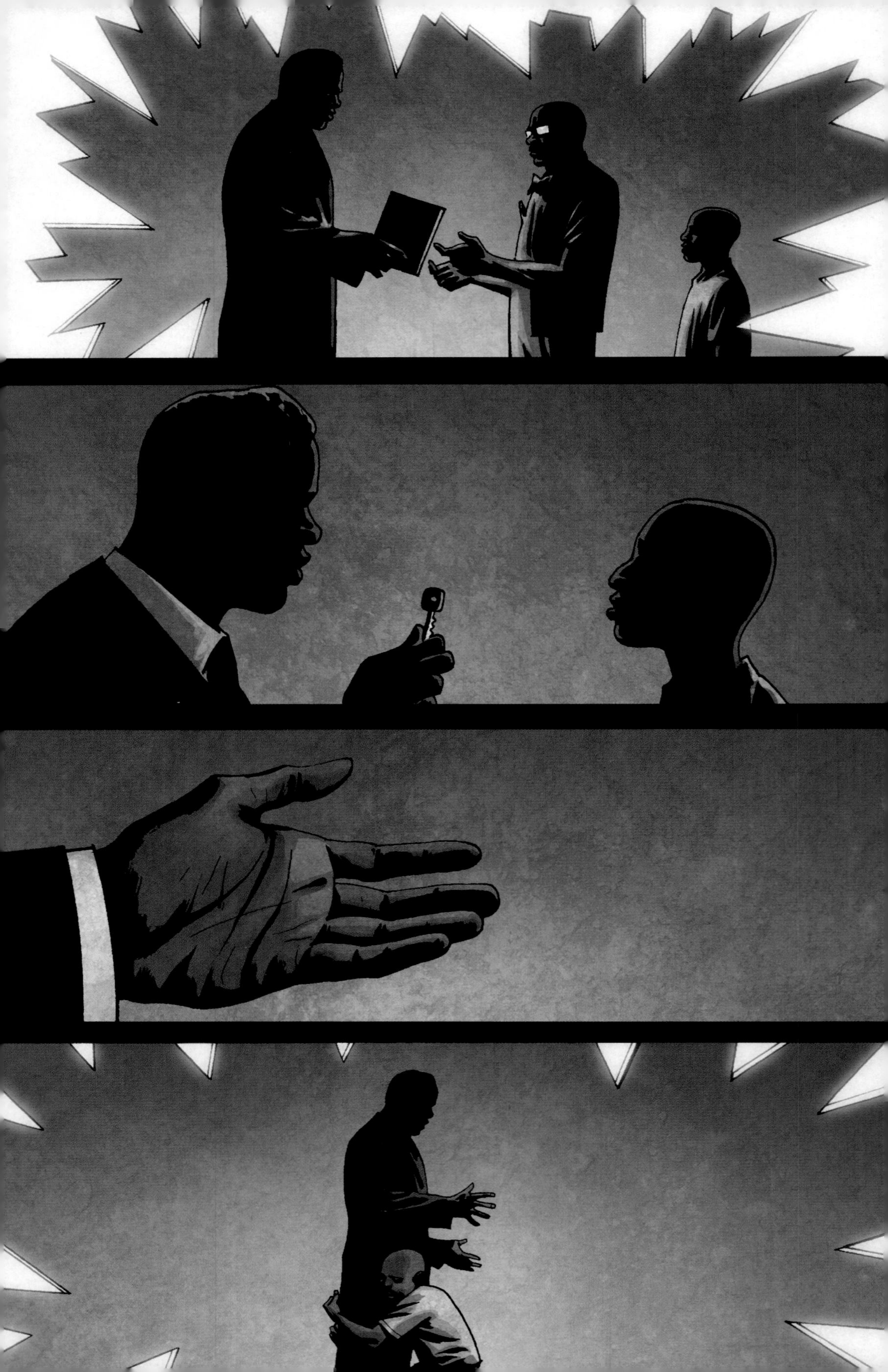

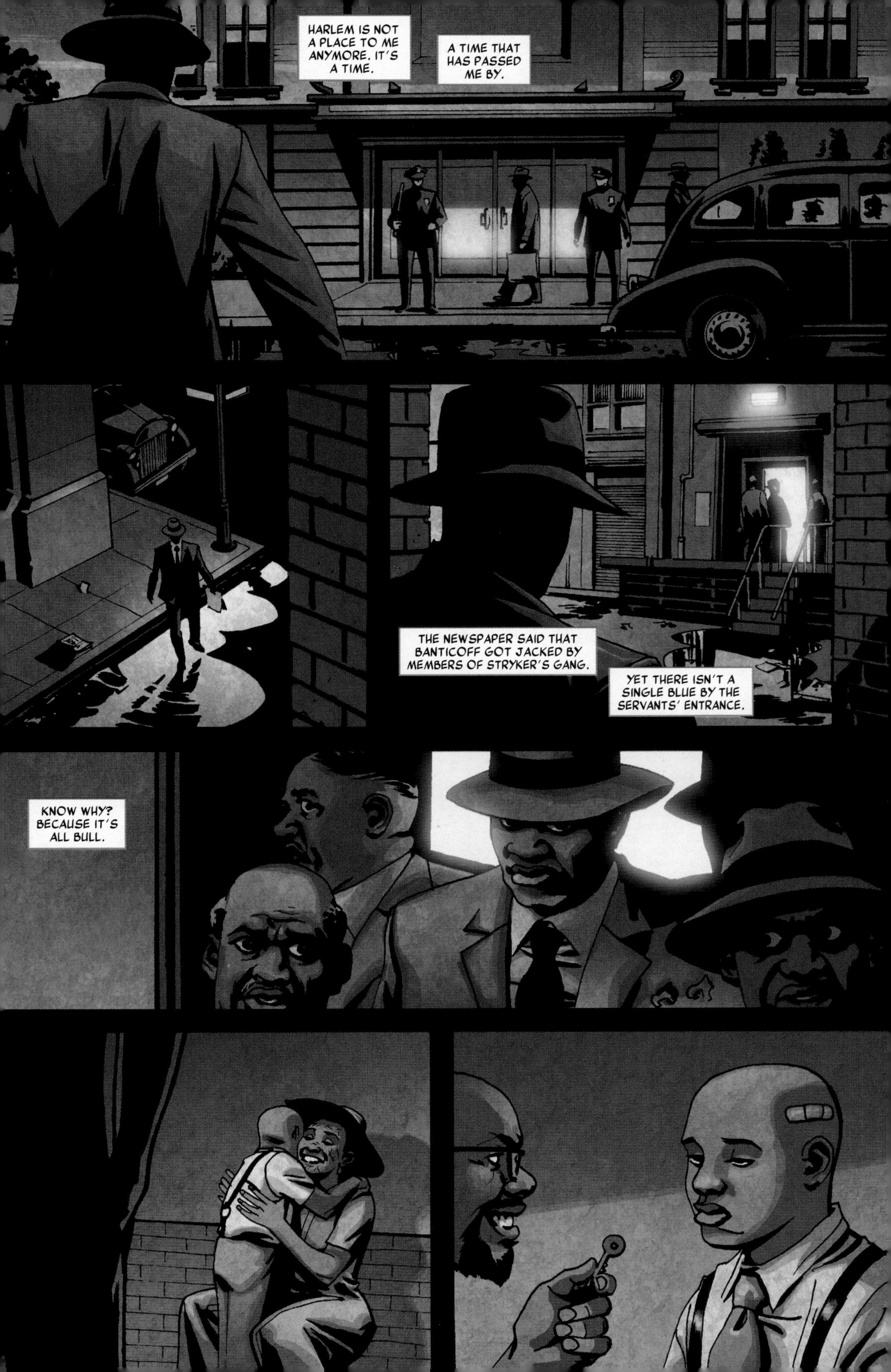
HARLEM IS NOT A PLACE TO ME ANYMORE. IT'S A TIME.
A TIME THAT HAS PASSED ME BY.
THE NEWSPAPER SAID THAT BANTICOFF GOT JACKED BY MEMBERS OF STRYKER'S GANG.
YET THERE ISN'T A SINGLE BLUE BY THE SERVANTS' ENTRANCE.
KNOW WHY? BECAUSE IT'S ALL BULL.

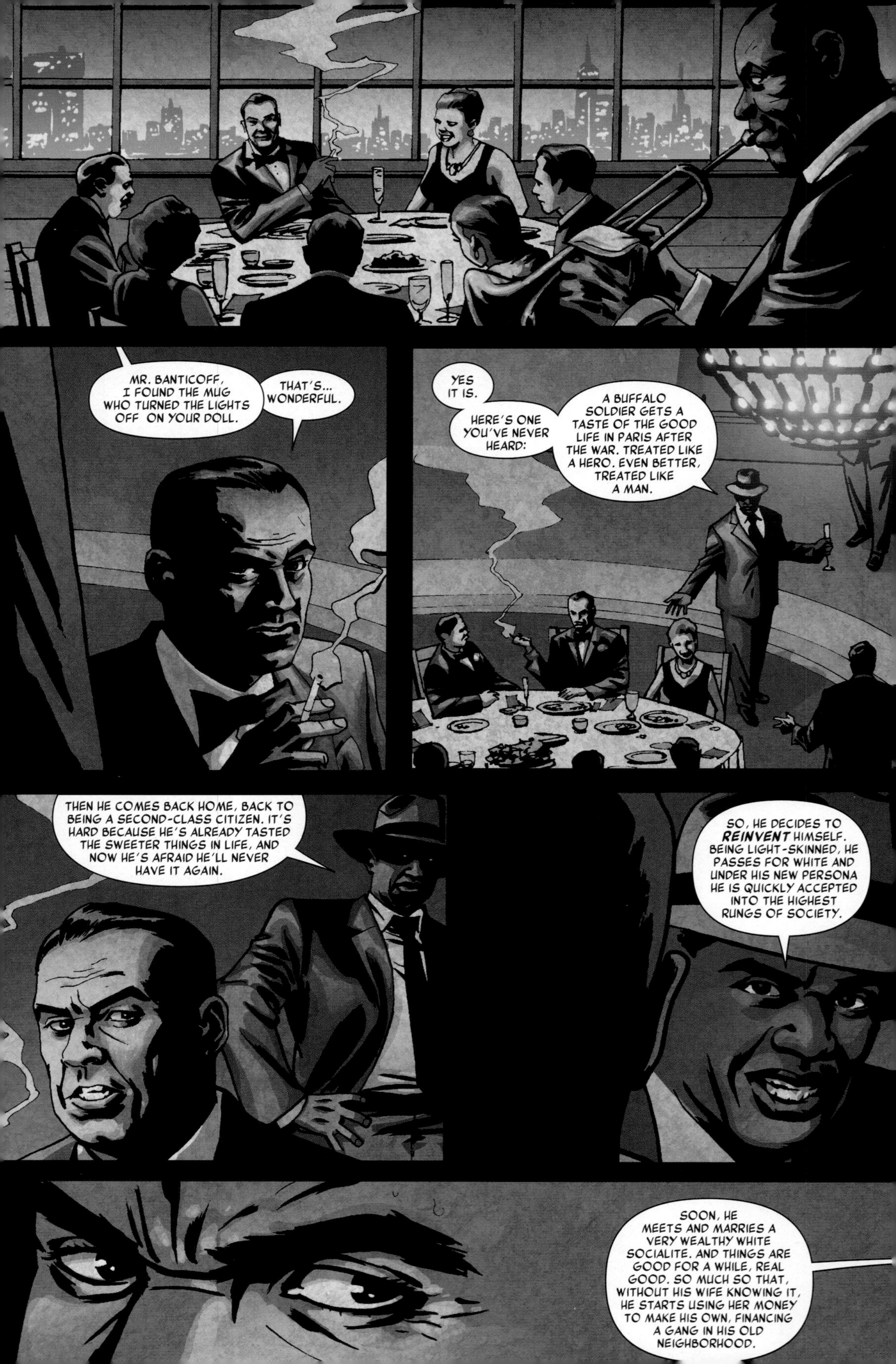
MR. BANTICOFF, I FOUND THE MUG WHO TURNED THE LIGHTS OFF ON YOUR DOLL.
THAT'S... WONDERFUL.
YES IT IS.
HERE'S ONE YOU'VE NEVER HEARD:
A BUFFALO SOLDIER GETS A TASTE OF THE GOOD LIFE IN PARIS AFTER THE WAR. TREATED LIKE A HERO. EVEN BETTER, TREATED LIKE A MAN.
THEN HE COMES BACK HOME, BACK TO BEING A SECOND-CLASS CITIZEN. IT'S HARD BECAUSE HE'S ALREADY TASTED THE SWEETER THINGS IN LIFE, AND NOW HE'S AFRAID HE'LL NEVER HAVE IT AGAIN.
SO, HE DECIDES TO *REINVENT* HIMSELF. BEING LIGHT-SKINNED, HE PASSES FOR WHITE AND UNDER HIS NEW PERSONA HE IS QUICKLY ACCEPTED INTO THE HIGHEST RUNGS OF SOCIETY.
SOON, HE MEETS AND MARRIES A VERY WEALTHY WHITE SOCIALITE. AND THINGS ARE GOOD FOR A WHILE, REAL GOOD. SO MUCH SO THAT, WITHOUT HIS WIFE KNOWING IT, HE STARTS USING HER MONEY TO MAKE HIS OWN, FINANCING A GANG IN HIS OLD NEIGHBORHOOD.

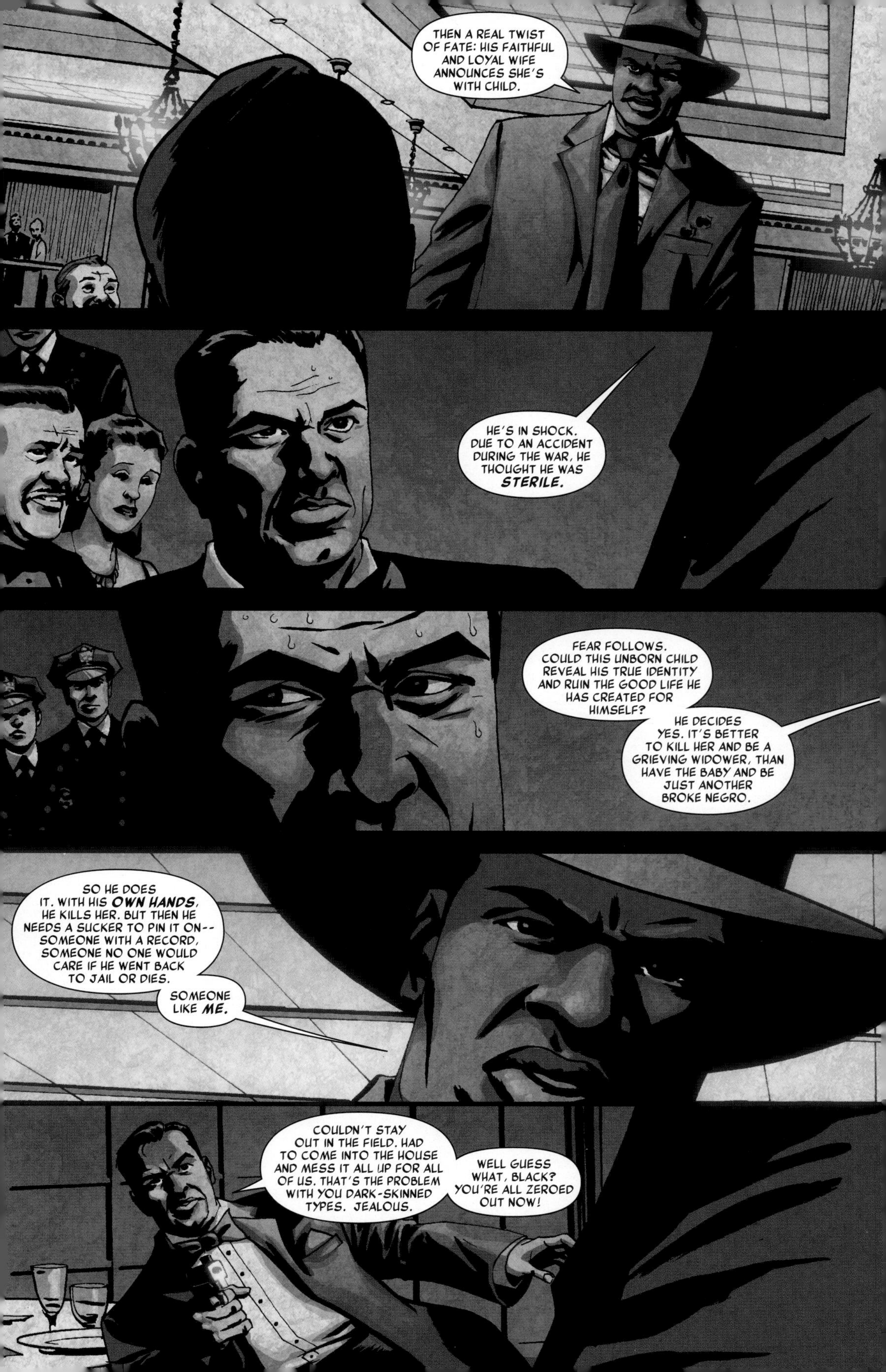
THEN A REAL TWIST OF FATE: HIS FAITHFUL AND LOYAL WIFE ANNOUNCES SHE'S WITH CHILD.
HE'S IN SHOCK. DUE TO AN ACCIDENT DURING THE WAR, HE THOUGHT HE WAS **STERILE.**
FEAR FOLLOWS. COULD THIS UNBORN CHILD REVEAL HIS TRUE IDENTITY AND RUIN THE GOOD LIFE HE HAS CREATED FOR HIMSELF?
HE DECIDES YES. IT'S BETTER TO KILL HER AND BE A GRIEVING WIDOWER, THAN HAVE THE BABY AND BE JUST ANOTHER BROKE NEGRO.
SO HE DOES IT. WITH HIS **OWN HANDS**, HE KILLS HER. BUT THEN HE NEEDS A SUCKER TO PIN IT ON-- SOMEONE WITH A RECORD, SOMEONE NO ONE WOULD CARE IF HE WENT BACK TO JAIL OR DIES.
SOMEONE LIKE **ME.**
COULDN'T STAY OUT IN THE FIELD. HAD TO COME INTO THE HOUSE AND MESS IT ALL UP FOR ALL OF US. THAT'S THE PROBLEM WITH YOU DARK-SKINNED TYPES. JEALOUS.
WELL GUESS WHAT, BLACK? YOU'RE ALL ZEROED OUT NOW!

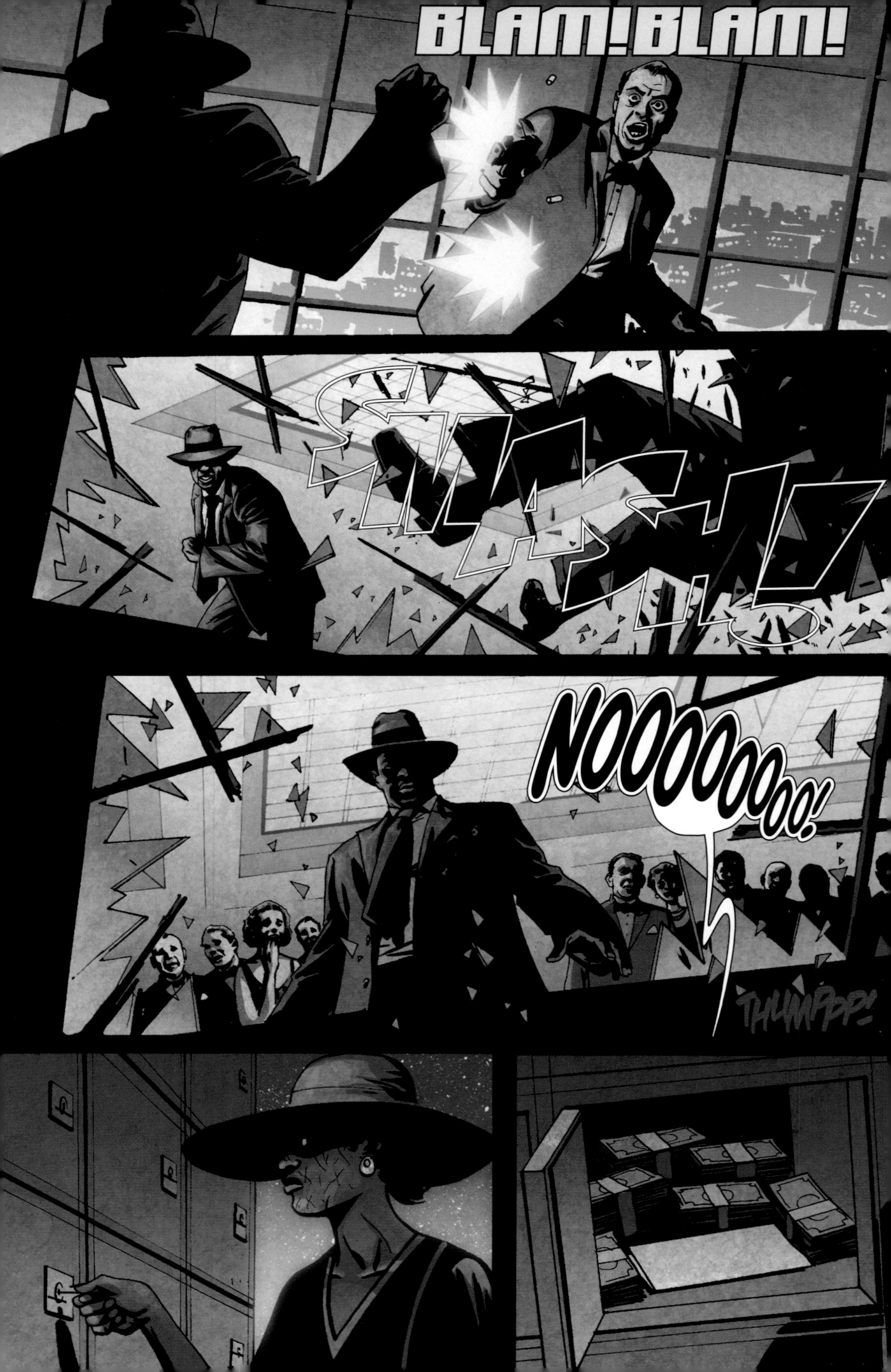
BLAM! BLAM!
SMASH!
NOOOOOOOOO!
THUMPPP!

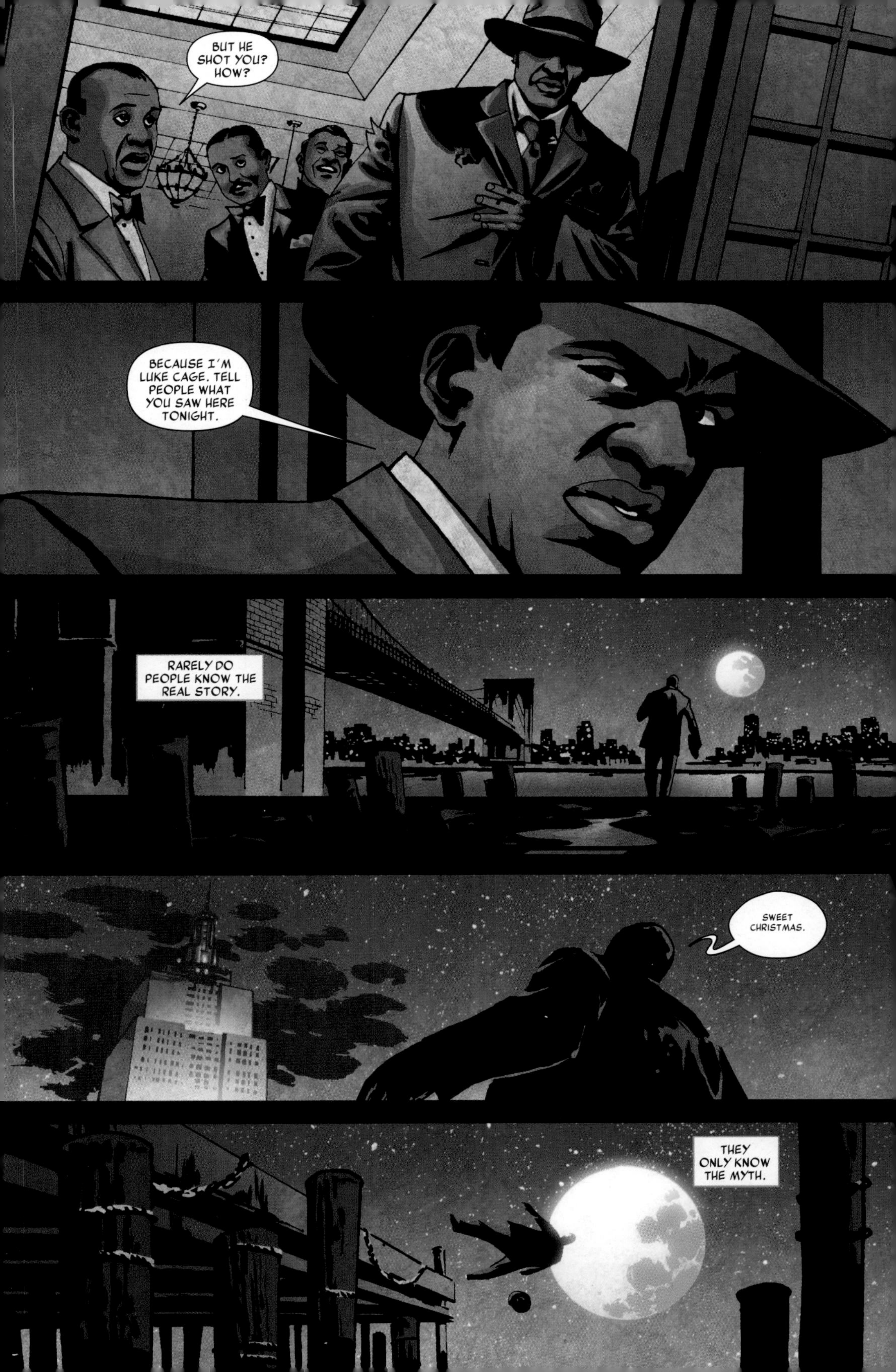
BUT HE SHOT YOU? HOW?
BECAUSE I'M LUKE CAGE. TELL PEOPLE WHAT YOU SAW HERE TONIGHT.
RARELY DO PEOPLE KNOW THE REAL STORY.
SWEET CHRISTMAS.
THEY ONLY KNOW THE MYTH.

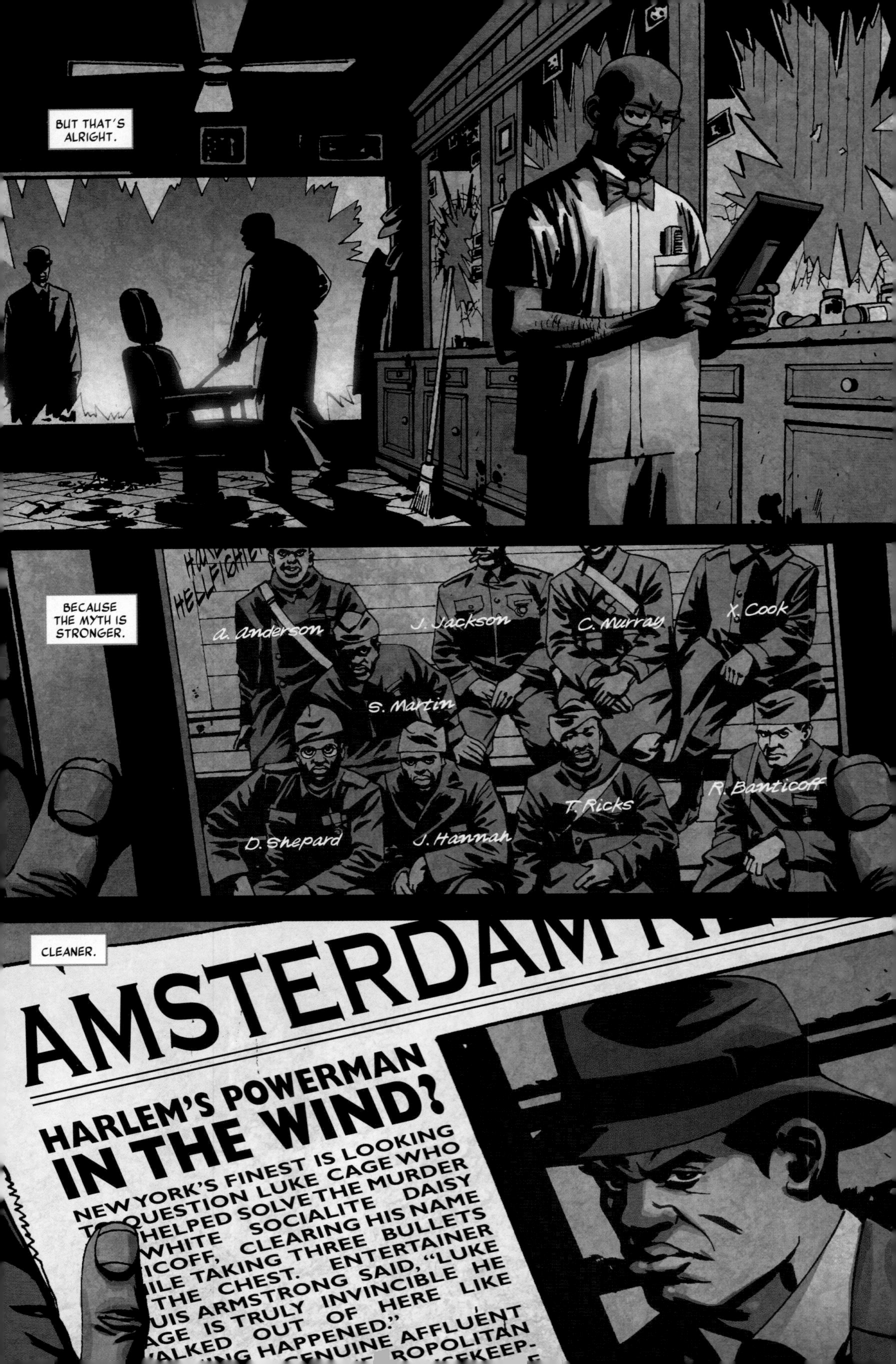

BUT THAT'S ALRIGHT.
BECAUSE THE MYTH IS STRONGER.
A. Anderson
J. Jackson
C. Murray
X. Cook
S. Martin
D. Shepard
J. Hannah
T. Ricks
R. Banticoff
CLEANER.
AMSTERDAM
HARLEM'S POWERMAN
IN THE WIND?
NEW YORK'S FINEST IS LOOKING
QUESTION LUKE CAGE WHO
HELPED SOLVE THE MURDER
WHITE SOCIALITE DAISY
ICOFF, CLEARING HIS NAME
ILE TAKING THREE BULLETS
THE CHEST. ENTERTAINER
UIS ARMSTRONG SAID, "LUKE
AGE IS TRULY INVINCIBLE HE
WALKED OUT OF HERE LIKE
HAPPENED."
GENUINE AFFLUENT
ROPOLITAN

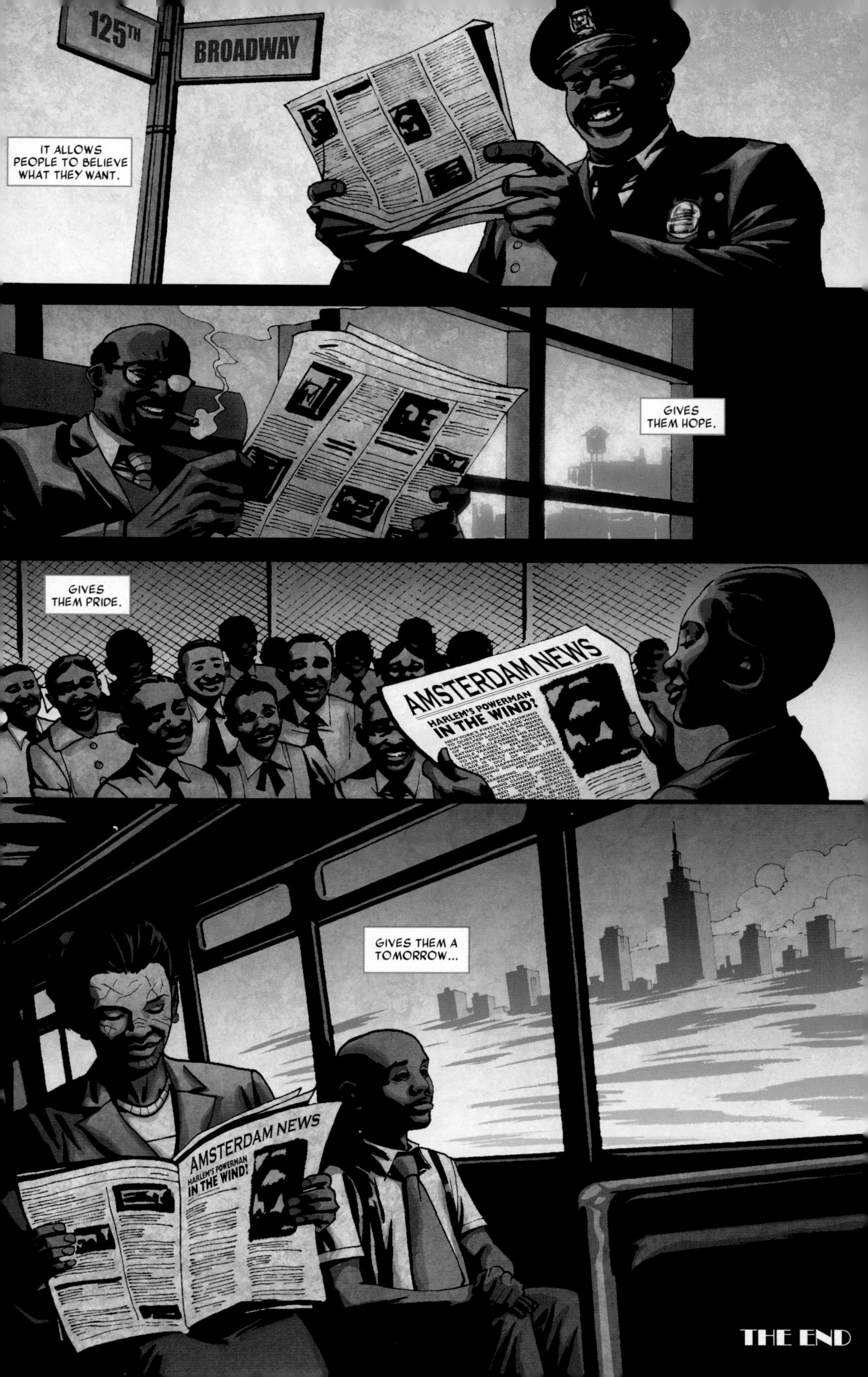

125TH
BROADWAY
IT ALLOWS PEOPLE TO BELIEVE WHAT THEY WANT.
GIVES THEM HOPE.
GIVES THEM PRIDE.
AMSTERDAM NEWS
HARLEM'S POWERMAN IN THE WIND?
GIVES THEM A TOMORROW...
AMSTERDAM NEWS
HARLEM'S POWERMAN IN THE WIND?
THE END

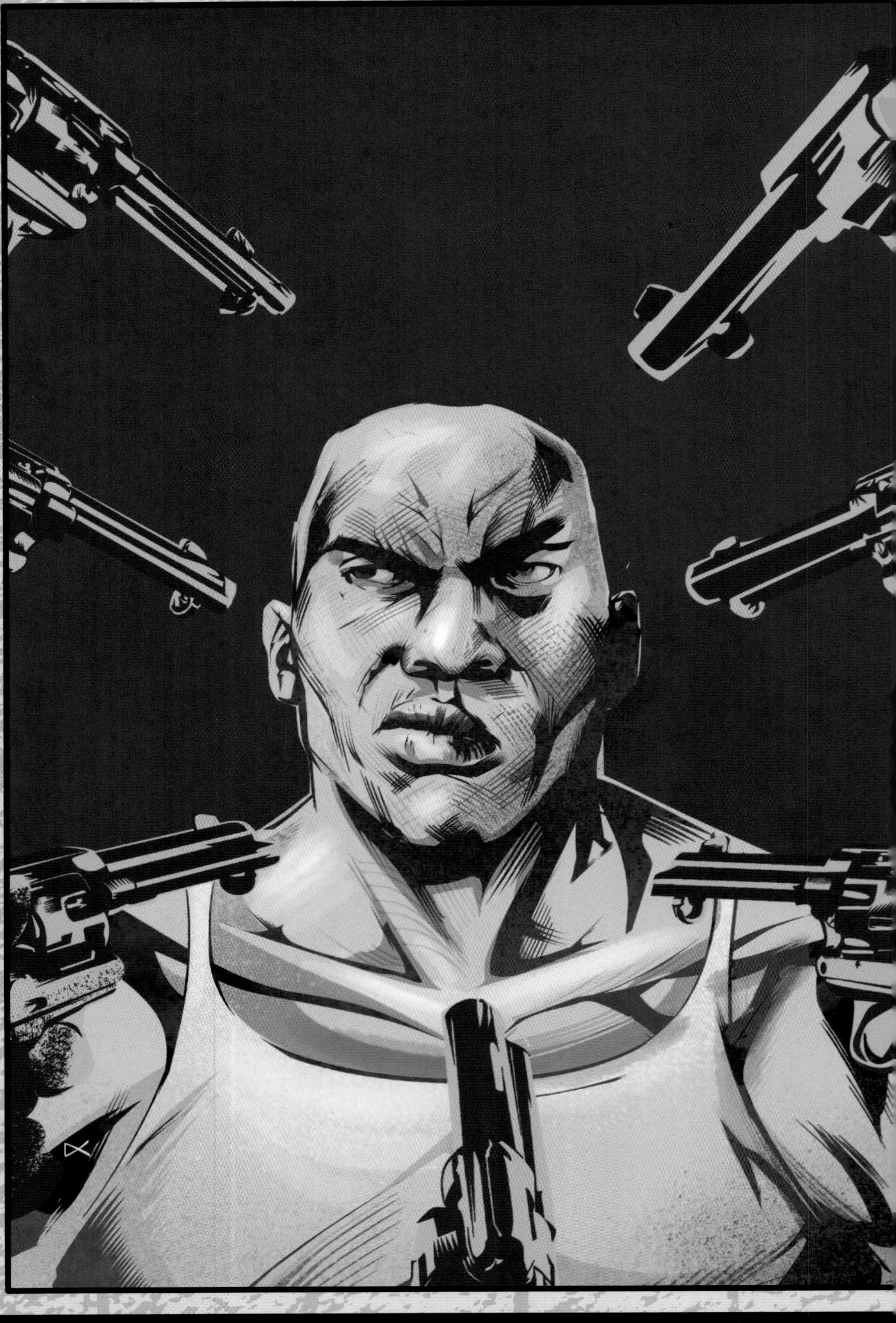

#1 VARIANT BY DENNIS CALERO

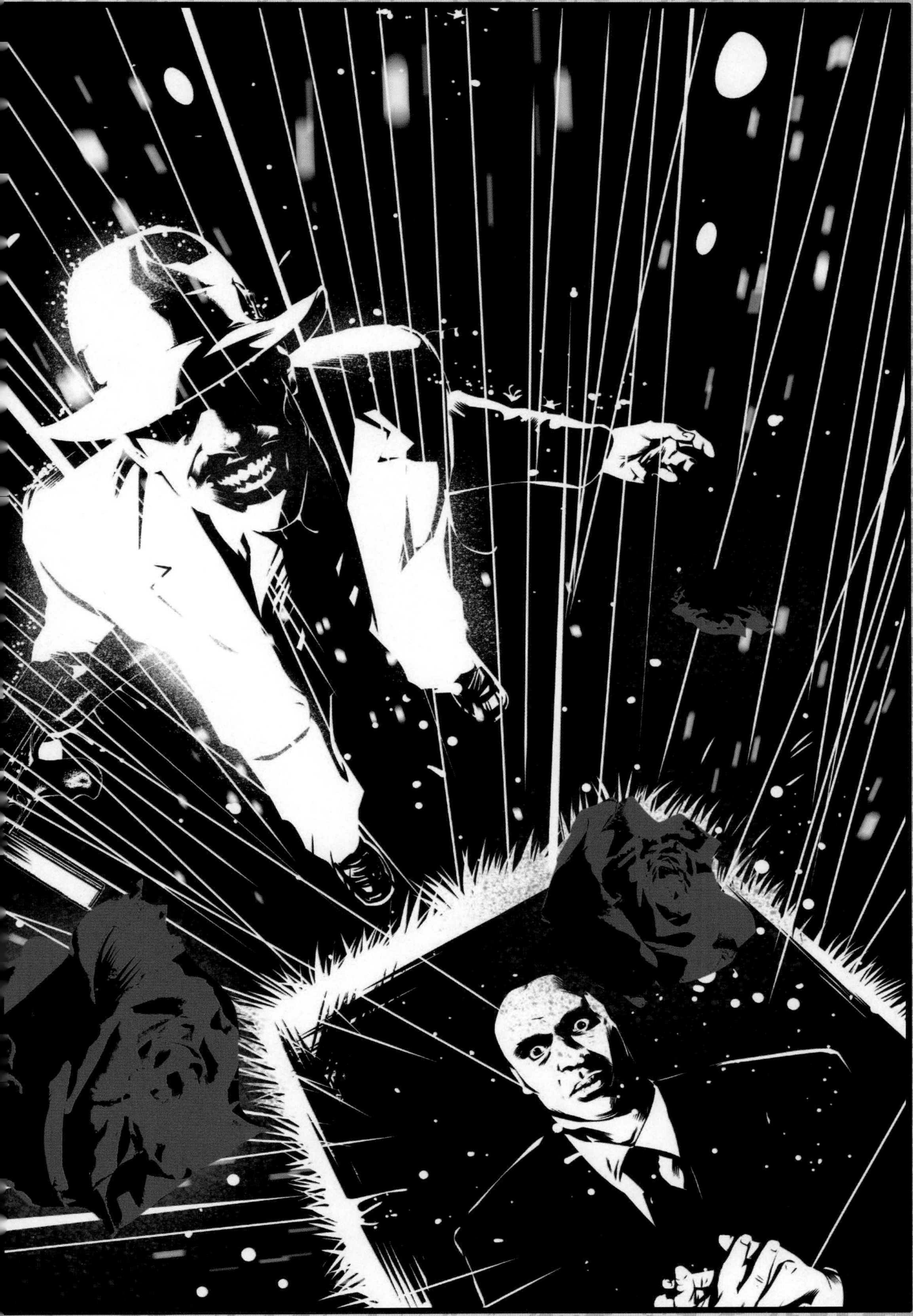

#2 VARIANT BY DENNIS CALERO

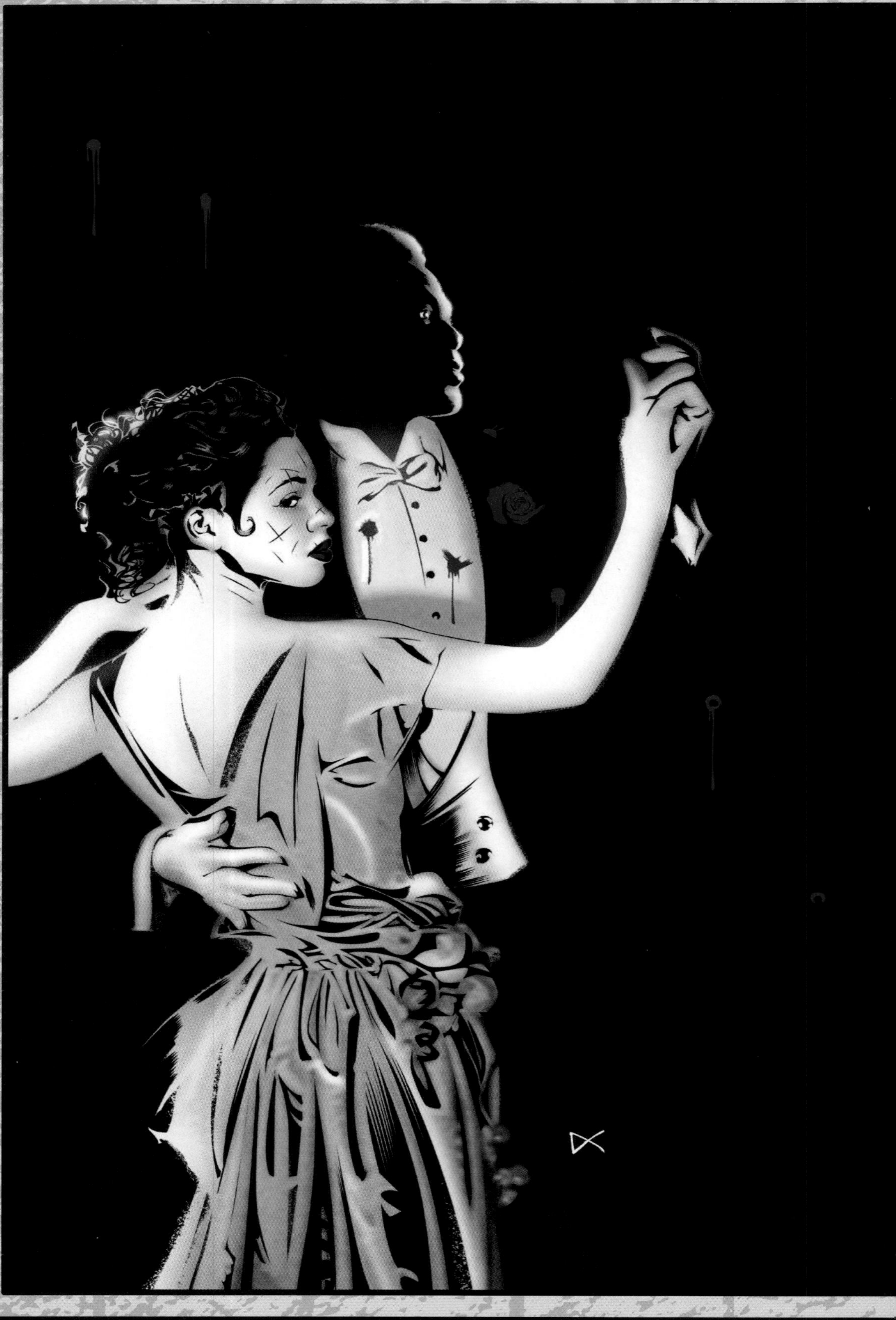

#3 VARIANT BY DENNIS CALERO

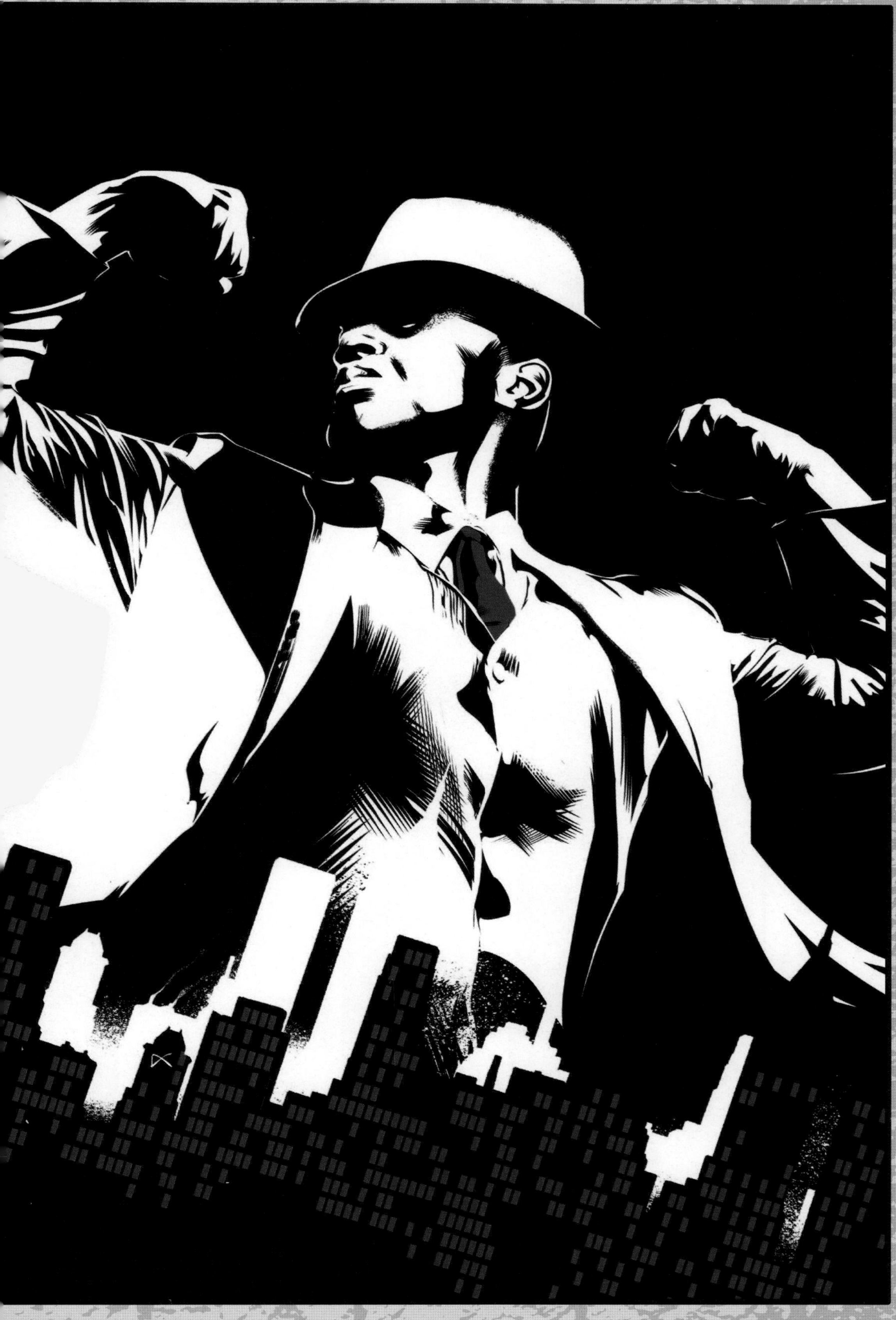

#4 VARIANT BY DENNIS CALERO

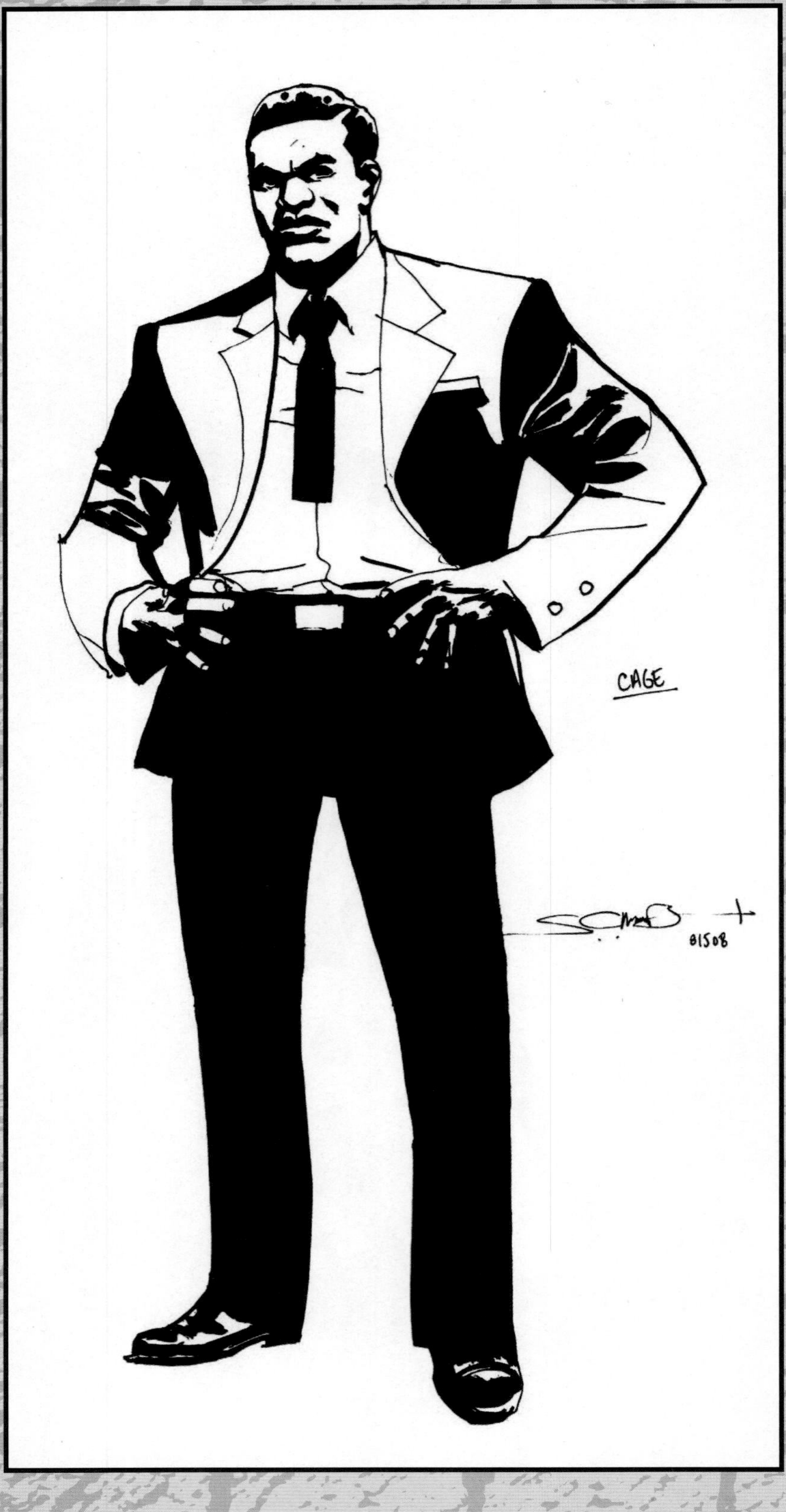
CAGE

CONCEPT ART BY SHAWN MARTINBROUGH

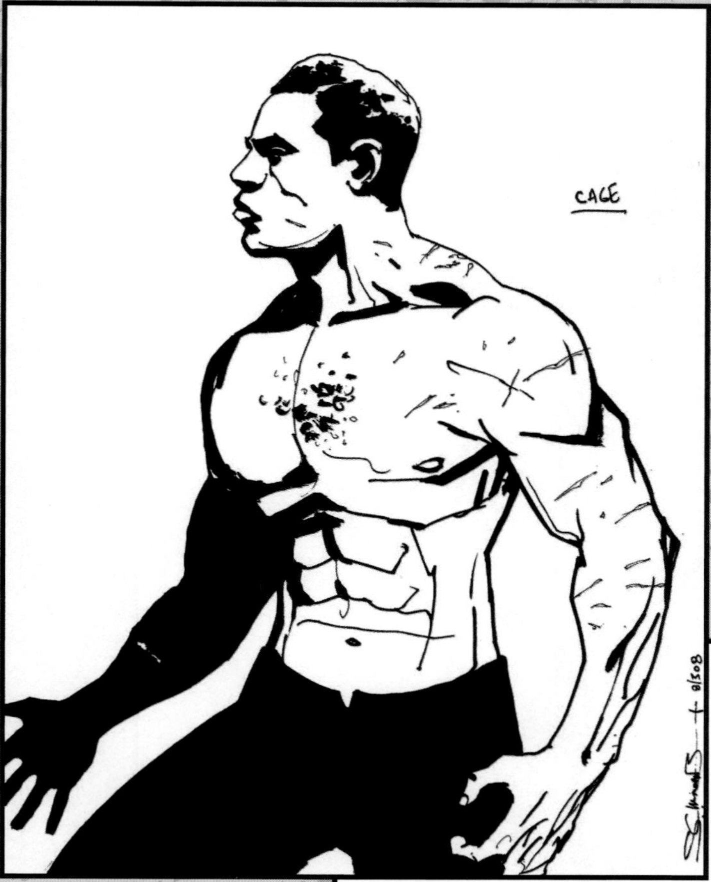
CAGE

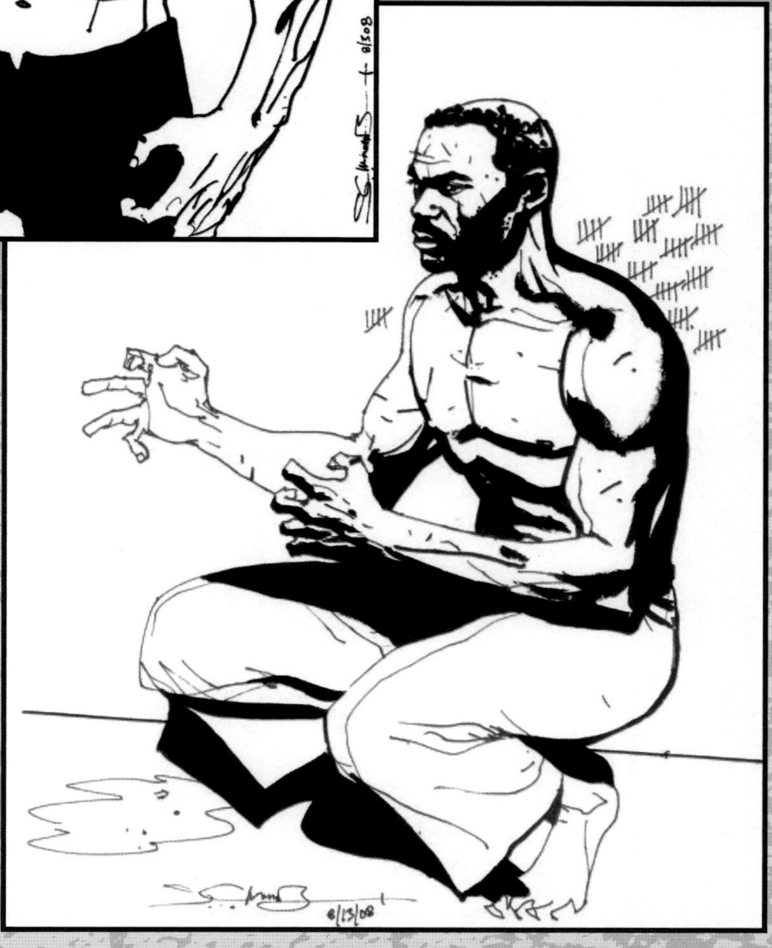

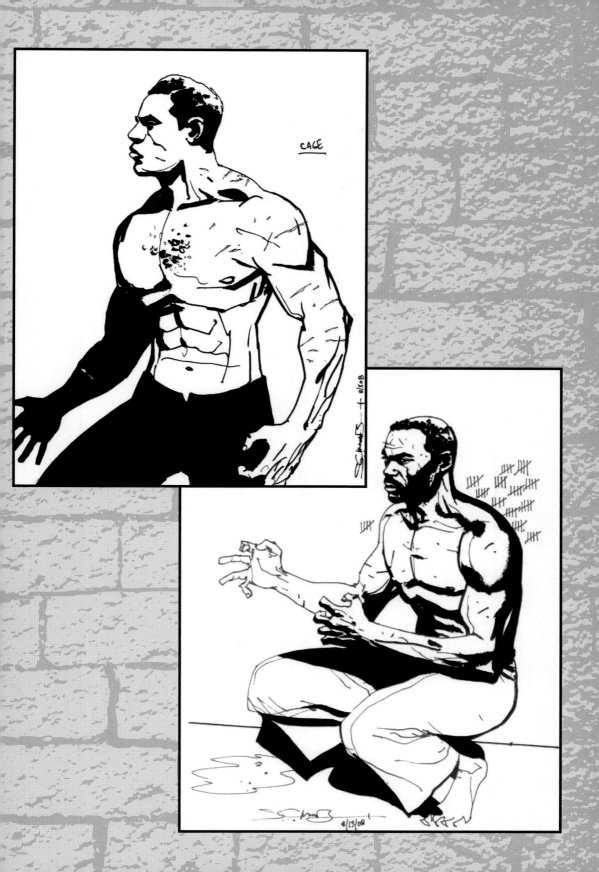

CONCEPT ART BY SHAWN MARTINBROUGH

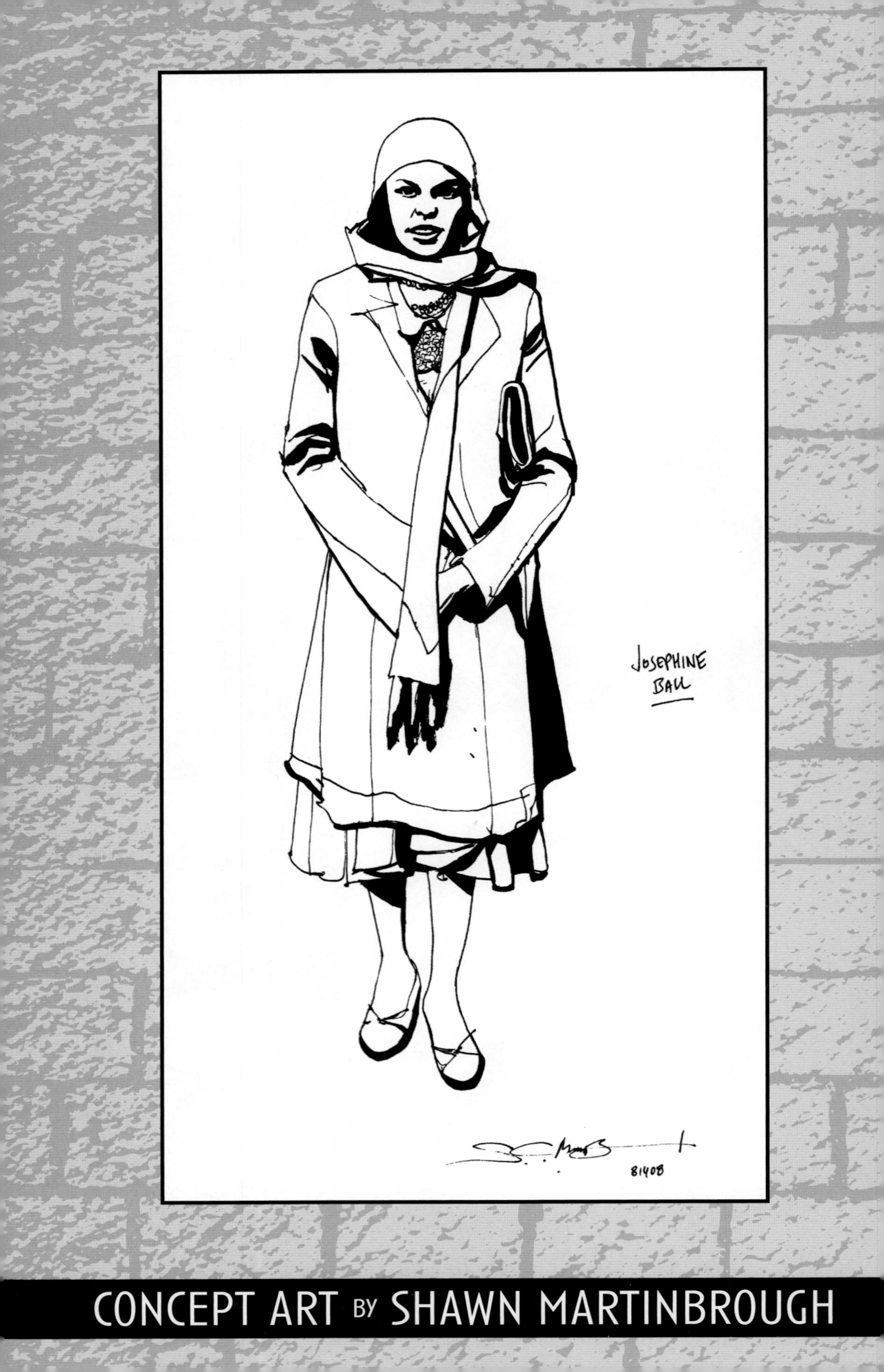
JOSEPHINE
BALL
81408

CONCEPT ART BY SHAWN MARTINBROUGH

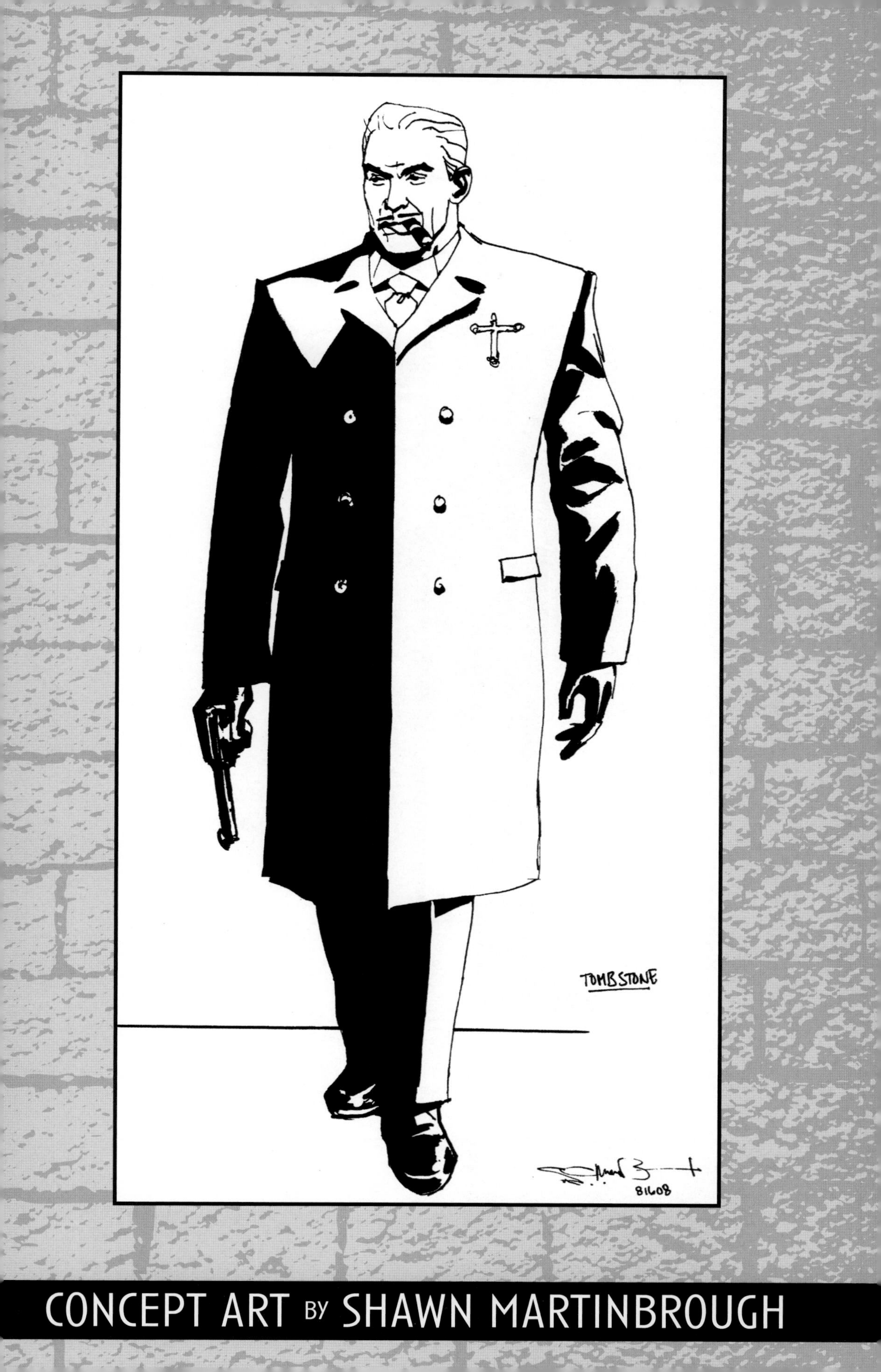
TOMBSTONE
81608

CONCEPT ART BY SHAWN MARTINBROUGH

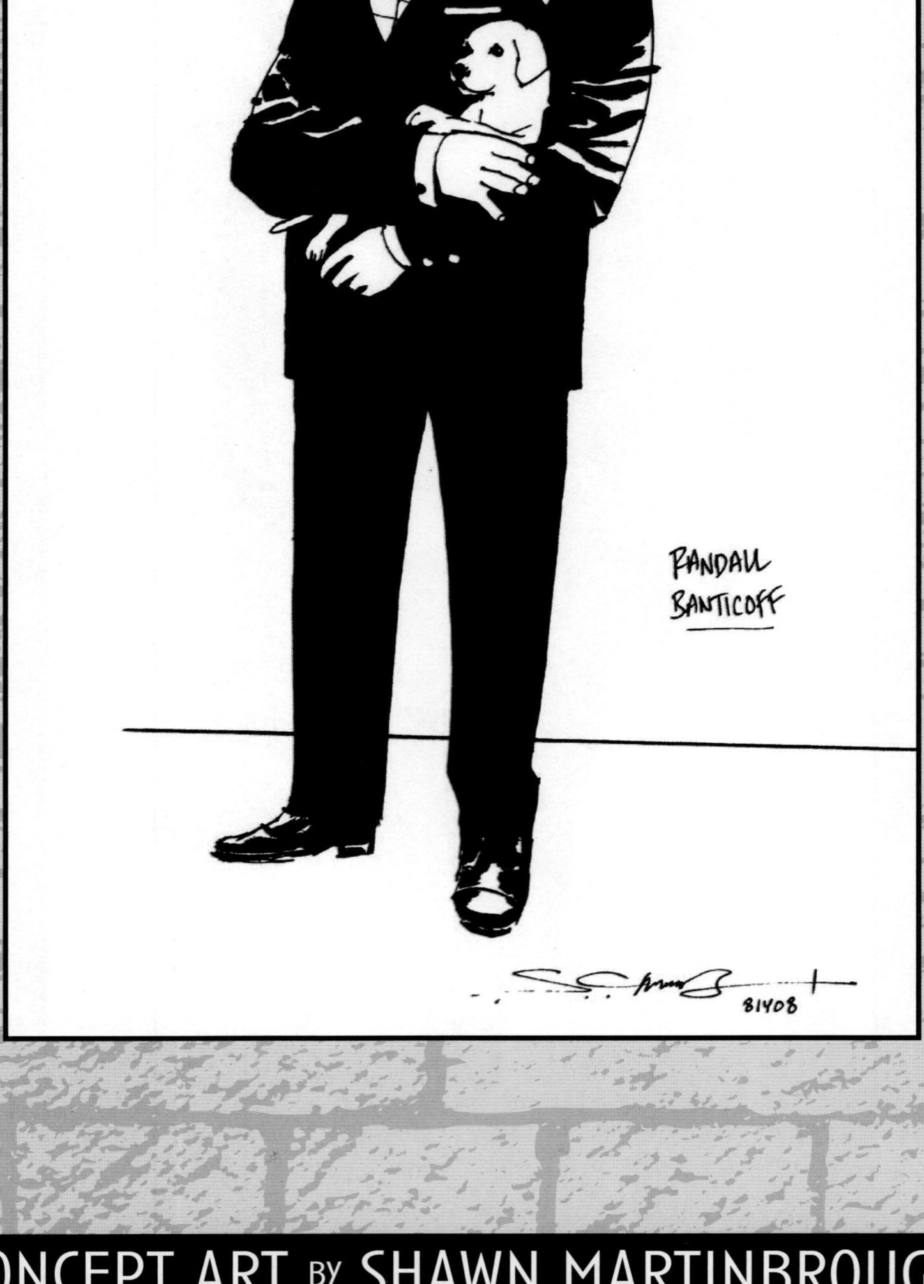
RANDALL
BANTICOFF
81408

CONCEPT ART BY SHAWN MARTINBROUGH

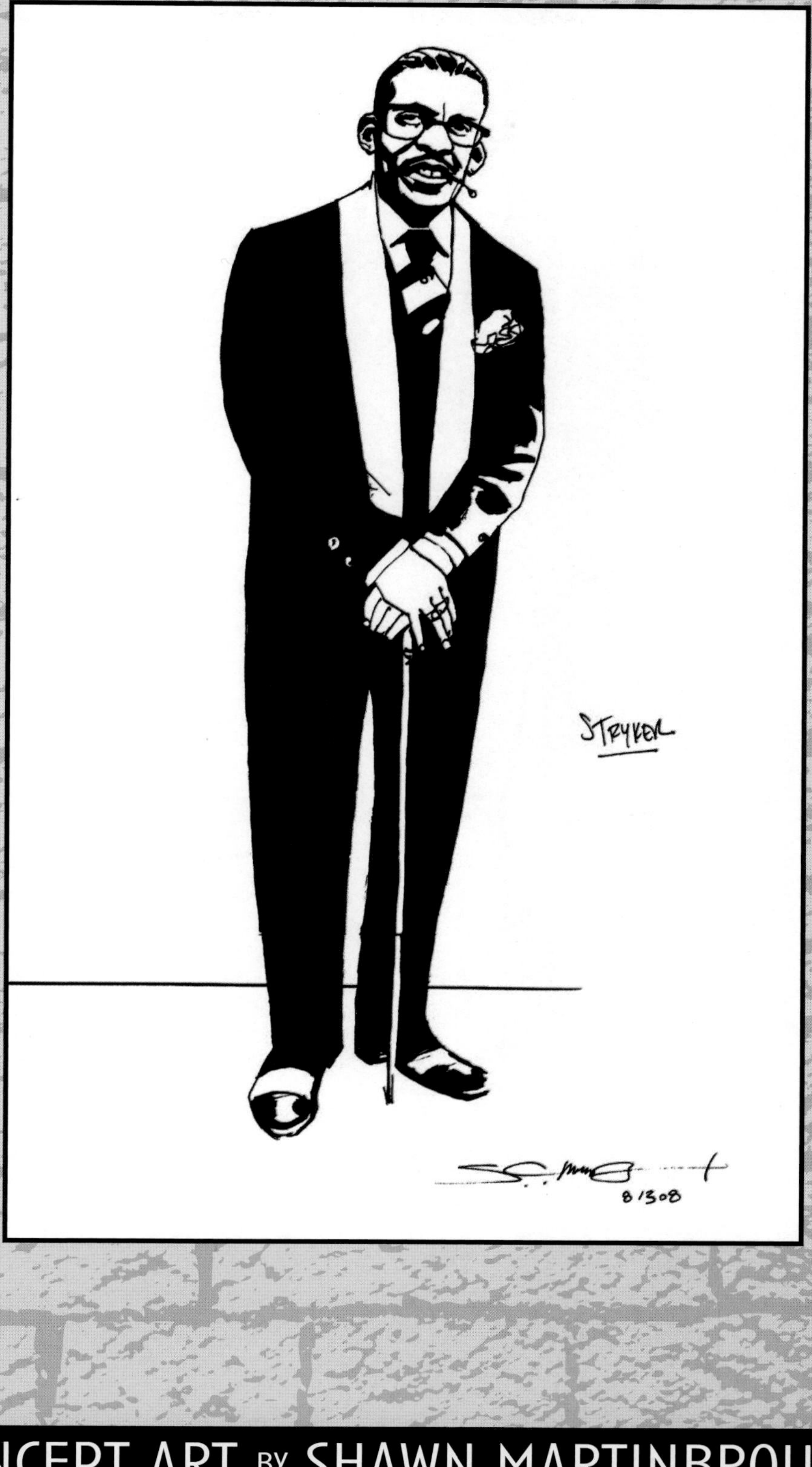
STRYKER
8/3/08

CONCEPT ART BY SHAWN MARTINBROUGH

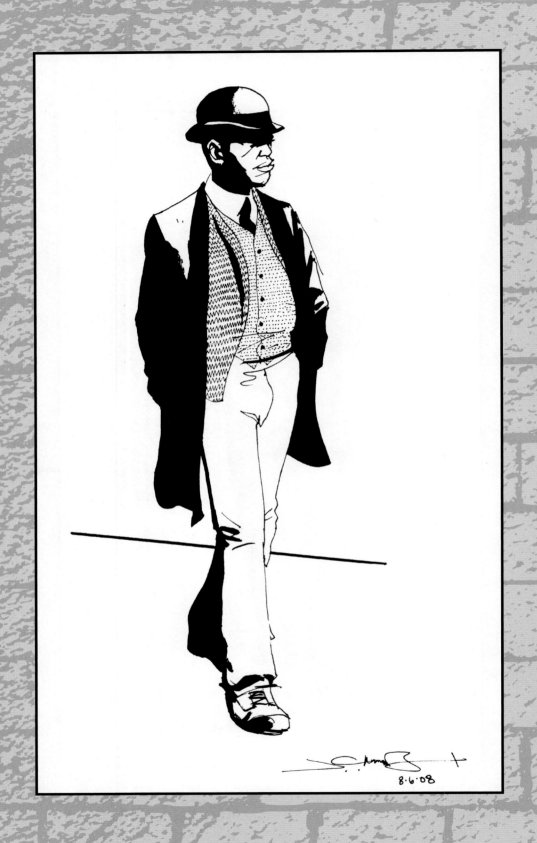

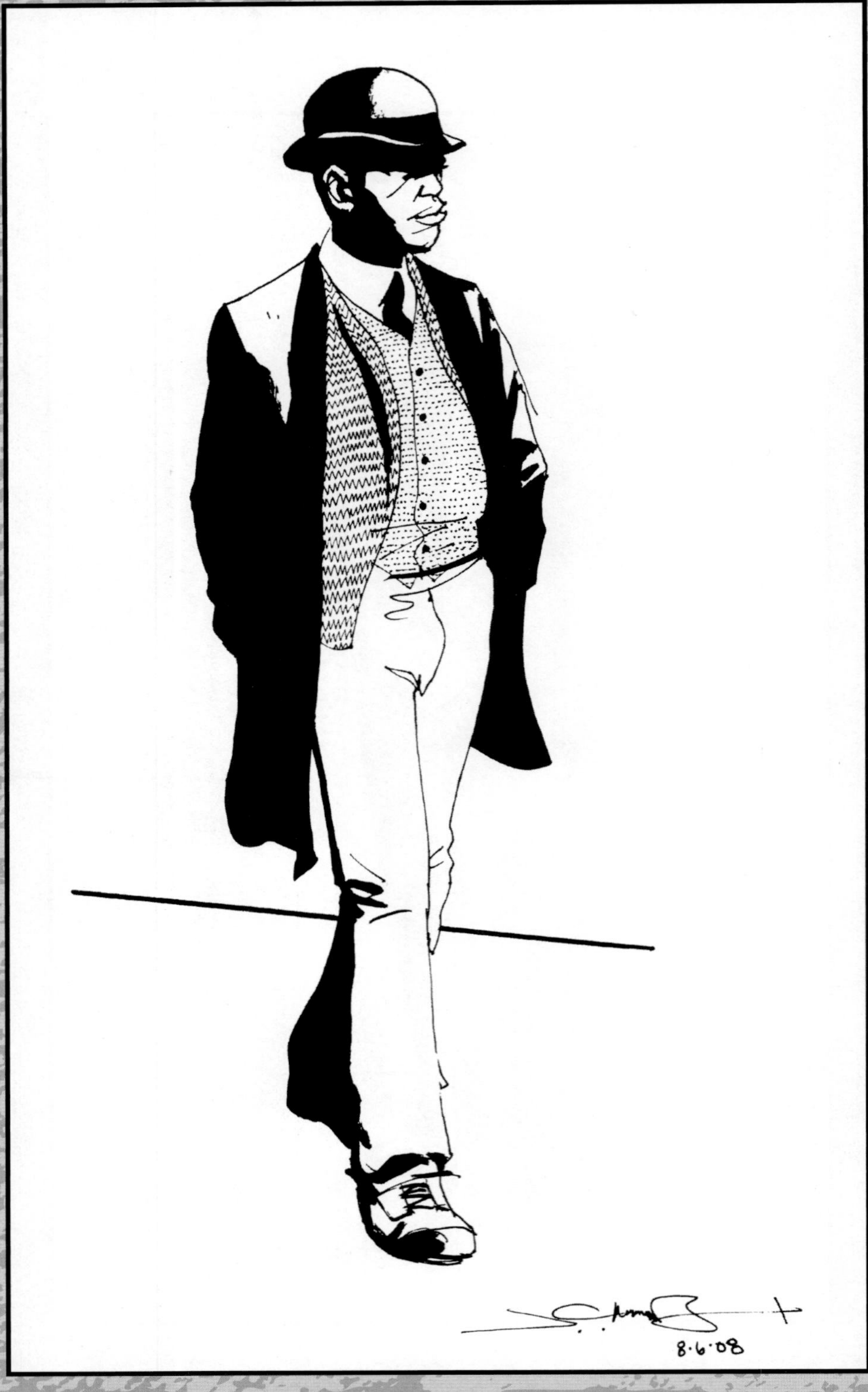
8·6·08

CONCEPT ART BY SHAWN MARTINBROUGH

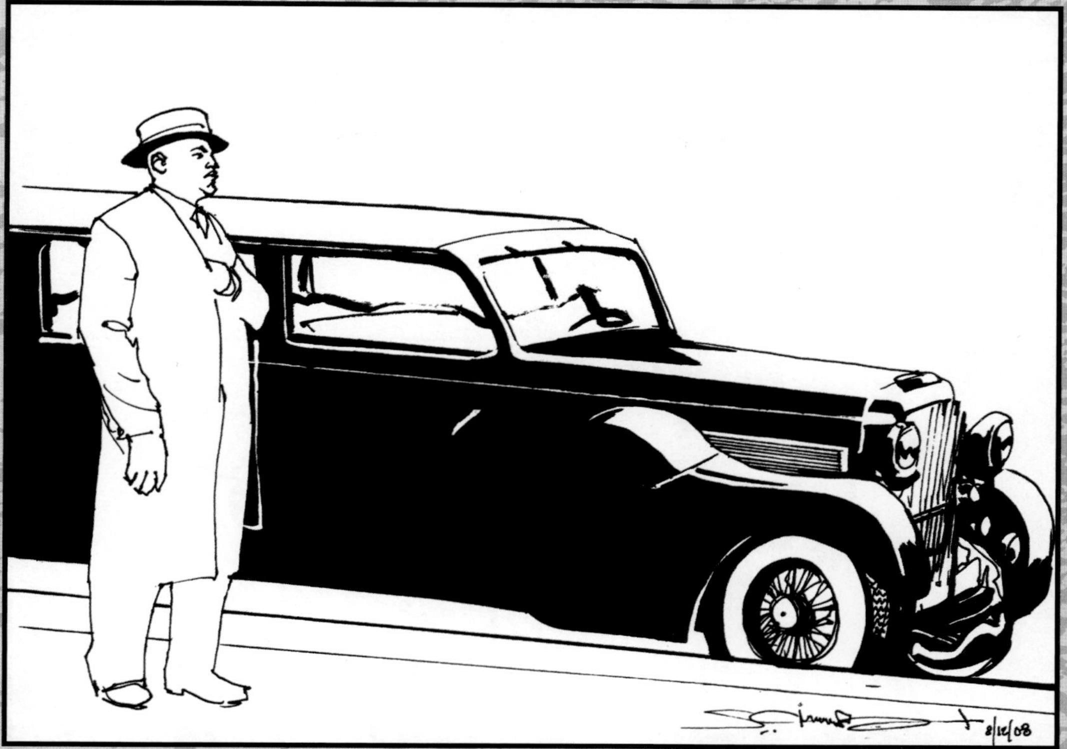

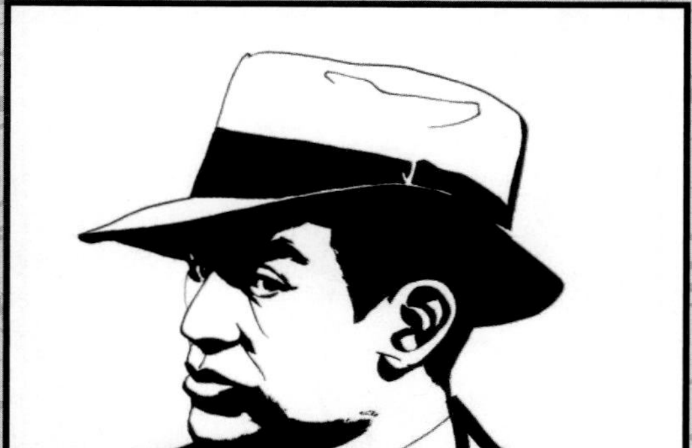
LANGSTON HUGHES
8/12/08

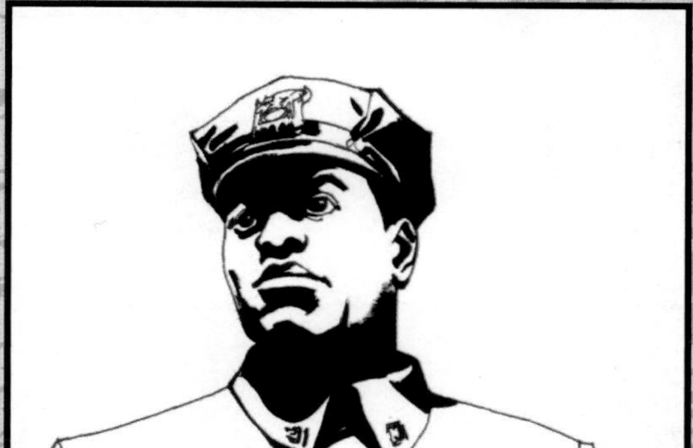
8/13/08

CONCEPT ART BY SHAWN MARTINBROUGH

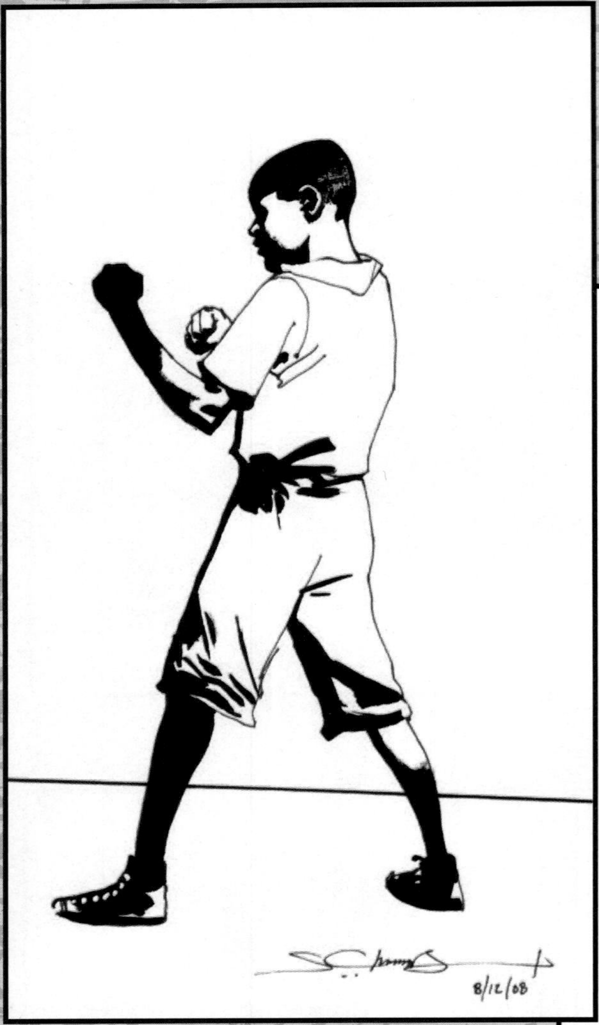
8/12/08

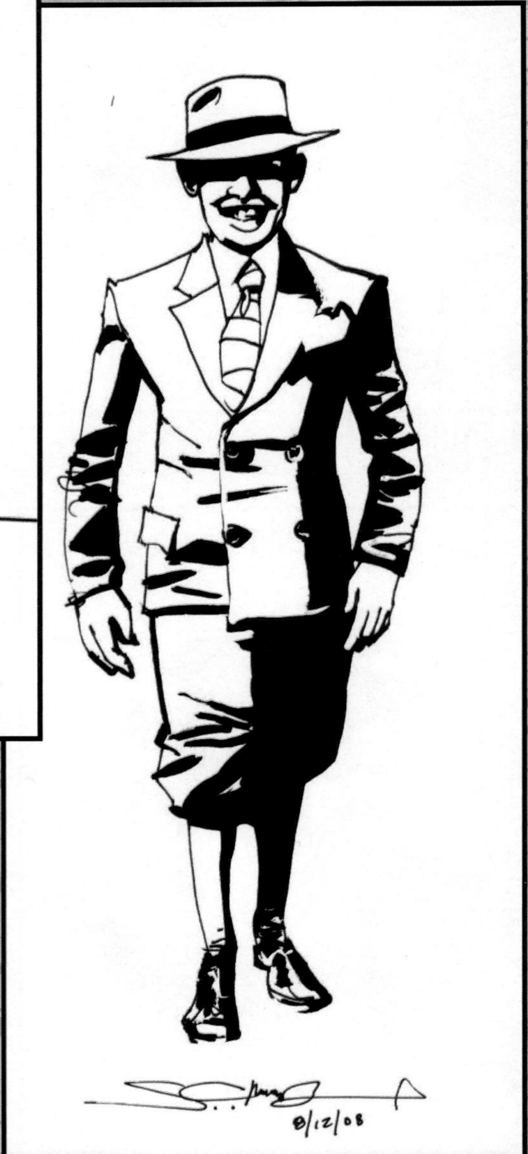
8/12/08

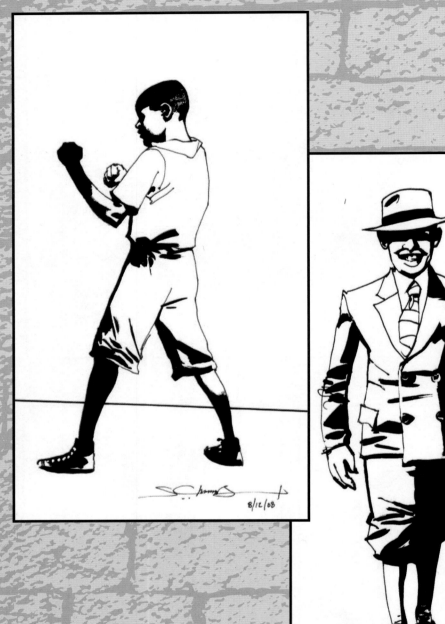

CONCEPT ART BY SHAWN MARTINBROUGH